Who Benefits from the Nonprofit Sector?

Who Benefits from
the Nonprofit Sector?

Edited by

Charles T. Clotfelter

THE UNIVERSITY OF CHICAGO PRESS

Chicago & London

CHARLES T. CLOTFELTER is professor of public policy studies and economics at Duke University. He is the author of *Federal Tax Policy and Charitable Giving* and co-author of *Economic Challenges in Higher Education*, both published by the University of Chicago Press.

The University of Chicago Press, Chicago 60637
The University of Chicago Press, Ltd., London
© 1992 by The University of Chicago
All rights reserved. Published 1992
Printed in the United States of America
01 00 99 98 97 96 95 94 93 92   5 4 3 2 1
ISBN (cloth): 0–226–11052–4

Library of Congress Cataloging-in-Publication Data

Who benefits from the nonprofit sector? / edited by Charles T.
  Clotfelter.
    p.   cm.
  Includes bibliographical references and index.
    1. Charities—Government policy—United States.   2. Corporations,
  Nonprofit—Government policy—United States.   3. Corporations,
  Nonprofit—Taxation—United States.   I. Clotfelter, Charles T.
  HV95.W53   1992
  361.7′0973—dc20   91–41221
                                                                  CIP

⊗The paper used in this publication meets the minimum requirements of the
American National Standard for Information Sciences—Permanence of Paper
for Printed Library Materials, ANSI Z39.48–1984.

Contents

Preface

Scholarly interest in the nonprofit sector has grown significantly in recent years. Research by historians, lawyers, social scientists, and humanists has appeared in a growing number of books and academic journal articles. One prominent component of this research has been contributed by economists, who have focused on such questions as the determinants of volunteer effort, the relative efficiency of for-profit and nonprofit firms, the socially desirable amount of fundraising, and the effect of tax policy on charitable contributions. Despite the growth of this economic research, it seemed to me that there was at least one important question that had not been addressed in any systematic manner, but could be with the use of conventional empirical analysis. This was the question of the distributional impact of our country's reliance on a large nonprofit sector to carry out important social functions. In other words, who are the beneficiaries of the services produced by nonprofit institutions? Although the issue of distributional impact rarely comes to the surface in policy debate—as when, for example, in the debate over favorable tax status private health clubs accused some YMCA's of catering to "yuppies" (Bailey 1989, 1)—it lies just below the surface in this as in many areas of public policy. Thus it is likely to be one among the important considerations whenever policies toward the nonprofit sector are debated.

The objective of the current volume is to present evidence bearing on this question of distributional impact. With the support of a grant from the Lilly Endowment, Duke's Center for the Study of Philanthropy and Voluntarism commissioned empirical papers to examine each of six major subsectors of the nonprofit sector. As a first step in this research, the authors gathered for a meeting in early 1990 to discuss the many empirical, theoretical, and methodological issues that confronted them in common. The major issues discussed there and the common assumptions adopted in the empirical chapters are discussed in the chapter 1. Drafts of these six chapters were presented and discussed at a conference at Duke on November 29–30, 1990. In addition to the authors, three economists were invited to act as commentators at the conference. These commentators were asked to reflect on the overall significance of the research presented at the conference. In addition, each commentator was asked to pay special attention to two of the chapters: Henry Aaron to the chapters on health and arts and culture; Estelle James to the chapters on social services and foundations; and Frank Levy to the chapters on education and religion. Following the conference, the authors revised their chapters in light of the comments offered by the commentators and other conference participants.

As a result of the coordination among authors both before and during the conference, the book has a cohesion that is seldom found in edited volumes. In each chapter the author briefly describes the institutional structure of a subsector, discusses the nature of the benefits produced by the nonprofit institutions in that subsector, presents information on the distribution of those benefits, and concludes by noting the implications of the findings. The three written commentaries that conclude the volume provide several perspectives useful for judging the importance of the empirical studies.

It would not have been possible to undertake this project without the support of the Lilly Endowment and the Center for the Study of Philanthropy and Voluntarism at Duke University. Also essential to the success of the project were the three staff assistants in the center who coordinated the many logistical and administrative details, Carole Stern, Beth Shulman, and Marshall Adesman. In the planning stages, I received helpful suggestions from a number of colleagues at Duke and elsewhere, and I am particularly grateful for the generous assistance given to me by Bradford Gray, Michael McPherson, Burton Weisbrod, and John Simon. I also received helpful comments on drafts from Elizabeth Boris, Donald Etheridge, Kathleen McCarthy, Ralph McCaughan, and Albert Rees. Finally, I think it is appropriate to recognize the participants at the conference itself. Although only the authors and commentators' words are recorded in the published volume, those who participated in the lively discussions at the conference contributed materially to the final product. Those participants included Dwight Burlingame, Dennis Coates, Joel Colton, John Day, Craufurd Goodwin, William Gentry, Virginia Hodgkinson, Rhonda Johnson, Alexander Keyssar, Helen Ladd, George Maddox, Richard Magat, Bruce Payne, Richard Schmalbeck, Steven Rathgeb Smith, Bob Smucker, Richard Stubbing, Dek Terrell, Natalie Webb, Rachel Willis, Julian Wolpert, Dennis Young, and Douglas Zinn.

C. T. C.

1

The Distributional Consequences of Nonprofit Activities

Charles T. Clotfelter

As this century enters its final decade, countries in all parts of the world are rethinking the roles traditionally played by government in providing social services. In the United States this rethinking has been encouraged by Presidents Reagan and Bush, who pushed for cuts in federal domestic spending and called for private voluntary action to assume greater responsibility for meeting social needs. In fact, the collection of institutions loosely referred to as the nonprofit sector has been playing an important part in education, health, and other social services from the nation's earliest days. To a degree unparalleled elsewhere, the nonprofit sector in the United States is enshrined in constitutional law, instrumental in the delivery of many essential social services, and inextricably bound up with broad social processes of change and governance.

The sector employs some ten percent of the nation's work force. Governments at all levels in this country have placed nonprofit organizations in a special position, exempting them from most taxation and encouraging their supporters in other ways. One of the most important of these is the income tax deduction for charitable contributions, for which much of the $90 billion donated annually is eligible. The nonprofit sector also relies on direct government support for a quarter of its income. By virtue of both their size and special treatment, nonprofit organizations have become an important subject of study for those interested in the implementation of public policy in this country.

In studying other institutions that affect public policy, economists and other policy analysts find it useful to examine at least two important aspects of performance: efficiency and distributional equity. The first of these two aspects has received considerable attention in the growing literature about nonprofit organizations. Several important analyses have evaluated the effect of such organizations on the efficiency of resource allocation. These studies have focused on the role of nonprofit organizations in providing services about which consumers are poorly informed or those which governments have for some reason failed to provide sufficient quantity.[1] In addition, there have been a number of empirical studies to determine the relative cost-effectiveness of using government, nonprofit, or for-profit institutions to produce and deliver certain kinds of services, often on a contract basis.[2] However, scholars have paid less attention to the second aspect—the distributional implications of our reliance on nonprofit institutions—this despite the fact that distributional considerations have always held a prominent position in American political debate.

This is not to say that observers of the nonprofit sector have never speculated on what might be the distributional impact of the sector's institutions and the voluntary donations that support them. They have, and for the most part the tenor of scholarly commentary suggests that the redistributive impact of the sector is minimal. In an essay on philanthropy, for example, William Vickrey put forth the hypothesis that most donors direct their gifts not toward the most disadvantaged in society but rather to those only slightly below them on the income ladder, concluding that "the role of philanthropy in redistribution is relatively slight" (Vickrey 1962, 44–45). Teresa Odendahl (1989, 246) is even more emphatic in arguing that such voluntary institutions result in little in the way of redistribution of resources: "The philanthropy of elites is not a system whereby the fortunate distribute resources to the less fortunate. Instead, philanthropy is primarily a system whereby the wealthy help to finance their own interests and institutions."

Similar arguments have been made about specific subsectors of the nonprofit world. For example, one commentator has said that "arts-funding is in practice an income-transfer program for the upper-middle class" (Bethell 1978, 136). Private health clubs have accused some YMCA's of catering to the affluent (Bailey 1989, 1). Still others have noted the "elitist" character of private universities (Shils 1973, 7). One paper compiled in the 1970s for the Commission on Private Philanthropy and Public Needs, popularly known as the Filer Commission, noted that "grants made directly for social change or to assist the powerless are dwarfed by the massive philanthropic contributions made annually in support of education, the

1. See, for example, Hansmann (1980) and Weisbrod (1988).
2. For studies of the relative efficiency of nonprofit organizations, see Savas (1982) or Schlesinger (1990). Taking the somewhat broader view that efficiency encompasses how social wants are satisfied, studies of the historical roots of nonprofit institutions can also be placed in the category of empirical work related to the efficiency of nonprofit organizations.

arts, health services and the like" (Carey 1977, 1110). And some scholars have argued that there is very little redistributive aspect to the biggest category of charitable giving, that directed to religious organizations (for example, see Schaefer 1968, 30). Moreover, the issue of distributional impact is bound up with the concern about the ultimate goal of nonprofit institutions. In this connection, the Donee Group report to the Filer Commission urged wider citizen involvement in governing boards and ways to "democratize" charitable giving in order for philanthropy to become "an advocate for those who are most in need" (Donee Group 1977, 57).

At the center of these and other related policy discussions is the question of who benefits from the nonprofit sector and public policies affecting the sector. Although few would argue that redistribution is the most important justification for maintaining nonprofit institutions, distributional impact remains one significant consideration, as it is in most areas of public policy. Such distributional concerns are certainly involved when Congress reexamines laws that will affect the size of the voluntary sector, such as the definition and taxation of "unrelated" business income earned by nonprofit organizations, or the establishment of limitations on the deductibility of charitable contributions. These concerns also arise on the local level in connection with granting property exemptions for nonprofit organizations. Despite the importance of these issues, however, we simply do not have a good idea about the sector's distributional consequences. Our lack of knowledge regarding these consequences invites empirical research. The purpose of this volume is to offer such research, using the conventional tools of empirical social science. Although they employ definitions and techniques unfamiliar to many readers, the studies have been written so as to be accessible to a broad audience. Taken together, the findings contained in the volume show that the distributional impact of the nonprofit sector can be characterized neither by the pro-poor charity of the Salvation Army nor by the affluent-orientation of some arts groups. Distributional impact differs by subsector and must be analyzed accordingly.

Before turning to the studies themselves, it is useful to introduce the topic in a general way and to discuss some of the methodological issues confronting all of the studies. The next section presents a brief descriptive overview of the nonprofit sector, noting the special tax treatment given to nonprofit institutions. The following section discusses the general approach taken by the papers in this volume to assess the distributional impact of nonprofit institutions. In particular, it deals with the methodological issues that are common to all of the papers and discusses the assumptions on which the analyses are based. There follow a short section describing the distribution of charitable contributions by income, a summary of the findings of these empirical studies, and a brief concluding section.

I. THE NONPROFIT SECTOR

Whether it is referred to as the "voluntary sector," the "private not-for-profit sector," or simply the nonprofit sector, there exists in this country a vast and diverse collection of religious groups, schools, hospitals, associations, and other nongovernmental organizations that fulfill a host of important functions. In size they range from the tiniest day-care center to the major research universities and established national charities. Some of them exist entirely for the benefit of their members, while others are devoted to helping others. Many of them operate quite independently of government, while others act as virtual extensions of government programs. In 1987 there were over one million separate nonprofit organizations in operation.

Probably the most important sign of recognition of the special role of nonprofit organizations in public law is the general exemption from federal income taxation; thus it is a useful approximation to equate "nonprofit" with "tax-exempt."[3] In fact, one useful way of categorizing nonprofit institutions is according to the gradations of tax treatment they receive. Table 1.1 defines three groups of tax-exempt organizations. The first two groups—including foundations and other charitable, religious, and educational organizations—constitute the so-called 501(c) (3) organizations, all of which are subject to provisions of the section of the Internal Revenue Code so numbered. The most important tax provision applying to these organizations is that contributions made to them may be deducted by donors in calculating their income tax. Institutions in the first group, foundations, are separated because they have traditionally been subject to more stringent tax provisions than other 501(c) (3) organizations. The special provisions applying to foundations are of two kinds. First, contributions to foundations have usually been subject to lower limits, as a percentage of a donor's income, and gifts of appreciated property have also been treated less favorably when given to foundations. Second,

---

3. Not all income generated by nonprofits is exempt from income taxation. Specifically, such an organization must pay tax on income that is deemed to be unrelated to its central charitable purpose. For a discussion of the relevant tax law and the issue of commercial activities of nonprofits, see articles in part two of Hodgkinson and Lyman (1989).

Charles T. Clotfelter

TABLE 1.1 Number of Tax-Exempt Organizations, 1987 (thousands)

Foundations	27.7
Churches and other charitable, educational and scientific organizations	
Churches and other religious bodies	346.1
Other	394.4
Other tax-exempt organizations	517.0
Total	1,285.2

SOURCE: Hodgkinson and Weitzman (1989, tables 1.2, 1.3, and 5.1; pp. 28, 29, and 121).

foundations themselves are subject to a number of rules, including a minimum payout requirement, stated as a percentage of investment assets, and regulations covering the governance and financial dealings of principal donors and their families.[4] In 1987 there were some 28,700 foundations in the United States. This number included a small number of widely recognized large private foundations such as Ford and Rockefeller, hundreds of others with assets in the millions, and a galaxy of miniatures. Further distinctions among foundations are discussed in chapter 7.

Numerically, the second and third groups of tax-exempt organizations listed in table 1.1 are much larger. The second group is composed of the organizations besides foundations eligible to receive tax-deductible contributions. Numerically most important here are the 346,000 churches and other individual religious bodies that are perhaps the most visible part of the country's nonprofit sector. This second group also includes some 394,000 other organizations, including private colleges and universities, hospitals, nursing homes, social welfare agencies, international relief agencies, museums, and other cultural institutions. The third group of organizations listed in the table, comprising over one-half million entities, is made up of organizations that generally do not receive the benefit of being able to receive tax-deductible contributions. By and large, these can be described as mutual-benefit organizations. They include groups such as civic clubs, fraternal societies, credit unions, business and labor associations, and farmers' cooperatives.[5] This book follows the practice in much of the research on the nonprofit sector by focusing entirely on the first two groups listed in table 1.1. While it is convenient to accept the distinction made in the tax law, this grouping is by no means pure. For example, organizations

4. For a description of the tax provisions applying to foundations, see Clotfelter (1985, 260–64).

5. In fact, contributions to several groups of non-501(c)(3) organizations are deductible: those to cemetery companies, veterans organizations, and corporations organized under an act of Congress (see Clotfelter 1985, table 1.1, 4–5).

5

in the first two groups certainly display some aspects of mutual-benefit groups, as Biddle discusses in chapter 4. By the same token, there are organizations in the excluded category that perform charitable functions. But, for the most part, the organizations that have been granted 501(c) (3) status generally have earned that special status by having certain characteristics that make them worthy of special attention.

In order to provide some descriptive background on the institutions that make up this sector, table 1.2 presents information on the sources of revenue and employment for each of six major subsectors. Overall, the charitable nonprofits summarized in this table employed some seven million workers, received volunteer services worth an additional 4.5 million worker-years, and brought in over $300 billion in revenue. Of this total revenue, fees and other private payments constituted the largest single source, followed by private donations and payments from government. Measured in terms of either total revenues or total work force, the health-related nonprofits constitute by far the largest subsector. At roughly half the size is the second largest subsector, education and research. Both the health and education subsectors are heavily dependent on fees by paying customers, with private payments accounting for at least half of total revenues in both cases. The second most important source of revenue for both of these subsectors was government, with private contributions ranking a distant third.

Religious organizations ranked third in total revenues, but they were by far the biggest recipients of charitable contributions, receiving about half of all such contributions. The religious subsector is distinctive in two other ways as well. First, like foundations and community chests, churches regularly transfer a significant portion of their income to nonprofit organizations in other subsectors. Second, the religious subsector accounts for a disproportionate share of contributed volunteer labor.

Social and legal services, comparable to what Salamon calls "human services" in chapter 5, constitute the next largest subsector. Institutions in this group are routinely used by governments, sometimes on a contract basis, to provide "public" services. It is not surprising that this is the only subsector for which government is the largest source of funds. In terms of the measures used in table 1.2, arts and culture and foundations are the smallest of the six subsectors shown, neither having gross revenues of more than $12 billion in 1987. Yet these two subsectors contain some of the most prominent nonprofit institutions in the country, and their activities have a profound effect on how the sector as a whole is perceived.

TABLE 1.2 Sources of Income and Employment in the Charitable Nonprofit Sector, 1987

	Sources of Funds ($ billions)							Employment (thousands)	
	Contributions	Private Sector	Government	Investment Income	Church	Other	Total	Paid Employees	Volunteers (FTE)
Health Services	10.5	78.3	54.8	1.7	8.2	2.8	156.3	3,367	817
Education/Research	8.3	38.7	12.8	4.0	4.3	1.9	70.0	1,666	516
Religious Organizations	43.6	3.1	—	0.9	-12.9	3.8	38.4	650	2,015
Social and Legal Services	11.3	4.0	12.1	0.9	0.3	0.6	29.2	1,196	819
Arts and Culture	6.3	1.1	1.2	0.4	0.1	0.8	9.9	122	240
Foundations	-5.5	3.8	—	7.7	—	—	6.0	22	84
Total	86.3[a]	125.2	80.9	15.6	0.0	9.9	317.6	7,024	4,528[b]

SOURCE: Hodgkinson and Weitzman (1989, tables 2.7 and 8.1, pp. 43 and 177).
[a]Includes $8.0 billion of contributions not allocated to any subsector.
[b]Includes 37,000 for international activities not allocated to any subsector.

It is worth noting the ways in which government policy affects the nonprofit sector. As has been mentioned, federal tax policy makes explicit concessions for nonprofit institutions, exempting their incomes from taxation and allowing donations to a subset of institutions to be deductible in the computation of personal and corporate income taxes and the estate tax. Similar concessions are contained in most state tax structures, and nonprofits are also typically exempted from paying state sales taxes. At the local level, nonprofits receive another important source of subsidy by being exempted from property taxation in most jurisdictions. These tax policies, along with other forms of favorable treatment, such as subsidized federal postal rates, are clear evidence of friendly public policy toward nonprofit institutions. Both the nature and the extent of these favorable policies make the performance of nonprofit institutions, including their distributional effects, a public policy issue.

II. Issues of Methodology

There is a long tradition in economics of attention to income distribution and the distributional effects of government policy. Particularly in the area of public finance, analysts have used theory and empirical tools to examine the ways in which taxes and government expenditures affect the well-being of households in different economic situations. Although there are a number of alternative schemes by which households can be grouped for these purposes—including age, race, region, and source of income—distribution is most commonly measured in terms of income class. Adopting this common approach, the studies in this volume examine the distributional pattern of the benefits produced by nonprofit institutions and thus, by implication, the distributional impact of policies that influence the scope of those institutions. The studies focus only on the "output" side of the nonprofit sector; they generally ignore any distributional effects arising from the financing of nonprofit institutions. Although these latter effects are certainly important in any overall assessment of the sector's distributional consequences, issues of financing seem sufficiently general that they can be dealt with separately, as they are later in this chapter.

The Basic Approach Taken in These Studies

This book is concerned with the distributional impact of our reliance on nonprofit institutions to carry out important social functions. Within the constraints imposed by data limitations, each of the empirical studies attempts to address two basic questions related to this impact. First, what

8

are the benefits produced by the nonprofit institutions in the subsector? Second, how are these benefits distributed across households of different incomes? Although these questions sound straightforward, answering them even in the presence of abundant data is by no means simple. The first question cannot be answered without asking the more basic question of what social functions nonprofit institutions serve in the first place. Only when their output is identified is it possible to proceed to the difficult question of valuing the benefits.

The valuation of benefits is an issue familiar in the subfield known as welfare economics. In theory, the value of a good or service is equal to the amount a person would be willing to pay for it. The net benefit to a consumer can be defined as this value minus any amount actually paid, or the consumer surplus. Applying this approach is fraught with difficulties, however, as the applied work in applied welfare economics makes clear. One obvious difficulty is placing dollar values on services for which there are no comparable services that are purchased in the market. What would be the theoretical value, for example, of a special exhibit of Italian Renaissance paintings or of the services supplied by a family planning clinic? A related problem arises with benefits that may be spread widely over the population or over more than one generation. For example, how would one value a foundation grant to support an adult literacy program or a university research project in high-energy physics? Another difficulty arises when the appreciation of a service is an "acquired taste." A young person's first symphony concert may be the least appreciated over a lifetime, though it may also be the most important one as well. In practice, conceptual difficulties such as these merely add to the general problem of inadequate information. In evaluations of the distributional effects of public expenditures, the distinction between expenditures and willingness-to-pay is often ignored.[6] Similarly, in the empirical work that follows, the best that can usually be done to measure benefits is simply to calculate per capita expenditures by income class.

The second task, assessing the distributional pattern of the benefits, requires knowledge of who uses the services produced by nonprofit organizations. Although it presents data problems of its own, this is generally a much more nearly attainable objective than the first. For this reason, the authors in this volume in most cases had to be content simply to identify

6. For example, Musgrave and Musgrave (1989, 246) use total expenditures in an assessment of overall fiscal incidence although they state that consumer surplus is the correct measure of the benefits of public programs (p. 136).

the nature of the benefits and estimate the pattern of usage across the population. While this is by no means a fully satisfactory answer to the question of distributional effect, it constitutes a step forward in our knowledge of the impact of nonprofit institutions.

Philanthropic Transfers and Production

A comprehensive assessment of the impact of the nonprofit sector on the distribution of income would certainly include more than just the benefits derived from the operations of nonprofit firms. In particular, one would want to take into account the effects of both financial contributions and volunteer services, since donors often are in different income classes from those of the beneficiaries of nonprofit services. In order to illustrate the sorts of redistribution that may occur, it is useful to consider five possible roles in which individuals may find themselves. These are shown in table 1.3 along with a description of the costs and benefits to the individual that arise directly as a result of each role. The first role shown is that of a beneficiary or client of a nonprofit organization, and it is this role that figures prominently in the present book. As noted above, each study would ideally examine the distribution of the net benefits, defined as the difference between the value of the service received and any fees paid.

The second role listed in the table, that of taxpayer, seems not to be directly relevant to the nonprofit sector. It is listed partly because government funds are an important source of revenue for nonprofits and partly because the role of taxpayer provides a useful contrast with the other roles shown in the table. To the individual in the role of taxpayer, the tax burden is a clear cost.[7] The benefits of government are many, but if they are not tied to tax payments on a quid pro quo basis, tax payments per se bring no direct benefit. In studies of tax incidence, therefore, it may be exceedingly hard to determine who bears the burden of a tax, but there is no doubt that that burden—viewed separately from the benefits of government—has a negative effect on those who bear it.

As donors and volunteers, individuals provide major sources of funding and labor for nonprofit institutions. Like the role of taxpayer, each of these roles carries a cost. In the case of financial contributions, the cost is the dollar amount of the gift less any tax savings that arise from using the

---

7. Taxes are said to be "shifted" if all or part of the attendant drop in potential consumption is borne by individuals other than those who actually make the tax payment. Thus the tax burden may not be equivalent to tax liability.

TABLE 1.3 Five Possible Roles for Individuals, with Associated Costs and Benefits of Each Role

Role	Participant's Cost	Participant's Direct Benefit
Beneficiary/client of nonprofit organization	Fee, if any	Value of output received
Taxpayer	Tax burden	None
Donor	Contribution (net cost)	Unmeasurable
Volunteer	Value of time	Unmeasurable
Employee	Wages and salaries available elsewhere	Wages and salaries

charitable tax deduction.[8] In the case of volunteering, there is a cost measured in terms of the value of the person's time.[9] Both of these roles are distinctly unlike that of the role of taxpayer in that the activities are voluntarily undertaken. As such, these activities must carry with them some form of benefit or satisfaction. It is possible, for example, that voluntary gifts of money or time may bring financial rewards, political power, or prestige. Even an act of purest altruism may be thought of as bringing its own rewards, although the amount and form of such benefit is a matter of debate.[10] It is the voluntary nature of giving that makes it difficult to apply to the problem posed in this book the standard models of fiscal incidence that are used in assessing the distributional impact of government taxes and expenditures. It is nevertheless important to keep in mind that there are probably distributional consequences that arise from the funding of nonprofit organizations as well as from their operation.

One other possible role through which nonprofit organizations might have a distributional impact is employment. For example, a foundation that paid its directors extraordinary fees would be exerting a "pro-rich" effect on the distribution of income, assuming those directors inhabited high-income classes. However, to the extent that nonprofit organizations pay their employees the market wage and the kinds of skills called for are not extremely rare in the labor force, the normal functioning of the labor

8. For a discussion of the net cost of making contributions, see, for example, Clotfelter (1985, 39–43).

9. For discussions of the valuation of time and volunteer labor supply, see Menchik and Weisbrod (1981) or Clotfelter (1985, chap. 4).

10. Sen (1977), for example, argues that to assume that the benefits of altruistic acts are always assumed to be at least as great as the costs is to assume away a form of giving that may well be important, namely sacrificial giving or acting out of commitment.

market will tend to minimize any distributional effects arising from employment. In those circumstances, those who work for nonprofit institutions will be paid about what they would be paid in comparable jobs in for-profit and government organizations.[11] For this reason, the studies in this book ignore any distributional effects that occur as a result of employment, though some of these probably are in fact at work.

Incremental Effects

What exactly is meant by "the" distributional consequences of a large sector of the economy? "Compared to what?" is an understandable response.[12] There is an implicit counterfactual situation used for comparison when a question of effect is asked—the situation that would have obtained in the absence of the factor in question. In the present case, it would be quite impossible and not very useful to try to use as a point of comparison a United States without a nonprofit sector. This sector is and has been too important a fact of life for such a comparison to be very interesting. But it would not be too difficult to imagine a sector that is slightly smaller or slightly larger than the one we have now. In that vein, the studies in this volume should be seen as relevant to the evaluation of incremental changes in the size of the nonprofit sector or its components. The research here can then be seen as bearing on policies that might lead to the expansion or contraction of the nonprofit sector. What would be the distributional effects of such incremental changes in the extent of the sector? Who would benefit and who would be hurt? One might also explore the effects of more specific policies, such as changes in certain programs that help to fund nonprofit institutions. In practice, data limitations make it impossible to dis-

---

11. Of central importance here is the elasticity of supply of labor of different varieties, which in turn depends on the scarcity of the skills being demanded by nonprofit firms. An expansion of nonprofit firms that occasioned an increase in the demand for clerks, for example, would be unlikely to affect the wage level of clerks and thus would have negligible distributional effects. Similar expansions leading to increases in the demand for professors or symphony musicians, however, might affect wages, especially in the short run. For a discussion of factor market effects in the context of higher education, see Nerlove (1972, S209).

12. In one of the two analogies that he offers in his commentary, Henry Aaron compares the nonprofit sector to a water pump in a car. He argues that determining the distributional impact of the nonprofit sector is as difficult as assessing the water pump's effect on the car's horsepower. If the water pump were missing, something else would be (and certainly has been in some models) inserted to perform its function. This certainly seems to be the case of nonprofit institutions as well. However, focusing on incremental changes allows one to ask a sensible question, namely, what would be the effect of a small change in the size of the water pump, or the size of the sector?

tinguish marginal as opposed to the average beneficiaries, so the practical application of the incremental concept requires the assumption that small changes in the size of nonprofit institutions would affect beneficiaries in a way that is reflected by data on the distribution of average benefits.

General Equilibrium Adjustments

Changes in the size of the nonprofit sector, even marginal changes, would likely be accompanied by other adjustments in the economy. For example, a reduction in the number of nonprofit day-care centers might lead to an increase in the capacity of the for-profit day-care industry. Or it might stimulate local governments to provide more day-care services. Adjustments of this sort are implicit in the notion of "crowding out" that has often appeared in the economic literature on charitable giving. If donors are interested in the total amount of a public good available, an increase in government provision of that good would be expected to result in a corresponding reduction, or crowding out, of charitable giving for that purpose.[13] There is in fact some evidence of this kind of adjustment, particularly reductions in philanthropic activity in the face of significant expansions of government services. For example, Ginzburg (1962, 74–79) reported that both the financing and functions of hospitals changed following the Depression, as the government assumed an increased responsibility for supporting the treatment of indigent patients. Whether the size of government, or the for-profit sector, would adjust in response to a change in the size of the nonprofit sector is uncertain, but it is surely a question that bears on an assessment of the distributional impact of changes in the nonprofit sector. If one assumes that increases in nonprofit services come about at the expense of government services, for example, it would be important to compare the incomes of those who use government services with the incomes of those who use services offered by nonprofits and to consider whether the characteristics of marginal clients would be the same as those of the average clients. Again, the limitations imposed by data may make it impossible to consider such factors thoroughly, but it is useful to keep the possibility in mind when assessing empirical findings.

In his commentary, Henry Aaron expresses doubt that empirical studies such as those presented here can adequately capture the distributional im-

---

13. For a theoretical treatment of crowding out in the case of altruistic giving, see Andreoni (1988).

pact of changes in the size of the nonprofit sector. He argues that any such changes probably would be compensated for by other sectors, just as a decline in output by General Motors would tend to be matched by increases in the output of other manufacturers. Knowing the income distribution of GM customers will not be very helpful in determining the distributional impact of a decline in GM output, owing to these likely adjustments by other suppliers. This argument seems especially apt when applied to subsectors where there exist comparable suppliers in the public or the for-profit sectors, such as health and education. Two characteristics of these subsectors increase the chance that variations in the size of the nonprofit sector will tend to be matched by countervailing variations in other sectors, with minimal impact on the distribution of benefits. First, to an extent greater than most organizations in the other subsectors, nonprofit institutions in health care and education tend to provide services that are quite similar to their government (and for-profit, in the case of health) counterparts. Second, they receive a significant share of their revenues in the form of earmarked government funds. To the extent that such funds will be spent on the same population regardless of provider, the clienteles of nonprofit providers tend to look more like those of other institutions using the same kinds of funds. This degree of similarity may exist as well in some human services institutions, but is decidedly not present in religion, the arts, and foundations. To summarize, the empirical studies in this book for the most part present evidence on the income level of current clients of nonprofit institutions. To what extent the distributional impact of changes in the nonprofit sector would parallel these existing patterns depends in part on whether there exist similar for-profit or government providers.

III. The Distribution of Charitable Contributions

Although the studies in this volume focus on the distribution of the outputs of nonprofit firms, their findings are obviously relevant to the larger question of the distributional impact of the entire philanthropic sector, which includes charitable giving. It is useful, therefore, to include here some summary information on such giving, especially on patterns of contributions by income level. The bulk of charitable contributions are made by living individuals; these amounted to some $80.8 billion in 1987. Much smaller in size were bequests, which totaled $6.6 billion, and corporate donations, which were $4.6 billion (Hodgkinson and Weitzman 1989, 71). Table 1.4 summarizes data on individual contributions taken from household sur-

TABLE 1.4 Patterns of Charitable Giving by Income

Income	Volunteers as % of all households 1989	Average Contribution, 1989		Percentage of Contribution to Religious Organizations	
		Total	As % of Income	1989	1987
Under $10,000	30	$ 186	2.5	67	82
$10,000–19,000	42	316	1.9	69	83
$20,000–29,999	56	560	2.1	64	69
$30,000–39,999	65	732	2.0	69	72
$40,000–49,999	67	702	1.5	71	64
$50,000–74,000	63	936	1.5	62	63
$75,000–99,999	62	2,575	2.9	72	63
$100,000 and over	74	2,512	2.4	66	51

SOURCE: Hodgkinson and Weitzman (1990, table 1.17, pp. 41–42).

veys in 1987 and 1989. The first column shows the percentage of households who reported doing any volunteer work during the year; this percentage generally rises with income. The next column shows average contributions for each income group and confirms the findings of other studies that contributions generally rise with income. Giving as a percentage of income, shown in the third column, has the familiar U-shape (see, for example, Clotfelter and Steuerle 1981).

The only aspect of the 1989 figures that do not appear to correspond to other data on giving is the split between religious and other giving. The table's last two columns show the percentage of contributions by income class reportedly made to religious organizations. Whereas the 1989 figures show little variation in this percentage among the income classes, figures based on a similar survey in 1987 show this percentage declining with income. In fact, all of the previous studies touching on this question indicate that the importance of religious giving does decline with income. One of these was a national survey on philanthropy taken in 1973. Data from that survey, which are based on the four major gifts made by respondents, are summarized in table 1.5. This table suggests that the distribution of gifts of the most affluent households is quite different from those of lower- and middle-income households. At higher income, giving to colleges, universities, and cultural institutions becomes much more prominent.[14]

14. Other sources of data on the distribution of contributions by type of donee are the 1962 *Statistics of Income* and a 1978 survey done by the Gallup Organization for CONVO, survey

TABLE 1.5 Percentage Distribution of Contributions, Major Donees, by Income, 1973

| Income | Religion | Education | | Combined Appeals | Medical and Health | Culture | Other Major | Not Identified[a] | Total |
		Higher	Other						
$0–9,000	59(%)	1(%)	0(%)	2(%)	3(%)	0(%)	2(%)	33(%)	100(%)
$10,000–19,999	67	1	0	3	3	0	4	22	100
$20,000–29,999	59	2	1	5	4	0	10	19	100
$30,000–49,999	42	5	7	6	3	3	6	28	100
$50,000–99,999	16	9	1	10	11	4	19	30	100
$100,000–199,999	10	14	5	9	10	5	6	41	100
$200,000–499,999	8	27	6	10	11	6	8	24	100
$500,000 or more	9	24	3	6	6	9	16	27	100
All	46	5	2	6	5	2	8	26	100

SOURCE: Morgan et al. (1977, table 38).
[a]Information as to donee was obtained only for the four major gifts of each donor; therefore additional giving could not be allocated to donee categories.

In considering the distributional impact of the voluntary sector as a whole, one would ideally want to consider these flows of charitable contributions as well as the benefits produced by nonprofit organizations. As implied by the discussion of table 1.3, however, information on voluntary contributions provides evidence on only part of their distributional impact. While the dollar amount of charitable contributions generally reflects the value of the benefit to the donee (except in cases where gifts are earmarked for purposes not highly valued by the donee), it does not reveal the extent to which donors might benefit from their own contributions.[15] If, despite this conceptual roadblock, one wanted to calculate a broader measure of distributional impact than that contained in the studies in this volume, one might use some simplifying assumption regarding the net value of contributions. One possible assumption would be that donors receive no benefit and thus that contributions can be treated in the same way as taxes in studies of fiscal incidence; another would be that donors receive benefits equal to the net dollar cost of their gifts. If the first assumption were adopted, one could compare the flows of contributions and tax revenues going to support nonprofit activities with the benefits flowing out. To give a rough idea of the pattern of those two sources of funding, table 1.6 presents estimates of the percentage distribution of federal income taxes, the major source of federal revenue, and contributions by five broad income classes. The figures show that households at higher income levels provide a disproportionate share of both of these sources of funding. Therefore, if it were found that the per-capital benefits of the services of nonprofit organizations were, say, equal across the income spectrum, the net distributional effect of the nonprofit sector would be pro-poor. However, if one were to adopt the alternative assumption that donors derive benefits from their gifts, such a conclusion would not be justified.

While information on the distribution of charitable contributions and tax revenues is useful in describing the sources of funding for the nonprofit sector, it is not sufficient for judging the overall distributional consequences of the voluntary sector of the economy. For that reason, the studies

---

GO 7993, July 1979. The former is based on itemized returns only and showed a marked decline in the percentage of giving to religious organizations. The latter included few high-income respondents but showed that the percentage of giving to religious organizations was smallest in the highest income class for which detailed data were given, the $20,000 to $50,000 class.

15. The benefit to the donee is the actual dollar value of the gifts, whereas the cost to the donor, shown in table 1.3, is the net-of-tax cost.

TABLE 1.6 Percentage Distribution of Households, Income, Federal
Income Taxes, and Contributions by Income Class, 1988

Income Class	Households	Income	Income taxes	Contributions
Under $10,000	17	5	1	3
$10,000 under 30,000	37	25	16	21
$30,000 under 50,000	25	25	21	24
$50,000 under 100,000	18	24	27	28
$100,000 and over	3	21	36	24
Total	100	100	100	100

SOURCE: U.S. Bureau of the Census, *Current Population Reports*, series P-60, no. 166, *Money Income and Property Status in the U.S. 1988*, table 3; Michael Strudler and Emily Ring, "Individual Income Tax Returns, Preliminary Data, 1988," *SOI Bulletin* 9 (Spring 1990): 15, 25; Hodgkinson and Weitzman (1990, 41–42).
NOTE: Calculations of contributions are based on average contributions from surveys for 1987 and 1989 reported in Hodgkinson and Weitzman by income class, except for the $100,000 and above class, for which itemized deductions in 1988 are used. Percentage distribution of income and income taxes are based on categories of adjusted gross income of taxpayers.

in this book focus on the distribution of the outputs of nonprofit organizations. Still, the studies do provide a great deal of new information about who the beneficiaries of nonprofit activities are and, thus, how the distribution of these benefits corresponds to the distribution of funding sources.

IV. Summary of the Findings

Despite the important simplifying assumptions employed in the empirical studies in this volume, it will soon be clear to any careful reader that the findings of these studies are still by no means simple. As in so many things, the closer one gets to the object of study, the more diversity one discovers. As subsectors within the nonprofit sector differ from each other, even more so do individual institutions within the subsectors. They differ in both function and clientele. Other factors also conspire to prevent easy summary of the findings, among them the difficulty of measuring outputs and the unevenness of data on the income level of beneficiaries. Nevertheless, these studies do bring together an unprecedented amount of information on the distributional aspects of nonprofit services.

David Salkever and Richard Frank's study of the massive health subsector ably illustrates how the diversity among institutions prevents easy generalization regarding the distributional pattern of benefits. This subsector is distinguished by the coexistence of nonprofit, government, and for-profit providers. And, as noted above, the nonprofits in this subsector rely to a great extent on revenues from patient fees, third-party insurance payments, and government health programs. Salkever and Frank look separately at community hospitals, nursing homes, mental health institutions, and programs providing alcohol and drug treatment. How the nonprofit providers compare to their public and for-profit private counterparts in serving low-income patients differs across these types of institutions. The authors find that the clienteles of nonprofit and for-profit community hospitals are similar but that hospitals run by state and local governments serve a higher proportion of uninsured or poor patients. Among nursing homes, nonprofits tend to have the lowest concentration of Medicaid, signifying low-income, patients among the three types of providers. In the mental health area, nonprofits lie between public and for-profit providers in their tendency to serve the uninsured and those under Medicaid, but in outpatient care their clientele tends to be more affluent than both public and for-profit providers. Among alcohol and drug treatment providers, public facilities again tend to lead in their tendency to serve the poor, with nonprofits taking a middle position among the three types.

With the exception of proprietary vocational schools, there are few for-profit educational institutions, so Saul Schwartz and Sandra Baum's chapter on the education subsector uses public institutions as the point of comparison with nonprofits. Their study looks first at elementary and secondary schools and then at colleges and universities. Evidence on the income level of elementary and secondary school students shows that those attending private nonprofit schools are on average somewhat more affluent than students in public schools, and this is especially true of non-Catholic nonprofit schools. Schwartz and Baum go beyond this comparison of clienteles to examine evidence on the educational effects on students of attending different types of schools. In particular, they compare school outcomes of students in public schools versus those in Catholic schools. They cite evidence that Catholic schools are associated with slightly higher achievement gains than public schools, although the differences are small and clouded by difficult issues of interpretation. There is also some evidence that Catholic schools may hold a special advantage for students from low-income families.

At the college level, Schwartz and Baum show that there are clear differences between public and private institutions in the average income level of students, though there are certainly affluent students who attend public institutions, just as there are poor students at the most expensive private colleges and universities. As in the case of health care, there is no readily available measure of educational benefits, but the authors do present measures of subsidies to students, defined as the difference between average instructional costs and the out-of-pocket costs borne by students and their families. Among students attending private institutions, the average amount of these subsidies falls with family income, owing to the pro-poor nature of scholarship programs. Once the lower college enrollment rates of the poor are factored into the equation, the private college subsidy per young person increases with income, though not as sharply as it would in the absence of need-based scholarship programs. By comparison, the subsidy available from public colleges and universities, per young person, also increases with family income, in line with earlier results by Hansen and Weisbrod (1969).

In contrast to the health and education subsectors, few institutions outside of the nonprofit sector resemble religious congregations. In his study, Jeff Biddle distinguishes two kinds of services produced by religious congregations: those provided to members of the congregation and those provided to others. The first of these are "clublike" services, which include most so-called sacramental activities. Biddle estimates that these activities account for about 70 percent of congregational spending, including most of the costs of buildings, maintenance, utilities, and staff salaries. Of the remaining 30 percent, Biddle estimates that about one-fifth is directed toward expenditures that benefit the poor. There is also some redistribution that occurs within congregations, with the relatively affluent subsidizing the less well-off, though the degree of such intracongregational redistribution is probably less when members are compared on the basis of lifetime income. When these forms of redistribution are taken together, Biddle concludes that neither the rich nor the poor consume a disproportionate share of the subsector's expenditures. One other form of redistribution that came up in discussion is that from the unreligious to the religious. Because the tax code allows expenditures for religious purposes to be deducted but not other forms of nonbusiness expenditures, it has a redistributive as well as an incentive effect.

Lester Salamon's chapter deals with the variagated subsector usually referred to as social services or human services. Organizations in this subsector provide such services as child day-care, job training and vocational rehabilitation, residential care, adoption services, foster care, legal services, and advocacy. Salamon's data come from a survey of 1,474 organizations in which the agencies were asked about the composition of their clienteles. Of all the agencies surveyed, 27 percent said that most of their clients were poor, defined as below the poverty line. Those most likely to focus primarily on the poor were in the areas of employment, training and income support (53 percent), and legal rights and advocacy (43 percent). Salamon uses these survey data to test several theories about the behavior of nonprofit organizations. Among his findings, one especially strong one is the high correlation between the agency's orientation toward the poor and the source of its funding, with those receiving federal aid more likely to focus on service to the poor. Like most of the organizations in the health and education subsectors, many of those in this subsector are profoundly influenced by their reliance on government funding.

In his chapter on nonprofit institutions in arts and culture, Dick Netzer examines data from several national surveys of attendance and participation related to the arts and other cultural institutions. There is good reason, he argues, to take survey data in this area with a grain of salt, but data from them can nevertheless be useful in examining patterns of participation across income classes. As might be expected, the proportion of households who take part in arts activities such as visiting museums and attending performances rises with income. In addition, the average number of visits also rises with income; these are highly income-elastic activities. This income effect is perhaps most evident in ballet and opera. Those with incomes of $50,000, which comprised only about 16 percent of all households, accounted for approximately one-third of ballet attendance and over 40 percent of opera attendance. Yet the survey data show that there was participation at all income levels, not just at the top. And when Netzer compares these participation patterns to the distribution of contributions and taxes paid, he finds no evidence that the affluent enjoy benefits that are disproportionate to their payments. There is little doubt that the distribution of benefits in this subsector favors the affluent more than in any other area. In passing, Netzer also notes the possibility that government subsidies to the arts may produce quite sizable benefits in the form of income for some star performers.

In no other subsector is it more difficult to identify the "clients" than it is in studying foundations. The externalities, the broad and ill-defined effects that certainly apply to some other institutions seem to predominate in the case of foundations. Partly because of the difficulty of assigning benefits in this case, Robert Margo's chapter was commissioned with the intention that it would take a somewhat more historical approach than the other essays, in that way allowing a longer perspective with which to judge effects. Margo uses data on foundation assets and grants to assess comparative rates of expenditure. His findings suggest, as has some previous work, that the payout requirements contained in the 1969 tax reform act had the effect of increasing average payout rates. He also examines the geographical distribution of foundation grants but notes the difficulty in matching the grants with their ultimate beneficiaries. After examining the stated purpose of a number of foundation grants, he concludes that few grants clearly benefit low-income groups directly, although there remains the possibility that grants may have important indirect benefits not immediately evident from a short description.

V. ANSWERS AND QUESTIONS

The purpose of these empirical studies is to examine the distributional effects of nonprofit institutions, or rather of our system of reliance on such institutions. This is not to say that redistribution is or should be the primary objective of the nonprofit sector or that its redistributive effects should be the principal criterion for judging policy toward the sector. Distributional effect is one relevant criterion, however. It is relevant to the larger question of whether we should keep or modify the rules by which we regulate, tax, and subsidize activities of the voluntary sector. These studies focus on quantifiable measures of distributional effect, largely based on identifying the clients of various nonprofit institutions. What is the usefulness of studies such as these? If one hopes to determine the ultimate effect on the income distribution of a change in the reliance on the nonprofit sector, complete with the effects that would result from the adjustments in demand and supply in the economy, the results of these studies will not be satisfactory. However, if knowing the first-round impact of marginal changes in the extent of nonprofit activities is useful in assessing current policy toward nonprofit institutions, these findings will be useful.

Three general conclusions emerge from these studies, taken together. First, there is great diversity within the nonprofit sector, and no overarching conclusions about distributional impact can be made. This said, a second finding is one stated in the negative: in no subsector is there evidence that benefits are dramatically skewed away from the poor and toward the affluent. Conversely, there is also evidence that relatively few nonprofit institutions serve the poor as a primary clientele. A third general conclusion is that an institution's source of funding appears to be important in determining the distribution of its benefits. Institutions which receive funding that is tied to certain objectives or recipients will tend to make expenditures reflecting those requirements.

Many questions remain, however. Most fundamentally, we have only the most rudimentary understanding of the outputs of nonprofit institutions—their forms, how broadly they are distributed, and how they should be valued. A second unanswered question relates to the general equilibrium effects that would likely accompany a change in policy toward the nonprofit sector. While theoretical models could be worked out on the order of tax incidence analysis, this approach is quite unlikely to yield satisfactory empirical answers. Another question has to do with how we treat charitable contributions in considering the distributional effects in the voluntary sector. Although contributions certainly provide an important source of funding, they are voluntarily made and thus presumably yield benefits of their own. What is the nature of these benefits, and how might they be compared to those received by the donees? Finally, the studies contained here raise the fundamental question of the nature of nonprofit organizations. For many institutions it is possible that this designation is little more than an accident of history and that tax laws and patterns of government funding have a greater impact on the organization's behavior than characteristics intrinsic to the nonprofit form. As questions such as these reveal, it is hard to study the issue of distributional effect without bumping into other basic issues about the objectives and behavior of these organizations.

2

Health Services

David S. Salkever and Richard G. Frank

According to official U.S. Government estimates (Health Care Financing Administration, Office of National Cost Estimates 1990), the personal health services sector (henceforth termed the health sector) accounted for 9.8 percent of the GNP in 1988.[1] The firms and organizations that make up this health sector are diverse. Many professionals (physicians, dentists, physical therapists, etc.) provide services through small for-profit firms. The same types of professional services, however, may also be provided by very large nonprofit organizations (for example, outpatient physician services provided by large urban hospitals). In some parts of the sector (such as psychiatric hospitals), state governments are important providers of services. In other parts of the sector (for example, outpatient treatment for mental illnesses), local governments play an important role through clinics which they operate. In still other parts of the sector (such as acute care hospitals), nonprofit providers predominate. These firms are also diverse in terms of the range of products and services they provide and the populations they serve.

Our examination of the role of nonprofit providers in the health sector will be, of necessity, quite selective. We focus on four types of services where nonprofit providers have an important share of the market: nonfederal community hospitals, nursing homes, alcohol and drug abuse treat-

Financial support from Grant no. HS 05614 from the Agency for Health Care Research and Policy, Grant no. AA 08364 from the National Intitute on Alcholism and Alcohol Abuse, Grant no. 44407 from the National Institute for Mental Health, and from the Center for the Study of Philanthropy and Voluntarism, Duke University, is gratefully acknowledged. We are indebted to Diane Ferro, Chuan-Fa Guo, and Alison Jones for their help in preparing this paper.

1. When research and construction expenditures reported separately in the U.S. government figures are included, the share of the GNP rises to 10.7.

ment services, and specialty mental health services.[2] Information about these four groups of providers is presented in table 2.1. Community hospitals are clearly largest of the four groups in terms of relative share of health sector spending and in terms of nonprofit market share. Nursing homes are the second largest in terms of their share of health sector spending (9.1 percent), but the market share of nonprofit nursing homes is relatively small (22.5 percent). The two smallest subsectors, specialty mental health services and alcohol and drug treatment services, are distinctive in that both show large nonprofit and public market shares and small for-profit market shares.[3]

We exclude from our analysis major portions of the health sector (for example, retail drug stores) where the role of nonprofit providers is negligible. Some types of services where nonprofit providers are important suppliers will be largely ignored because of data limitations; for example, while nonprofit hospitals provide an important fraction of outpatient medical services through their outpatient clinics and emergency rooms, we do not focus on these services because detailed data on the patients served and finances of hospital outpatient and emergency services are not generally available.

It is also worth noting that nonprofit firms in the health sector constitute a very large share of the total activity by nonprofits in the economy as a whole. For example, of the total current operating expenditures of $261.5 billion by nonprofit firms in 1987, 51.3 percent was accounted for by nonprofit firms in the health sector (Hodgkinson and Weitzman 1989, table 3, p. 43).

The role of nonprofit firms in the health sector has attracted considerable attention from policymakers, legislators, and the courts in the past

2. For the purposes of our analysis, community hospitals are defined to include all hospitals where the average length of an inpatient stay is less than 30 days; excluded are all federal hospitals, hospitals that specialize in psychiatric treatment, hospitals that specialize in alcoholism and chemical dependency treatment, chronic disease hospitals, and units of institutions (such as prison hospitals or college infirmaries). Our definition of community hospitals corresponds to that of the American Hospital Association (1988). Specialty mental health services include psychiatric specialty hospitals, psychiatric units of general hospitals, and other nonhospital clinics and facilities specializing in mental health services. (Private psychiatric practices are not included.) Alcohol and drug treatment providers include hospitals, clinics, and other organized treatment programs; private practitioners are not included.

3. Note that there are considerable overlaps among these four groups of providers. For example, a community hospital that has a specialized psychiatric inpatient unit and an alcohol detoxification service would be included in three of our four groups (all but nursing homes).

TABLE 2.1 Size of Subsectors Relative to the Total Health Sector and Nonprofit Market Shares within each Subsector

	Community Hospitals		Nursing Homes	Specialty Mental Health Services				Alcohol and Drug Treatment
	Total	Inpatient		Total	Inpatient	Outpatient	Partial	
Percent of Health Sector Spending	38.1	31.1	9.1	4.3	NA	NA	NA	0.8
					Market Share (%) of:			
Nonprofit	72.8	73.0	22.5	NA	48.8	62.3	70.8	59.0
For-profit	8.6	8.8	69.3	NA	10.8	0.8	1.3	11.7
Public	18.6	18.2	8.2	NA	40.4	36.9	27.9	29.2
Market Share Measure	Adjusted Inpatient Days	Inpatient Days	Inpatient Days		Inpatient Discharge	Patients	Patients	Patients

SOURCES AND EXPLANATION OF DATA: Health sector spending (i.e., spending on personal health care in 1986 and 1987), community hospital spending (i.e., community hospital revenues in 1987), and expenditures on nursing homes for 1987 are taken from Health Care Financing Administration, Office of National Cost Estimates (1990, 7). Inpatient day figures (adjusted and unadjusted) for community hospitals are reported in American Hospital Association (1988, 7). (Adjusted inpatient days are inpatient days inflated to reflect the fraction of outpatient revenues in total patient revenues). Nursing home inpatient days are reported in National Center for Health Statistics, E. Hing, E. Sekscenski, and G. Strahan (1989, 8). Specialty mental health expenditures for 1986 are reported in National Institute of Mental Health (1990, 55). Fiscal 1987 revenues for alcohol and drug treatment units are estimated from reported revenues in National Institute on Drug Abuse and National Institute on Alcohol Abuse and Alcoholism (1989) adjusted to include an estimate of revenues (based on numbers of clients) for units with missing revenue data. Data on public providers for acute care hospitals and specialty mental health services do not include federal facilities; nursing home and alcohol and drug treatment unit data do include federal facilities.

several years for diverse reasons. "Privatization" of health services has occurred through the shrinking of public sector providers and the shifting of patients primarily to nonprofit providers. While this trend has been most dramatic in mental health services, it has also occurred to a lesser degree in general hospital services. What are the implications of this shift? Are nonprofit firms providing the same types of services to the same populations that were previously provided by public facilities or does privatization bring with it a decline in the supply of "community services" and a decline in access to care for the uninsured?[4]

A second reason for concern with the nonprofits' role is the growth in private and public third-party financing over the past several decades. From 1960 to 1987, the percent of personal health care spending paid for directly by patients out-of-pocket dropped from 55.9 to 23.6 percent (Health Care Financing Administration, Office of National Cost Estimates 1990, table 16, p. 31). This meant that many nonpaying patients became paying patients, so the charitable role of the nonprofits and the importance of philanthropy as a revenue source eroded. Accordingly, the propriety of continuing tax-exempt status for nonprofit providers was called into question. The scrutiny of nonprofit tax exemptions was further encouraged by health care providers branching out into other businesses (for instance, health clubs, pharmacies, motels) with the resulting claims of unfair competition by their for-profit competitors in these other businesses (Lumsdon 1991). The clearest manifestation of concern with the rationale for preferred tax treatment is the "Charity Care and Hospital Tax-Exempt Status Reform Act" (H.R. 5686) which was introduced on September 24, 1990, by Congressman Roybal.[5]

A third concern relates to the recent appearance of more vigorous competition, and cost containment pressures in the health sector have caused observers to wonder whether the cross-subsidization of "good works" that nonprofits were presumed to practice could in fact be long maintained. If

4. The usage of the term "community services" in the current policy discussions is generally consistent with the standard economic notion of public goods. A consensus as to precisely which services fall into this category, however, has yet to be achieved. A detailed recent effort to delineate these services in the case of hospitals is reported in General Accounting Office (1990).

5. This bill proposes computing the value of tax advantages received by each nonprofit hospital and requiring hospitals to provide dollar volumes of uncompensated community services in proportion to this value; hospitals that failed to meet this requirement would be subjected to a special excise tax.

not, and if nonprofit and for-profit providers converged in behavior, once again the justification for tax-exempt status would be called into question.

I. CONCEPTUAL APPROACH

For the purposes of our analysis, the beneficiaries of nonprofit health services providers are defined as the recipients of services subsidized by these providers, where subsidy is taken to mean that the marginal revenue received by the provider for a particular service is less than its marginal cost. The reader should note an important distinction relative to other major portions of the nonprofit sector discussed in this volume: the great majority of the clients of nonprofit health services providers are not beneficiaries according to this definition. While these clients presumably derive consumer surplus from their purchases, it is reasonable to presume that they (or their insurers) are paying prices for these services that are not below marginal cost. In contrast, services provided to beneficiaries (as defined above) must be subsidized through private donations, use of the provider's own financial reserves, or cross-subsidization by nonbeneficiaries.[6]

An an empirical matter, applying our definition of beneficiaries is not entirely straightforward. Accurate measurement of marginal costs of services would seem to require application of econometric methods; such an exercise is beyond the scope of this chapter. Instead, we simply assume that average cost is roughly equal to marginal cost; this assumption is supported by the general result in econometric studies in the health sector that economies and diseconomies of scale are small or nonexistent (Friedman and Pauly 1983).

We also will apply our definition on a group rather than individual basis where the group is defined by the source of payment for services.[7] We focus on groups for whom average payments for services are substantially below costs. In particular, we examine distributional characteristics of uninsured clients and of clients covered by Medicaid or by other public programs

6. One might also view persons whose services are financed by a government grant to the nonprofit provider as a beneficiary according to our definition when the amount of the grant is independent of the number of people served. We discuss this situation in more detail below.

7. Because the types of services rendered in the health sector are very heterogeneous, it is not feasible for providers to apply price schedules that accommodate much of this heterogeneity. Some individual clients with problems that are complex and costly to treat receive services the cost of which substantially exceeds their billed charges. We do not attempt to identify these individuals in our analysis. While some might argue that nonprofit providers are less likely to avoid serving these clients (that is, they are less likely to "cream-skim"), the data available to us do not permit an investigation of this possibility.

which do not pay the providers amounts sufficient to cover the incremental costs of services.[8]

It has long been asserted that Medicaid programs have been paying below-average costs for hospital services. Casual examination of data on Medicaid expenditures and average costs per hospital day suggest that in 1981 Medicaid programs paid rates that were on average approximately 70 percent of average costs (U.S. Department of Health and Human Services 1983). The cost function estimates by Friedman and Pauly (1983) imply that marginal costs are between 85 and 90 percent of average costs. This suggests that Medicaid rates are below both average and marginal costs. Most systematic evidence is presented by Hadley and Feder (1985). They show that in 1982, markups of revenues over average per diem costs for Medicaid patients amounted to 89.7 percent. This offers support for the view that services to Medicaid patients often involve subsidy by institutions providing that care. Evidence for subsidies to persons covered under other public programs, however, is less substantial. In particular, while one might conjecture that state and local public indigent care program funding is below costs, systematic evidence on this point is not, to our knowledge, available.

Care for uninsured persons is typically financed through charity funds, through cross-subsidization by other groups of patients, or by providers absorbing losses directly. While these persons may in fact pay for a portion of the cost of their treatment, evidence cited below suggests this portion is quite small.

It should also be noted that the general public may be "beneficiaries" of nonprofit providers in the sense that these providers may supply some services that could be viewed as public goods (for example, standby treatment capacity, admission for treatment of public inebriates who would otherwise cause public nuisance). For these public goods, distributional questions are much less relevant, since most people in the community place presumably some value on these services and since they are not charged directly for them. Thus, we devote little attention to distributional aspects of providing these public goods.

The counterfactual situations that we use for defining the impact of the nonprofit sector are described by a change in ownership status (from non-

---

8. A third possible beneficiary group are the individuals noted in footnote 6. By defining beneficiaries in terms of groups, we also do not differentiate between persons within the same insurance pool whose benefits exceed premiums and those whose benefits do not exceed premiums. Thus, the former individuals are not defined as beneficiaries in our analysis.

profit to for-profit or from nonprofit to government) of a small segment of the nonprofit providers' market share. It is assumed that this marginal change in ownership status would have no effect on the quantity and quality of services received by "nonbeneficiary" groups (whose payments cover the incremental costs of their services) and that the principal effect of the ownership shift is to alter the supply of services rendered to beneficiary groups. We assume a persistent state of excess demand for services by people in these beneficiary groups so that providers do not face any demand-side constraints in deciding how much and what kinds of services to provide to them.[9] We also assume that any change in the degree of cross-subsidization by nonbeneficiary groups as a result of this ownership change has no (or negligible) effect on the quantity and quality of services purchased by the individuals in these nonbeneficiary groups.[10]

The consequences of a marginal change in ownership status can be divided into direct and indirect effects. We estimate the direct effect to be the response of the provider whose ownership status changes in supplying services to beneficiary groups, assuming no change in the behavior of other providers. Our estimate of this direct effect is based on simple comparisons of nonprofit versus for-profit versus government providers in serving these beneficiary groups. The indirect effects are the responses of other providers, whose ownership status is unchanged, to the direct effects just described. These indirect effects have been addressed in the literature on "crowding-out," and we shall review the results of this literature and their implications in section 7. As will be clear from that review, most of the relevant "crowding-out" studies examine indirect effects in the private sector; information on public sector responses is more limited.[11]

Stated in summary terms, our analysis focuses on the implications of changes in ownership for the supply of subsidized care to beneficiaries where the subsidies are provided by the suppliers themselves. If there are differences in the propensity of for-profit versus nonprofit versus public

9. Note the difference between these assumptions and the standard "differential incidence" analysis, where changes in financing arrangements are assumed to have no effect on the quantities of services consumed.

10. The distributional impact on nonbeneficiaries of changes in the extent of cross-subsidization are also ignored in our analysis.

11. Our distinction between direct and indirect effects is obviously related to the distinction between partial and general equilibrium effects. The latter, however, are the ultimate result of a sequence that includes direct effects, first-order indirect effects, feedback effects from the first-order indirect effects, and so on. The literature on "crowding-out" generally does not address these ultimate general equilibrium effects.

firms to use the economic rents available to them to subsidize care for beneficiaries, changes in the ownership distribution of suppliers will affect the flow of this subsidized care. (We exclude consideration of tax subsidies paid by the general public to the providers; we assume the supply of these subsidies is not strongly dependent on the ownership of the suppliers to whom they are paid.)[12]

II. Income Levels of Uninsured Persons and Medicaid Recipients

The data presented below comparing nonprofit versus for-profit versus government providers in serving beneficiary groups generally do not contain descriptive information on the characteristics of individuals within these beneficiary groups. Therefore, to understand the distributional significance of serving these beneficiary groups, we first present information (in table 2.2) on income levels of individuals in these groups. As would be expected, these data show that in 1987 almost four-fifths of persons under 65 who report Medicaid coverage are below the poverty line, with the remainder of these persons divided almost equally between the near-poor (income between one and two times the poverty line) and the nonpoor. Among persons with only Medicaid coverage (81.9 percent of all persons with Medicaid coverage in March 1987), the concentration among the poor is greater and the relative share of the nonpoor if much smaller. Comparing 1984 with 1987 data suggests that Medicaid became more concentrated among the poor over this three-year-period. For the uninsured under age 65, the data suggest that approximately one-third are below the poverty line, while almost 30 percent are near poor. Comparing the data in the 1984 to 1987 period suggests a modest increase in the share of nonpoor among the uninsured. Note, however, that only 15 percent of the general population under age 65 is poor and less than 20 percent are near poor.

---

12. The reader should also note the contrast between our approach and the implicit assumption which is the basis for the commentary by Henry Aaron. In particular, Aaron simply assumes that the supply of these subsidies will not be affected by changes in ownership and, therefore, he logically concludes that comparisons by ownership type of the level of these supplier-financed subsidies currently provided is not informative. (See, for example, his water-pump analogy and the comments following it.) In our view, Aaron's implicit assumption is inconsistent with the data presented. A more extreme interpretation of Aaron's comments is that he implicitly assumes no change in aggregate (tax-financed plus supplier-financed) subsidies can occur in response to ownership changes because any change in supplier-financed subsidies is always exactly offset by tax-financed subsidies. This assumption of complete "crowd-out" is clearly not supported by the empirical literature on the subject.

TABLE 2.2 Percentage Distribution of Uninsured Persons and Persons
Covered by Medicaid by Income Status Relative to Poverty-level Income
(Persons Age 0–64 Only)

	Ratio of Family Income to Poverty Level			
	Under 1.0	1.0 to 2.0	2.0 and Over	Total
March 1986 Current Population Survey Data				
Uninsured	33.0	29.7	37.3	100.0
General Population	15.1	18.5	66.3	100.0
March 1987 Current Population Survey Data				
Uninsured	29.7	29.6	40.7	100.0
Medicaid	79.1	11.5	9.4	100.0
Medicaid Only	85.5	9.8	4.8	100.0
1984 National Health Interview Survey Data				
Uninsured	40.3	30.7	29.0	100.0
Medicaid Only	74.9	13.6	11.5	100.0

SOURCES: March 1987 data are computed from Congressional Research Service (1988),
tables A-11 and A-12, pp. 305–6. (Income from this source is defined as "pre-welfare" income.) Data for 1984 are computed from Jones and Salkever (1988, 27); data for March
1986 are computed from General Accounting Office (1989, table 2.3, p. 19).

Thus, relative to other groups in the population, the groups identified as
beneficiaries are clearly concentrated among the poor and near-poor.[13]

III. COMMUNITY HOSPITALS

By far, the largest group of nonprofit firms within the economy is the private nonprofit (or "voluntary") hospitals. Figures presented by Weisbrod
(1988, 179–81) indicate that these hospitals accounted for more than 40
percent of all employees and more than 45 percent of all expenses among
tax-exempt service firms in 1977. Data for 1985 (Hodgkinson and Weitzman 1989, 46) indicate that hospitals incur 51 percent of all personnel
expenses reported by 501(c) (3) tax-exempt organizations and 49.7 percent of all current operating expenses of these organizations. These hospitals are also, of course, the most important type of nonprofit firm within
the health sector. Hospitals in general accounted for 44.3 percent of per-

13. Persons over age 65 were excluded from the data in table 2.2 since they accounted in
March 1987 for less than 1 percent of the uninsured, only 14 percent of persons with Medi-
caid coverage, and virtually none of the persons with Medicaid coverage only (Congressional
Research Service 1988, 306).

TABLE 2.3 Ownership Structure of U.S. Community Hospitals, 1988

	Hospitals	Beds (000)	Admissions (000)	Expenses ($ mil)
Nonprofit	3,242	668	22,939	124,703
For-profit	790	104	3,090	15,545
Government (nonfederal)	1,501	175	5,424	28,474
Total	5,533	947	31,453	168,722

SOURCE: American Hospital Association, *Hospital Statistics,* 1989–90 edition.

sonal health services expenditures in 1988 (Health Care Financing Administration, Office of National Cost Estimates 1990, 25). Within that total for all hospitals, federal hospitals accounted for 7 percent of revenues, nonfederal community hospitals accounted for 86.1 percent, and other nonfederal hospitals accounted for the remaining 6.9 percent (Health Care Financing Administration, Office of National Cost Estimates 1990, 7). The principal source of hospital care to the general population is clearly the nonfederal "community" hospital. Information on these hospitals reported in table 2.3 demonstrates the dominant position of private nonprofit firms within this group of hospitals. They account for 58.6 percent of community hospitals, 70.5 percent of beds, 72.9 percent of admissions, and 73.9 percent of expenses.

Also note that nonfederal government hospitals are the second largest ownership group among community hospitals and are nearly twice as large in aggregate as the for-profit community hospitals. (Almost all of such government hospitals are local government facilities.) Relative shares have been changing, however. In 1983, nonfederal government hospitals accounted for 18.5 percent of all community hospital expenses while by 1988 their share fell to 16.9 percent. Over the same five years, the for-profit share of expenses increased from 7.9 percent to 9.2 percent, while the nonprofit share rose by 0.4 percent.[14]

"Uncompensated Care" and Medicaid Revenues

The provision of care to beneficiaries, whom we have defined to be uninsured persons and Medicaid recipients, can be measured in several different ways. One approach is to examine the dollar volume of charges for

14. Both the slow decline in the public hospital share and the more rapid rise in the forprofit share have been the source of concern over the implications of "privatization."

services rendered to patients who are uninsured or covered by Medicaid. Data on the dollar volume of charges for services rendered to these patients, however, are not readily available at the national level. Thus, the dollar volume of "uncompensated care" (bad debt plus charges to charity care patients) is typically used to measure services to the uninsured. While some bad debt is accounted for by insured persons who fail to pay out-of-pocket charges not covered by their insurance, empirical evidence suggests that the bulk of bad debt is incurred by persons with no insurance.[15] In the case of Medicaid patients, the dollar volume of actual revenues from Medicaid can be used at least to measure relative differences in services by hospital ownership, even though our maintained hypothesis is that the Medicaid revenues actually received do not cover incremental costs of these services.

National data for 1987 that compare public and private nonfederal hospitals show that uncompensated care accounts for 14 percent of total charges to patients in public hospitals but only 4.8 percent of charges in private hospitals (Health Care Financing Administration, Office of National Cost Estimates 1990, 6). Community hospitals, as defined here, account for 92.6 percent of spending by nonfederal hospitals. Nonprofit hospitals comprise almost 90 percent of spending in private community hospitals. Therefore, the large public versus private differential in uncompensated care percentages reflects primarily differences between nonprofit and public community hospitals.

The large public-private differential in provision of uncompensated care was also reported in several previous national studies based on a 1982 American Hospital Association survey. In particular, Sulvetta (1985) has estimated that the public hospital percentage of charges for uncompensated care is roughly three times the corresponding percentage for private hospitals. Feder and Hadley (1987) used the same survey data to compare public versus private major teaching hospitals. (Virtually all of the latter hospitals are private nonprofits.) They found that uncompensated care accounted for 15.8 percent of gross charges for public teaching hospitals and only about 4.5 percent for their private counterparts. In contrast, Medicaid charges as a percentage of gross patient charges were only about 60 percent higher for the public teaching hospitals (19.5 percent) than for the

15. For example, in a study carried out by the staff of the Maryland Health Services Cost Review Commission, 59 percent of the total bad debt from a 1986 sample of patients' hospital bills were accounted for by patients classified as having no insurance (State of Maryland 1986).

34

private hospitals.[16] A third study using the same data, by Sloan, Valvona, and Mullner (1986) compared public teaching, public nonteaching, non-profit teaching, nonprofit nonteaching, and for-profit hospitals in terms of ratios of uncompensated care charges to total charges. Results indicated that the ratio for public teaching hospitals was 3.03 times the ratio for nonprofit teaching hospitals and 1.96 times the ratio for public nonteaching hospitals. Relative to nonprofit teaching hospitals and for-profit hospitals, the uncompensated care charge ratio for public teaching hospitals was respectively 3.52 and 4.23 times as large.

Several studies have compared the distribution of revenues by funding source and uncompensated care across ownership categories within individual states. Lewin, Eckels, and Miller (1988) compared for-profit and nonprofit hospitals in California (1984), Florida (1985), North Carolina (1984), Tennessee (1985), and Virginia (1985) in terms of percentage of costs accounted for by uncompensated care. They found that nonprofits reported roughly twice as high a percentage of uncompensated care, except in California, where the differential was in the same direction but the non-profit excess over the for-profit share was only 15 percent. More recent comparative data for California have been presented in Seidman and Pollack (forthcoming) and in previously unreported work by Seidman shown in table 2.4. Seidman and Pollack distinguish, within the nonfederal public sector, between county hospitals and district hospitals. The distinction is important legally since only county hospitals are required by state law to provide indigent care. Moreover, there are important locational differences; district hospitals tend to be in more rural areas. Seidman's results, shown in table 2.4, document that county public hospitals, whether teaching or nonteaching, provide a considerably larger fraction of uncompensated care and a much larger fraction of services to Medicaid recipients. Among nonteaching hospitals, differences between nonprofit, for-profit, and district hospitals are very small. It is also notable that the teaching versus nonteaching distinction within nonprofit hospitals is much more important in the distribution of Medicaid (that is, Medi-Cal) services than in the distribution of uncompensated care.[17]

---

16. Feder and Hadley (1987) reported data for private hospitals separately according to whether the hospital was the "flagship" for the affiliated medical school's program versus simply being affiliated with the medical school. All hospitals in their study were members of the Council of Teaching Hospitals.

17. Seidman and Pollack (1991) report parallel results for uncompensated care for 1987; they do not examine Medicaid charges.

TABLE 2.4 Bad Debt Charity Care Charges and Medicaid Charges as Percentages of Total Charges in California Hospitals for Fiscal Years Ending Between 6/30/87 and 6/29/88

	Bad Debt and Charity Care	Medicaid
Teaching		
Nonprofit	3.9	18.3
County Public	25.8	35.1
Nonteaching		
Nonprofit	3.1	9.9
County Public	9.4	31.2
For-profit	2.9	10.4
District Public	3.3	10.3

SOURCE: Robert L. Seidman, (no date) unpublished tabulations from the hospital financial data files of the California Health Facilities Commission.

Regression analyses controlling for a variety of explanatory variables have also been carried out to measure the *ceteris paribus* difference that ownership makes to the volume of uncompensated care relative to the total volume of care. Generally, these studies have produced weaker evidence for that type of control matters than have the descriptive studies reviewed here. This has been interpreted as reflecting systematic locational differences by ownership types; for example, for-profit hospitals tend to locate in communities that have smaller uncompensated care problems to begin with.[18]

Comparing Hospitals in Terms of Patients Served

Several studies have compared nonprofit, for-profit, and public hospitals in terms of the distribution of patients served or the distribution of days of inpatient care provided across various insurance coverage groups. In these comparisons, some patients may be reported as charity care cases, but many of them are classified as self-pay simply because on admission the hospital knows they are not insured but does not know whether or not

18. Efforts to allow for this form of selectivity bias by making ownership endogenous present difficult statistical problems, such as finding plausible identifying restrictions and avoiding negative results for the predicted ownership variable because of poor fit in the first-stage ownership regression.

they will be able to pay their bill. There is empirical evidence (see note 15) that self-pay patients do account for a large portion of bad debt; although the percentage of such patients who do in fact pay their bill is generally not reported in the literature, the study cited in (note 15) indicated it was only 3 percent.

Frank, Salkever, and Mullan (1990) used data from the U.S. National Hospital Discharge Survey (NHDS) for the years 1980–84 to compare percentages of patients classified into the following primary payor source categories: self-pay and charity, Medicaid, Medicare, and other. Nonprofit hospitals were separated into secular and religiously affiliated institutions. Their principal results for 1984 with respect to self-paying/charity and Medicaid discharges are reproduced in table 2.5. (Results for earlier years were quite similar.) The results indicate that the highest percentages of self-paying and charity patients are treated in public hospitals with the lowest percentages in for-profit hospitals. Nonprofit hospitals report percentages slightly above the for-profit figures. The pattern of results for Medicaid discharges was similar. To explore the possibility that differences in the quantity of care existed across payor groupings for the same types of cases, and that these differences varied by ownership type, the authors also compared the ratio of actual to expected length of stay for self-paying/charity patients and for Medicaid patients relative to the analogous ratio for other patients. They found that for self-paying/charity patients, actual relative to expected length of stay tended to be especially low for the for-profit hospitals and highest for the public hospitals, with both groupings of nonprofit hospitals being intermediate in this regard. Analogous comparisons for Medicaid patients also suggested more of a tendency toward shorter lengths of stay in for-profit hospitals, but the differentials by ownership were much smaller than for the self-paying/charity patients. Given the in-

TABLE 2.5 Percentages of Discharges Accounted for by Self-Paying Charity Patients and Medicaid Patients in Acute Care Hospitals, 1984

	Self-paying Charity	Medicaid
For-profit	4.3	6.9
Nonprofit, religiously affiliated	6.6	7.9
Nonprofit secular	6.4	9.7
Nonfederal public	11.6	13.2

SOURCE: Tabulated from the public use tapes of the U.S. National Hospital Discharge Survey, 1984.

formation from table 2.2 on income characteristics of uninsured persons (who presumably account for most of the self-paying/charity patients) and Medicaid recipients, the results reported in this study imply that low-income beneficiaries are largest relative to the total patient population in public hospitals and smallest in for-profit hospitals whether their share is measured in terms of numbers of discharges or days of inpatient care.[19]

An alternative data source that provides much less detailed information on the medical problems treated and treatments received but much greater information on the economic status of individual patients is the U.S. National Health Interview Survey (NHIS). We used data from the 1984 NHIS to examine the distribution of admissions to acute care hospitals by several different personal characteristics, including insurance coverage, labor force status (for adults), and poverty status.[20] The results, presented in table 2.6, indicate that public hospitals had considerably higher shares of admissions of uninsured patients and patients covered only by Medicaid. In comparing nonprofits and for-profits, we observe lower uninsured percentages for the nonprofits but higher Medicaid percentages. The results for the uninsured is surprising in view of the evidence from the NHDS reported above. When patients are classified by labor force status, we observe an increasing percentage of the unemployed as one moves from for-profit to nonprofit to public hospitals. Finally, our results show that public hospital patients are also disproportionately poor. It is interesting that the poor do not make up a higher proportion of patients for nonprofits than for-profits while nonprofits do report a higher proportion of near-poor patients.

Summary of Results for Community Hospitals

In summary, when one looks at insurance characteristics of patients served, there is a fair amount of evidence that nonprofit hospitals serve slightly larger fractions of the uninsured and Medicaid patients than do for-profit hospitals, but contrary findings are not lacking. There is also evidence that nonprofit teaching hospitals devote a larger fraction of their resources to serving the uninsured and Medicaid recipients than nonprofit and for-profit nonteaching hospitals. Among nonteaching hospitals, the differences

19. Days of inpatient care are simply equal to number of discharges multiplied by average length of stay.

20. The NHDS and NHIS data sets do not use the community hospital designation described earlier. There is, however, a close correspondence between the acute care hospital designation used in these surveys and the community hospital designation.

TABLE 2.6 Percentage Distribution of Acute Care
Hospital Admissions by Selected Patient Attributes
and Hospital Ownership, 1984

	Public	Nonprofit	For-profit
Insurance Status			
Uninsured	16.5	8.1	10.5
Medicaid Only	10.5	6.7	4.4
All Other	73.0	85.2	85.2
Total	100.0	100.0	100.0
Employment Status			
Employed	35.0	38.4	40.6
Unemployed	6.3	4.9	3.0
Not in Labor Force	58.7	56.7	56.4
Total	100.0	100.0	100.0
Income Relative to Poverty			
Poor	28.8	16.7	18.7
Near-Poor[a]	26.5	25.5	22.0
Nonpoor	43.7	57.8	59.3
Total	100.0	100.0	100.0

SOURCE: Tabulated from the public use tapes of the U.S. National Health Interview Survey, 1984.

[a]Near-poor is defined as household income between one and two times the poverty level.

between nonprofit and for-profit institutions are very small. Public hospitals on average provide a disproportionately large share of services to the uninsured and to Medicaid recipients. Even within this group, however, considerable variation exists between teaching and nonteaching facilities. Based on the California experience, it appears that smaller public district hospitals behave more like private nonteaching hospitals than like other larger public hospitals. Of course, as noted, one must be careful in interpreting the comparisons reported here as evidence of behavioral differences due to ownership, since differences in market conditions (which may themselves affect hospital location or choice of ownership form) are not controlled.

IV. THE NURSING HOME SECTOR

In comparison to the case of community hospitals, nonprofit firms play a more modest role in the nursing home subsector. According to the 1985 National Nursing Home Survey (NNHS), private nonprofit nursing homes accounted for 19.7 percent of homes, 22.8 percent of beds, and 22.9 percent of current residents of nursing homes (National Center for Health Statistics, Hing, Sekscenski, and Strahan 1989, table 1, p. 7). Government facilities accounted for less than 10 percent on all three measures, and for-profit homes accounted for at least two-thirds of the market.[21]

Differences between private nonprofit and for-profit homes are not dramatic. Nonprofits tend to be slightly larger (97.6 versus 78.4 beds), to have higher labor inputs (and a more highly skilled mix of labor inputs) per day of care rendered, and to charge higher prices. (These differences are also observed when one controls for the level of care—skilled versus intermediate—for which the home is certified.) Differences in some patient characteristics are, however, substantial. Nonprofit homes have higher proportions of very elderly residents than proprietaries (48.0 versus 38.4 percent) and higher proportions of residents who have been in the nursing home five years or more (20.5 versus 16.8 percent).[22]

We used data from the 1985 NNHS to compare nonprofit, proprietary, and public homes in terms of funding sources and types of insurance coverage of their patients. Comparisons of funding sources for current residents (patients in the nursing home at the time of the survey) for the month prior to the survey date are reported in table 2.7. These figures should be reasonable estimates of the total distribution of funding since length of stay is long and patient turnover is low. These data indicate that a very small proportion of funding for patients is charity care (that is, in-kind donations of care) provided by the homes themselves. They also show that very little funding for nonprofit homes comes from private charitable programs (only 0.59 percent).

There is no evidence that nonprofit homes are more willing than for-profit homes to serve patients funded under Medicaid and other public programs. The relevance of the Medicaid results in the context of our discussion of "beneficiaries" is problematic, however. There is little evidence to suggest that Medicaid patients in nursing homes are being cross-subsidized or supported by other revenue sources (such as donations); indeed the very large share of Medicaid patients in the for-profit homes

21. There is regional variation in these ownership patterns, however, with nonprofits having a much larger share of the market in the northeastern and north central regions of the country (Weisbrod 1988, 83).

22. Data cited in this paragraph are from National Center for Health Statistics, Hing, Sekscenski, and Strahan 1989, tables 3, and 9–12, p. 9 and pp. 15–18.

TABLE 2.7 Percentage Distribution of Funding Sources for the Prior Month's Care for Current Residents of Nursing Homes by Ownership Type, 1985

	For-profit	Nonprofit	Public
Own Financial Resources of Patient or Family	46.3	57.7	37.3
Medicare	0.9	0.7	0.4
Medicaid	43.2	33.8	51.1
State-funded Indigent Care Programs	1.6	0.5	0.6
Other Government Assistance	2.2	1.0	3.1
Private Foundations and Nonprofit Agencies	0.0	0.6	0.0
VA Contract Funds	1.0	0.2	2.1
Charity Care	0.2	0.7	0.0
Other	0.9	0.6	1.0
Unknown	3.7	4.2	4.5
Total	100.0	100.0	100.0

SOURCE: Weighted estimates based on data from the Current Residents file of the National Nursing Home survey. A small number of records (less than 2 percent) were excluded because reported funding summed to more than 100 percent of charges.

strongly suggests that the incremental revenues from serving this group of patients are above the corresponding incremental costs.[23]

V. THE MENTAL HEALTH SECTOR

The specialty mental health sector, as we view it, consists of organized care settings that specialize in the treatment of mental disorders. These include psychiatric hospitals, mental health clinics, distinct part psychiatric units of general hospitals, and freestanding partial hospitalization programs. Excluded are office-based providers of mental health care, schools, general hospitals (without separate psychiatric units), and health clinics, each of which supplies substantial amounts of mental health care.

The mental health sector is very much a three-sector economy, although the shares of each sector have been changing. Over the past fifteen years, the share of psychiatric inpatient beds in the public sector has declined

23. Estimates analogous to those in table 2.7 were also developed for distribution of current residents by primary payment source during the month of their admission to the nursing home and for primary payment source in the final month of care for residents discharged in the month before the survey. Results were quite similar to those reported in table 2.7.

steadily while the shares of beds in for-profit psychiatric hospitals and general hospital psychiatric units have grown dramatically. For example, between 1970 and 1986 the share of total psychiatric beds in private for-profit psychiatric hospitals grew from 1 percent to 10 percent. The share of beds in general hospital psychiatric units went from 4 percent in 1970 to 20 percent in 1986. At the same time, the public psychiatric hospital remains an important supplier of mental health care, accounting for roughly 50 percent of psychiatric hospital beds.[24]

Table 2.8 provides information on market shares for different types of providers and ownership categories in the inpatient and outpatient services markets. Data on inpatient beds and cases indicate a relatively large market share for for-profit firms among private psychiatric hospitals but a more limited role for these firms in providing general hospital psychiatric services.[25] Data on outpatient market shares show that in contrast to their substantial share of the inpatient market, for-profit psychiatric hospitals play a more limited role in the outpatient care subsector, including partial hospitalization programs.[26] One possible reason for this is the strict limits placed on outpatient mental health care by most insurance plans (public and private).

In examining data on patients and revenues for specialty mental health providers to determine the nature of beneficiaries (as previously defined), several important facts regarding public funding sources should be borne in mind. First, as in the case of community hospital care, there is a strong presumption that Medicaid patients are beneficiaries since Medicaid payment levels are limited and limits on numbers and types of services covered are strict. (It is also important to note that Medicaid does not cover inpatient services in psychiatric hospitals for persons between the age of twenty-one and sixty-four.) Second, revenues from government grants and contracts often are not strictly tied to numbers of patients served, so the marginal revenue for these patients may be quite low even though the costs of treating these patients, as a group, are largely covered by public funding.

24. These estimates of market share exclude Residential Treatment Centers for Emotionally Disturbed Children and focus on hospital beds.

25. When dealing with a chronic illness (such as most mental disorders), cases are counted as the sum of the number of patients in residence at the beginning of a year and new admissions during the year.

26. Partial hospitalization is organized in much the same way as inpatient psychiatric care. That is, it furnishes a very structured environment for the patient. However, the patient returns to a community residence after each day's treatment, which usually lasts four to eight hours.

TABLE 2.8 Market Shares in the Specialty Mental Health Services Sector, 1986

	Inpatient Services	
	Beds	Cases
State and County Mental Hospitals	119,033	445,181
Private Psychiatric Hospitals		
For-profit	21,859	185,716
Nonprofit	8,342	72,539
General Hospital Psychiatric Units	43,255	883,119
For-profit	2,698	NA
Nonprofit	32,322	NA
Public	8,235	NA
Residential Treatment Centers for Emotionally Disturbed Children	24,874	203,851
Multiservice Mental Health Organizations	21,150	217,961
	Outpatient Services	
	Outpatient Cases	Partial Hospital Cases
State and County Mental Hospitals	146,361	13,440
Private Psychiatric Hospitals		
For-profit	52,794	3,954
Nonprofit	159,451	8,830
General Hospitals	902,785	38,597
Residential Treatment Centers for Emotionally Disturbed Children	96,304	10,569
Freestanding Outpatient Clinics	786,964	—
Freestanding Partial Hospitalization Programs	—	22,132
Multiservice Mental Health Organizations	2,896,449	246,605

SOURCE: Tabulations from the 1986 Inventory of Mental Health Organizations, National Institute of Mental Health.

To identify patients whose services are covered by these grants as beneficiaries, one must assume that, in the absence of nonprofit providers, direct government provision or public grants and contracts to for-profit providers would, in fact, have resulted in fewer of these patients being served. Empirical support for this assumption is not available.

Table 2.9 presents information on the relative importance of these public revenue sources by provider ownership. It is interesting to note that for-profit providers have a lower Medicaid share than do nonprofit providers across all three types of programs. In contrast to the results for community hospital care, however, nonprofit providers also surpass public providers

TABLE 2.9 Revenue Shares (%) for
Medicaid and for Other Public Grants
and Contracts for Specialty Mental
Health Providers

	Medicaid	Other Public Grants and Contracts
Inpatient		
For-profit	12	9
Nonprofit	15	35
Public	10	79
Outpatient		
For-profit	9	12
Nonprofit	20	54
Public	12	75
Partial Hospitalization		
For-profit	11	22
Nonprofit	21	58
Public	14	73

SOURCE: Tabulations from the 1986 Inventory of
Mental Health Organizations, National Institute of
Mental Health.

in their Medicaid revenue shares. The importance of revenue from other public grants and contracts varies consistently in the expected directions. For-profit providers have limited revenue shares from these sources, public providers rely heavily on them, and nonprofit providers are intermediate between these two extremes.

Comparisons by ownership of the distribution of patients by insurance status are presented in table 2.10. Results in the table are estimates based on tabulations of the 1986 Client/Patient Sample Survey of Mental Health Organizations conducted by the National Institute of Mental Health.[27] In examining results for inpatients, it is important to recall that state Medi-

27. The Client Sample Survey is a two-stage, stratified sample survey. Patients were sampled following stratification by facility type, program type (inpatient, outpatient, and partial hospital care), and geographic region of the nation. Seventy-nine percent of the programs sampled responded. The resulting usable sample consisted of approximately seventeen thousand patients treated in roughly one thousand, nine hundred treatment programs. Individual patient records were merged with the characteristics of the facility and program in which they received mental health care based on information from the 1986 Inventory of Mental Health Organizations. We are grateful to Wayne Johnson and Marilyn Rosenstein for making the data available and for assistance in using and interpreting the data.

TABLE 2.10 Percentage Distribution of Patients by Insurance, Ownership, and Type of Service, 1986

	Medicare/ Private Insurance	Medicaid	No Insurance	Other	Total
		Inpatient			
For-profit	85.5	2.8	3.9	7.5	100.0
Nonprofit	54.3	27.7	10.9	7.1	100.0
Public	23.7	10.2	52.6	23.6	100.0
		Outpatient			
For-profit	19.9	35.7	40.8	3.6	100.0
Nonprofit	27.8	15.1	40.9	16.2	100.0
Public	19.9	19.0	55.0	6.2	100.0
		Partial Hospitalization			
For-profit	67.9	14.3	6.3	11.4	100.0
Nonprofit	21.1	32.9	30.0	15.9	100.0
Public	14.6	28.7	37.5	19.2	100.0

SOURCE: Tabulations from the 1986 Client/Patient Sample Survey of Mental Health Organizations, National Institute of Mental Health.

caid programs are prohibited from reimbursing psychiatric hospitals for treating Medicaid patients between the ages of twenty-one and sixty-four. Thus, the larger Medicaid inpatient share for nonprofits may reflect primarily that nonprofit psychiatric specialty beds are mainly in general hospitals (which can receive Medicaid funding), while public and for-profit psychiatric beds are mainly in specialty psychiatric hospitals. Other inpatient differences are striking, however. Uninsured patients clearly constitute a larger share of all inpatients for nonprofit providers relative to for-profit providers, but the share in public programs in substantially above both private sector figures. Patients funded by "other" sources (mainly public programs and workers' compensation) are also relatively more important in the public sector.

The results for outpatient services indicate that nonprofit and for-profit providers treat essentially the same portion of uninsured patients, with both falling short of the public providers' percentage. Our results also indicate that for-profit programs treat a larger share of Medicaid patients than do nonprofit or public programs; this result is somewhat puzzling in view of the findings on revenue shares in table 2.9. The two findings taken together suggest that for-profit programs provide relatively shorter and less expensive treatment for Medicaid recipients; another possibility is that these patients are referred to other programs when the limits on their covered Medicaid services are reached.

The distribution of patients in partial hospital programs by insurance type shows nonprofit providers with the largest Medicaid share and public providers with the largest uninsured share. Corresponding shares for for-profit providers are considerably smaller.

While data are not available on income levels of patients in general, or on income levels of the groups of patients we have identified as beneficiaries, information is available on the distribution of patients by educational attainment across ownership categories of providers. (Educational attainment can be viewed as relevant to distributional issues because it is at least a rough proxy for permanent income or wealth.) The data on inpatient programs in table 2.11 suggest few differences between nonprofit and for-profit hospitals. Nonprofit providers report a slightly lower percentage in the highest education group than do for-profits. Public providers treat a larger portion of patients with lower levels of educational attainment. On the outpatient side, for-profit providers treat a larger portion of cases where the person completed a high school education or less (82 percent versus 79 percent for nonprofits). Once again, public providers supply substantially more care to individuals with lower levels of education. The

TABLE 2.11 Percentage Distribution of Patients by Educational Attainment and Provider Ownership

	1–11 yrs.	12 yrs.	13–16 yrs.	17 + yrs.	Total
			Inpatient		
For-profit	39.0	33.8	21.3	5.9	100.0
Nonprofit	38.1	37.0	21.8	3.0	100.0
Public	44.7	35.7	17.0	2.6	100.0
			Outpatient		
For-profit	58.3	24.3	12.8	4.7	100.0
Nonprofit	45.4	33.3	18.8	2.5	100.0
Public	52.8	29.3	16.8	1.1	100.0
		Partial Hospitalization			
For-profit	31.2	50.0	19.0	0.9	100.0
Nonprofit	46.5	38.7	13.1	1.7	100.0
Public	46.5	34.9	16.6	2.1	100.0

SOURCE: Tabulations from the 1986 Client/Patient Sample Survey of Mental Health Organizations, National Institute of Mental Health.

pattern in partial hospitalization programs is less pronounced. For-profit organizations treat a larger share of patients with a higher education level than nonprofits (19 percent versus 15 percent) and a comparable share to public programs (19 percent).

VI. ALCOHOL AND DRUG TREATMENT FACILITIES

Treatment for alcoholism and for drug addiction is provided by a variety of types of facilities in the United States: general hospitals, alcoholism hospitals, psychiatric hospitals, other specialized hospitals, community mental health centers, halfway houses, other residential nonhospital facilities, outpatient clinics, etc. The principal source of data on these providers we have used is the 1987 National Drug and Alcoholism Treatment Unit Survey (NDATUS) conducted by the National Institute on Drug Abuse (NIDA) and the National Institute on Alcohol Abuse and Alcoholism (NIAAA). According to this survey, 6,866 facilities were providing alcoholism and drug treatment services in 1987 to 614,123 clients. Outpatient facilities accounted for 37.6 percent of all facilities and 49.9 percent of all clients. Hospitals accounted for an additional 18 percent of facilities and 14.6 percent of clients. Data on 935 community mental health centers were reported and accounted for 14.5 percent of all clients. Halfway houses and other nonhospital residential facilities accounted for 23.2 percent of facilities and 10.2 percent of clients.[28]

Private nonprofit facilities are the most important ownership type of provider in the alcoholism and drug treatment sector, accounting for 65.6 percent of facilities and 59 percent of all clients. State and local government facilities are also relatively important, accounting for 17.5 percent of facilities and 24.9 percent of clients. Private for-profit facilities constitute 14.3 percent and 11.7 percent of facilities and clients, respectively, while the federal treatment programs (which are excluded from discussion here) make up the relatively small remainder (2.6 percent of all facilities and 4.3 percent of clients).

We used the NDATUS survey data to compare the different ownership types of facilities along several different dimensions, distinguishing in our comparison between alcohol-only, drug-only, and combined alcohol/drug

---

28. There is overlap between the facilities on whom data are reported in this section and the facilities reported on in the previous section on mental health services. This is particularly true for hospitals, community mental health centers, and other outpatient facilities; in contrast, data on halfway houses and other residential providers are generally not reported in the National Institute of Mental Health survey data discussed in the preceding section.

treatment programs. (Drug-treatment-only providers accounted for 54.6 percent of total revenues, alcohol-only providers accounted for 25 percent, and combined treatment facilities accounted for 20.4 percent.) Since the NDATUS survey data are limited in the detail they provide on provider revenue sources and patient characteristics, evidence concerning distributional impacts is even more indirect here than in previous sections.

Information on revenue sources is provided in table 2.12. While the NDATUS survey does not specifically report Medicaid revenues, it does identify public third-party payments, which include Medicaid, Medicare, and the CHAMPUS program for military dependents. Given the relative sizes of these different public third-party programs, and the demographic patterns of alcoholism and drug abuse in the population, it is reasonable to assume that a large portion of the public third-party funding is from Medicaid in particular. For the largest service category, drug-treatment-only, nonprofit providers have the highest revenue share from public third parties. For alcoholism treatment providers, the corresponding nonprofit share (10.0 percent) is slightly below the public provider share but still above the for-profit provider share (6.7 percent). In contrast, for the smallest group of providers, combined alcohol and drug treatment, the for-profit providers report the largest share of public third-party revenues.

Donations are, of course, a potential revenue source for subsidizing care to beneficiaries (as defined here). The data in table 2.12 indicate that donations are a very small share of total revenues for nonprofit providers. (As expected, donations are negligible for for-profit and public providers.) Finally, note that the "other" category includes a variety of public grant and contract funding sources. Revenues from these sources are quite important to nonprofit providers. While these revenues are presumably used to fund care to many indigent and low-income persons, we have already noted that these persons may not be properly viewed as beneficiaries if the public revenues in fact cover the costs of serving these persons.

Additional, albeit indirect, evidence concerning provision of subsidized services is presented in table 2.13. In the case of alcoholism and combined treatment services, for-profit providers report the lowest percent accepting Medicaid patients, while public providers report the highest rates. In the case of drug-treatment-only providers, the order is reversed. Further, more detailed information is obviously needed to reconcile the differences between these findings and the suggestion, based on the data in table 2.12, that for-profit providers have smaller shares of Medicaid revenues, except in the case of combined treatment providers.

TABLE 2.12 Percentage Distribution of Revenues by Funding Source for Alcoholism and Drug Treatment Providers

	Public Third Party	Private Insurance/ Client Fees	Private Donations	Other	Total
		Alcoholism Services			
For-profit	6.7	87.3	0.1	5.9	100.0
Nonprofit	10.0	40.9	2.5	46.6	100.0
Public	11.4	8.8	0.2	79.6	100.0
		Drug Abuse Services			
For-profit	10.8	76.0	0.2	13.2	100.0
Nonprofit	16.3	11.8	3.1	68.8	100.0
Public	8.9	4.0	0.0	87.1	100.0
		Combined Services			
For-profit	12.1	81.7	0.2	6.0	100.0
Nonprofit	8.0	51.7	3.1	37.2	100.0
Public	4.8	22.6	0.4	72.2	100.0

SOURCE: Tabulated from the 1987 National Drug and Alcoholism Treatment Unit Survey, National Institute on Drug Abuse and National Institute on Alcohol Abuse and Alcoholism.

The use of sliding scale fees (with lower charges to patients whose ability to pay is lower) might be viewed as evidence of cross-subsidization to finance care to (presumably indigent or near-poor) beneficiaries. That interpretation, along with the data in table 2.13 showing a high percentage of nonprofit providers using sliding scale fees, suggests that the beneficiaries of cross-subsidization by nonprofits may indeed be numerous. Nonetheless, the fact that a large fraction of for-profit providers report using sliding scale fees reminds us that this practice may also be consistent with profit maximization (Kessel 1958).

In terms of patient characteristics, the only information available from the NDATUS survey is the racial distribution of patients. While information on race is potentially relevant to income distribution concerns in view of existing differences in income by race, it would have been preferable to have data on the racial distribution of patients for specific beneficiary groups (that is, Medicaid and uninsured patients); such data are not available. The data in table 2.14 do show consistent patterns of differences, however. For drug abuse patients, in all but one instance (outpatients of drug-abuse-treatment-only providers) the percentage of nonwhite patients is highest for the public providers. Similarly, for alcoholism patients, in all

TABLE 2.13 Percentages of Alcoholism and Drug
Treatment Facilities Accepting Medicaid Patients
and Percentages Reporting Use of Sliding Scale Fees

	Medicaid Accepted	Sliding Scale Fees
Alcoholism Services		
For-profit	15.5	54.4
Nonprofit	22.4	72.0
Public	44.9	75.5
Drug Abuse Services		
For-profit	50.0	25.0
Nonprofit	33.3	77.5
Public	29.0	47.3
Combined Services		
For-profit	18.3	33.0
Nonprofit	33.4	70.7
Public	48.0	75.9

SOURCE: Tabulated from the 1987 National Drug and Alcoholism Treatment Unit Survey, National Institute on Drug Abuse and
National Institute on Alcohol Abuse and Alcoholism.

but one instance (alcoholism services outpatients of combined services providers), the percentage of nonwhite patients was lowest for the for-profit
providers. These findings at least suggest that, on the whole, patients
served by for-profit providers have higher incomes, patients served by public providers have the lowest incomes, and patients served by nonprofit
providers (some of whom are beneficiaries) presumably have income levels
between these other two groups.

VII. Interaction between the Sectors and Indirect Effects

The analysis presented thus far can be used for "back-of-the-envelope"
estimates of what we have called the direct effects of an incremental shift
in ownership shares within the health sector. As previously noted, the impact of this shift may include indirect effects, that is, behavioral responses
of other providers to a change in the overall ownership shares within the
markets in which they function. We now turn to consideration of these
possible behavioral responses, focusing in particular on empirical evidence
pertaining to "crowding-out" and interactions between ownership forms

TABLE 2.14 Percentage Distribution of Drug Abuse and Alcoholism Patients by Race, Facility Type, and Ownership

	Inpatients				Outpatients			
	White	Non-White	Other/ Unknown	Total	White	Non-White	Other Unknown	Total
A. DRUG ABUSE PATIENTS								
Drug Abuse Service Providers								
For-profit	59.3	40.7	0.0	100.0	59.2	37.4	3.4	100.0
Nonprofit	38.1	60.0	1.9	100.0	46.4	50.6	3.0	100.0
Public	27.6	72.3	0.1	100.0	39.5	49.5	11.1	100.0
Combined Service Providers								
For-profit	70.3	26.3	3.4	100.0	71.1	26.6	2.4	100.0
Nonprofit	64.1	33.4	2.5	100.0	70.1	26.7	3.2	100.0
Public	49.6	47.2	3.2	100.0	60.4	30.7	8.8	100.0
B. ALCOHOLISM PATIENTS								
Alcoholism Service Providers								
For-profit	82.9	17.0	0.1	100.0	64.5	31.1	4.4	100.0
Nonprofit	67.0	30.4	2.6	100.0	62.9	34.0	3.1	100.0
Public	62.4	33.9	3.7	100.0	55.5	40.4	4.1	100.0
Combined Service Providers								
For-profit	77.8	19.8	2.5	100.0	76.1	22.3	1.7	100.0
Nonprofit	72.4	24.5	3.1	100.0	75.4	19.8	4.8	100.0
Public	60.7	33.3	6.0	100.0	67.8	26.8	5.5	100.0

SOURCE: Tabulated from the 1987 National Drug and Alcoholism Treatment Unit Survey, National Institute on Drug Abuse and National Institute on Alcohol Abuse and Alcoholism.

in the supply of uncompensated care. Most of the evidence that exists on these issues derives from research on the hospital subsector.

Thorpe and Phelps (1988) use data from private nonprofit hospitals in the state of New York to study the supply of indigent care in these hospitals. They estimate regression models where the dependent variable is specified as the logarithm of annual uncompensated care costs in each hospital. The independent variables included: the share of total hospital discharges in a county that are accounted for by public hospitals, an indicator of market structure,[29] and a set of other variables explaining the types of insurance held by county residents and the characteristics of each hospital. The estimated coefficient for the variable measuring the share of discharges from public hospitals was consistently estimated to have a negative impact on the level of uncompensated care costs in nonprofit hospitals.[30] This finding lends support to the hypothesis that public hospitals crowd out indigent care supplied by nonprofit facilities. The coefficient estimates for the market structure indicator suggest that in markets that are relatively more concentrated, nonprofit providers supply higher levels of indigent care. While the market structure is not directly measured in terms of the supply of charity care, the finding could be viewed as supporting the existence of some "private" crowding-out, that is, the hypothesis that when other private hospitals are more numerous, the amount of indigent care supplied by each individual nonprofit hospital is less.

Sloan, Morrisey, and Valvona (1988) analyzed the percentage of self-paying (that is, uninsured) patients served by hospitals in selected years between 1980 and 1985. Explanatory variables included hospital characteristics (for example, ownership and teaching status), and county characteristics (employment, Medicaid enrollment, and hospital market structure). Regression models were estimated using the hospital as the unit of analysis and provide some evidence relating to public and private crowding-out. The authors report a significant negative effect on the percentage of self-paying patients for a binary variable indicating the presence of an "other public hospital" in the county. In contrast, a binary variable indicating that a hospital was "the only hospital in the county" showed no significant effect. These results, taken together, suggest that reducing the

29. The Herfindahl index was used in this analysis. This index is defined as the sum of the squared values of the market shares for all hospitals within a single market. (Thus, if there were two hospitals of equal size in a market, the index value would be $(1/2)^2 + (1/2)^2 = 1/2$.)

30. The significance of the coefficient varied considerably with the estimation method employed.

size of the public hospital sector may result in some increased supply of charity care by nonprofit hospitals. The evidence on the consequences of increased competition among privately owned hospitals (both nonprofits and for-profits) is not clear from theses studies.

Our research on hospitals in Florida during the 1980–84 period (Frank, Salkever, and Mitchell 1990) was similar to these earlier studies in that most of the charity care supply functions include market structure variables rather than direct measures of charity care supply by other hospitals. Estimated coefficients for these market structure variables were generally consistent with the conclusion that charity care supply was reduced when the share of beds in other hospitals was greater; however these coefficients were generally not significantly different from zero. It is worth noting that the share of for-profit beds had a negative and significant impact on charity care supply by nonprofit hospitals in several specifications. One specification did directly test crowding out by replacing market structure variables with measures of charity care supply by other hospitals. Results were again weakly consistent with the crowding-out hypothesis.

Finally, in a study of general hospitals in Maryland for the years 1980–84 (Frank and Salkever 1988), we found very weak evidence of crowding-out. We did, however, find evidence of rivalry; that is, nonprofit hospitals appear to supply more indigent care when the supply of indigent care by other nonprofits in the same county increases. When we measure the impact of the supply of indigent care by public psychiatric hospitals on the supply of indigent psychiatric care by nonprofit general hospitals, we find a significant negative effect that is robust to specification changes (Frank and Salkever 1990). This implies that public mental hospitals crowd out a portion of the indigent psychiatric care supplied by nonprofit hospitals (but the magnitude of the crowd-out effect is relatively small).

In summary, the empirical evidence of indirect effects reported to date in the literature suggests, at most, modest crowding-out of charity care by public providers. The very limited evidence on the relationship between for-profit and nonprofit hospitals offers evidence that the presence of for-profit hospitals in a market leads to reduced supply of indigent care by nonprofit facilities. Taking this evidence in conjunction with the evidence on direct effects presented in section 3, it appears that growth in the non-profit share of the hospital market at the expense of public hospitals would probably result in a net reduction of the aggregate supply of hospital care to the indigent. If nonprofit hospital growth came at the expense of for-profit providers, the result would be a net increase in indigent hospital care. This would occur because nonprofit facilities supply more indigent care than similar for-profit organizations and because the presence of for-profit hospitals leads to reductions in the nonprofits' supply of care to the indigent.

VIII. Conclusions

As we noted at the outset, nonprofit firms in the health sector are indeed diverse; thus, it is not surprising that results of comparisons among firms by ownership type are also diverse. While the data presented quite consistently show differences between for-profit and public providers in services to presumed beneficiary groups (namely, Medicaid recipients and the uninsured), where the nonprofit firm falls between the for-profit and the public providers varies considerably. In the case of nursing homes, there are very few salient differences between for-profit and nonprofit providers. (It is also true, however, that for-profit versus public differences are somewhat less pronounced for nursing homes than for other types of health care providers.) In the case of outpatient mental health services and drug abuse programs, nonprofit firms fall closer to the public end of the spectrum. This is perhaps not surprising since these nonprofit firms also derive a large share of their funding from the public sector. More generally, it is striking that across the entire nonprofit health sector the role of philanthropy as a revenue source is quite modest. Hodgkinson and Weitzman (1989, table 8.2, pp. 180–81) report that only 6.7 percent of total revenues for nonprofit health services providers derived from private contributions in 1987. Moreover, this percentage has been declining since 1977. The implication of this funding pattern, in an era of public fiscal restraint and increasing cost-control and competitive pressures from private third-party payers, seems to be that the services to those who are unable to pay will fluctuate with public sector revenues (since cross-subsidization by other patient groups paying charges in excess of costs is diminishing).[31] If the flow of public revenues is substantially reduced, will private philanthropy respond? While there are anecdotal reports of increased efforts to raise donations by nonprofit hospitals, evidence of the response of donors to these increased efforts has yet to be documented.

---

31. As evidence on this point, it is pertinent to note that in our study of nonprofit hospitals in Florida (Frank, Salkever, and Mitchell 1990), we found that the excess of Medicare prospective per case payment levels over each hospital's predicted per case cost was strongly and positively related to the supply of indigent care by the hospital.

3

Education

Saul Schwartz and Sandy Baum

In the field of education, the nonprofit sector supplements a public sector that makes elementary, secondary, and postsecondary schooling widely available. This chapter examines, along several dimensions, the character- istics of students attending nonprofit and public schools. ⎯

Most locally controlled and publicly funded school systems require that families send their children to the schools nearest them. Thus parents, when they choose a place to live, implicitly choose elementary and second- ary schools for their children. About 10 percent of young children in the United States attend private schools explicitly chosen by their parents. Many private schools are affiliated with the Roman Catholic Church, but these are complemented by a number of unaffiliated religious schools and elite preparatory schools.

About 20 percent of postsecondary students attend private, nonprofit colleges and universities. In general, the range of different types of postsec- ondary institutions is much greater than the range of elementary and sec- ondary schools. Within postsecondary education, the nonprofit sector pro- vides an alternative to the large and diverse public sector and to a small, but growing, set of for-profit schools.[1]

Students from low-income families are less likely than others to attend private nonprofit schools. Table 3.1 shows the distribution of public and private school enrollment by income class. In the top section, secondary schools are divided into four categories. The first two columns represent the two categories of school, public and Catholic, that contain almost all high schools in the United States. The third column represents "other-

---

1. The existence of many different types of postsecondary institutions does not guarantee that all students will be *able* to choose freely among the institutions. Most schools do not accept all those who apply and not all students can afford all schools for which they are qualified. The primary mechanism for promoting more choice has been student aid programs at the federal, state, and institutional levels.

TABLE 3.1 The Distribution of Enrollment by Family Income among Secondary and Postsecondary Students by Type of Institution

SECONDARY SCHOOLS

| Annual Family Income in 1980 | Weighted Percentage of Students in Each Category of Family Income | | | |
	Public	Catholic	Other Private	Elite Private
Less than $7,000	8(%)	2(%)	2(%)	1(%)
$ 7,000–$11,999	13	7	7	1
$12,000–$15,999	18	15	16	4
$16,000–$19,999	20	18	16	7
$20,000–$24,999	18	21	20	6
$25,000–$37,999	13	18	12	13
$38,000 or more	10	19	27	69
Total	100%	100%	100%	100%
Unweighted Number of Respondents	19,569	2,102	419	273

POSTSECONDARY INSTITUTIONS

| Annual Family Income in 1985 | Weighted Percentage of Students in Each Category of Family Income | | |
	Public	Private Nonprofit	Proprietary
Less than $12,000	13(%)	11(%)	29(%)
$12,000–$19,999	12	9	18
$20,000–$29,999	17	14	20
$30,000–$39,999	18	16	16
$40,000–$49,999	15	14	8
$50,000–$74,999	17	21	8
$75,000–$100,000	4	7	1
More than $100,000	3	9	1
Total	100%	100%	100%

SOURCES: Upper section (Coleman and Hoffer 1987, 30); lower section calculations done by the authors from the National Postsecondary Student Aid Survey (U.S. Department of Education 1987a).

private" schools, while the fourth column isolates a small number of elite private secondary schools.[2]

The top section shows that the families of those who attend private secondary schools have higher incomes, on average, than the families of those

2. Table 3.1 is based on data from the longitudinal High School and Beyond Survey (U.S. Department of Education 1981), which surveyed about sixty thousand high school students

who attend public schools. But it is also clear that the private schools, with the exception of the elite private schools, are not the exclusive preserve of the wealthy; substantial proportions of Catholic-school students come from low-income families.

The lower section of table 3.1 describes the distribution of income among students at public colleges and students at private nonprofit colleges and universities. Here again, while students at private nonprofit schools are more likely to come from higher-income families, this tendency is not overwhelming. Substantial numbers of low-income students attend private colleges and universities, and substantial numbers of high-income students attend public colleges and universities.

The distinction between public schools and private nonprofit schools is important because there is reason to believe that institutional form is crucial in shaping the nature of what institutions do. Private schools, whose survival depends on the satisfaction of their customers, may be more likely to respond quickly and effectively to the demands of those customers. Public schools, whose operation depends on the satisfaction of the government officials (representing the society at large), as well as on the satisfaction of the immediate consumers of their product, may not be able to respond as quickly and flexibly as private schools.

One implication of such a view is that differences in institutional form may imply differences in average scholastic performance. Private schools may be "better" than public schools. If so, increasing the current levels of public subsidies to private schools might increase the number of students attending private schools and thus increase the average level of educational quality.[3] Private schools might also be "worse" than public schools. Free from public control, for example, they might strive to inculcate values that are inconsistent with societal norms.

We will focus here on the hypothesis that private schools are more effec-

---

from about one thousand high schools in 1980. The survey was then readministered to subsamples of the base year sample in 1982, 1984, and 1986. "Other-private" and "high performance" private schools were defined and oversampled in the design of the survey. Details of the design and implementation of the HS&B are available in any of the HS&B codebooks available from the National Center for Education Statistics. For our purposes, one variable definition is especially important. Throughout this chapter (as in most research using the HS&B), the "family income" variable is based on the responses of the students, not their parents, and thus may be subject to significant measurement error.

3. These are two conceptually different points. Private schools might be "better" than public schools for the students currently attending private schools but *not* be "better" for the students who are induced to attend by increased public subsidies of private education.

tive than public schools in fostering one set of positive outcomes—higher achievement, higher earnings, and greater educational attainment. Examining differences between public and private schools in the transmission of values or in curriculum is beyond the scope of this study.

A second and related reason that analyzing private schools in comparison to public schools might be important is that private and public schools might have differential effects on different income groups. There is some evidence, for example, that private secondary schools are more effective than public schools in increasing the achievement of low-income students.

Given the possible importance of institutional form, this chapter attempts to summarize research directed at answering two questions. First, are the benefits of private nonprofit education different from the benefits of public education? And, second, how does the distribution of those benefits, by income class, differ between the two sectors? In the remainder of this introduction, we describe some of the essential institutional characteristics of American education, beginning with elementary and secondary education.

According to Murnane (1984, 275), American elementary and secondary schools form "an education system requiring universal participation of students but permitting extensive choice among schooling alternatives, with the range and quality of the options very sensitive to family income." For most Americans, the local public school system is the only form of schooling that is both readily available and easily affordable. In 1988, 88 percent of the eighth-grade population was enrolled in public schools. But in many areas, Catholic and other religious schools will admit most students willing and able to pay a modest tuition. Of the eighth-grade population in 1988, 8 percent were enrolled in Catholic schools, and 4 percent were enrolled in other private, usually religiously oriented, schools. Independent schools—those "elite private schools which are members of the National Association of Independent Schools"—are an option for a very small number of affluent families; about 1 percent of the eighth-grade population was enrolled in independent schools in 1988.[4]

For the well-to-do, the range of schooling options is wide. For eighth graders whose families were in the top quartile of socioeconomic status in

4. These percentages and definitions are drawn from *A Profile of the American Eighth Grader: NELS:88 Student Descriptive Summary* (U.S. Department of Education 1990). The standard errors applicable to these estimates from the NELS (National Education Longitudinal Study of 1988) are small (usually less than 1 percentage point); the standard errors are reported on p. E-10 of the above report.

1988, 78 percent attended public schools, 19 percent were in Catholic and other religious schools, and 3.5 percent were in the elite private schools. Among those whose family incomes were in the lowest quartile, 96 percent attended public schools, 4 percent attended Catholic and other religious schools, and virtually none attended the elite private schools.

Enrollment in postsecondary institutions reached an all-time high of 12.5 million students in the fall of 1987 despite a decline in the number of 18–24-year-olds that began in 1980 (U.S. Department of Education 1989).

Of these, 2.6 million or 20 percent were enrolled in private nonprofit institutions. Another 2 percent attended proprietary schools. Thus, the nonprofit sector clearly plays a much larger role in higher education than it does in elementary and secondary education. Furthermore, the importance of the nonprofit sector may be greater than its share of enrollments might suggest.

Many of the most prestigious research universities and the vast majority of well-respected liberal arts colleges are in the nonprofit sector. In the 1989 ranking of institutions by *U.S. News and World Report,* twenty of the twenty-five top-ranked national universities were private nonprofit institutions. All of the top liberal arts colleges and 87 percent of the top regional colleges and universities listed in that magazine were in the non-profit sector.[5]

That some parents and students are willing to pay relatively high private school tuition suggests that these students and their parents, at least, also perceive the nonprofit sector as delivering a product that is of higher value than its public counterpart. In 1987–88, for example, the average yearly cost of attendance (including tuition, fees, room and board) was $13,330 at private universities and $4,760 at public universities (College Board 1988, 11).

These generalizations, however, obscure the fact that there is considerable diversity among nonprofit postsecondary institutions. The schools at the top of the *U.S. News and World Report* list have very high average SAT scores and accept far fewer than half of their applicants, but most non-profit colleges are considerably less well-known and do not have very selec-

5. "America's Best Colleges," *U.S. News and World Report,* October 16, 1989, 107:53–58. These rankings reflect a combination of objective data with the views of a broad spectrum of academic administrators. Although these rankings are often dismissed as unscientific, they seem to correspond to widely held views of college quality. Bruce Johnstone, for example, asserts that "a disproportionate number of the nation's leading business executives, physicians, lawyers, and political and governmental leaders have come out of private higher education" (Johnstone 1986, 115).

tive admissions policies. The prominence of the relatively few highly selective private institutions creates the perception of a public/private quality distinction which, in fact, may not be generally applicable.

In the sections that follow, we review previous efforts to measure the level and distribution of the benefits of education, defining the benefits as higher achievement, higher earnings, and greater educational attainment. We begin by discussing secondary education in section I, followed by post-secondary education in section II. The last part of section II contains an analysis of the distribution of subsidies to college students.

I. The Distribution of the Benefits of Secondary Education

Coleman and Hoffer (1987) argue that the existing structure of American elementary and secondary schools has resulted, in part, from two central and sometimes conflicting orientations. The first orientation sees education as an extension of the family, as a way of reinforcing the particular values and viewpoints of the family. This orientation is especially appealing for families whose values differ from those of the society at large and who therefore feel that their values are "at risk" of not being transferred across generations.

The other conception is that of "the school as emancipator of the child from the family" (Coleman and Hoffer 1987, 5). For a child born into a low-income family, for example, school can be a way of compensating for the inability or unwillingness of the family to provide educational support. In general, the school can create a "level playing field" on which performance can come to depend more on the characteristics of the students and less on the characteristics of their families. From this vantage point, the school is a common ground where all students, regardless of family background, can move into the mainstream of American society. Furthermore, the school can also be a place where students of widely differing family backgrounds are exposed to basic societal values.

These issues have the most force in the disproportionately black and Hispanic low-income population. Unlike other minority groups, these families are less able to afford alternatives to public schools. Since these children come into the schools with the greatest initial disadvantage, they have the most to gain from the creation of a level playing field.

Both orientations assume that all schools perform the most basic function of schooling—teaching reading, writing, and arithmetic. Furthermore, both orientations assume that all schools prepare some students for college, some for vocational programs, and the remainder for immediate entry into the labor market. These more mundane goals are the easiest to measure. Differences in high school dropout rates measure the extent to which schools are differentially successful in bringing their students through to graduation. Achievement tests may assess cognitive skill levels fairly reliably. Differences in college enrollment rates indicate the extent to which schools prepare their students for admission to college.

But these comparisons cannot address the basic argument that lies at the heart of any discussion of the relative merits of public and private education. It is not enough for private schools to do a better job of imparting cognitive skills or to do a better job of preparing their students for the post–high school labor market. If the goal of the society were to submerge differences arising from family background, then allowing families to choose schools that reinforce those differences would clearly be counterproductive. But if the goal of the society were to allow choice, to encourage the maximum degree of diversity in educational offerings, then a single schooling system for all members of a community would be counterproductive.

The current debate about educational quality skirts these sensitive issues by focusing on the practical benefits of schooling. By this view, schools can be judged by their success in improving the cognitive skills and educational attainment of American students. From this perspective, one organizational form for schools is better than another if that form leads to higher cognitive skills, regardless of how that organizational form affects the values of its students.

In this section, we focus on the measurable outcomes of secondary schooling—dropout rates, achievement test scores, and college attendance rates. In particular, we analyze the level and distribution of these outcomes among students who attended the two largest groups of schools, public and Catholic secondary schools. As the preceding discussion implies, these particular outcomes are certainly not the only ones that are relevant to judgments concerning the relative merits of public versus private education, but they are the only outcomes for which we have direct measures.

There are two kinds of differences that will dominate our discussion. The first is whether Catholic schools are better, on average, than public schools: do Catholic high school students have lower dropout rates, higher gains in achievement in their high school years, and higher rates of postsecondary enrollment than comparable public high school students? A second question is whether different income classes have different outcomes *within* each sector. For example, among Catholic high school students, is achievement gain inversely related to family income or family socioeconomic status? And is that relationship stronger or weaker than in the public sector? Before summarizing the evidence on these questions, we briefly review two methodological issues related to these questions.

Parents often choose the schools that their children attend. This fact creates a potential problem, called "selectivity bias," in measuring the effect of schools on students. When looking at two distinct groups, such as Catholic high school students and public high school students, in which group membership is chosen rather than random, researchers must recognize the possibility that differences in the two groups may be a function not of the different *experiences* of the two groups but rather a function of the different *characteristics* of the two groups. In the current case, the differences between Catholic high school students and public high schools students may be due not to differences between Catholic and public high schools but rather to differences between the kinds of families that send their children to Catholic and public schools.

To ameliorate the potential selectivity bias, researchers try to account for differences in observable characteristics before coming to any conclusion about relative effectiveness. But unobservable differences are also potential sources of selection bias. If, for example, the parents of Catholic students feel more strongly about education than the parents of public high school students (and if those feelings are positively correlated with schooling outcomes), then differences between Catholic and public high school students may be spuriously attributed to the schools, even after the researchers have statistically controlled for all observable differences in background characteristics.

Coleman, Hoffer, and Kilgore (1982a, 1982b, and 1982c) found that Catholic-school students had higher achievement test scores than public-school students, both before and after adjusting for differences in the observed characteristics of the two groups. This finding generated considerable debate and the possibility that the Coleman et al. findings were affected by selectivity bias played no small role in that debate.

Another question addressed here is whether Catholic schools are differentially better for low-income students. Coleman and his colleagues believe that the answer to this question is "yes," and they have labeled the difference a "common school effect" (Coleman, Hoffer, and Kilgore 1982a, 1982b, 1982c; Hoffer, Greeley, and Coleman 1985; and Coleman and Hoffer 1987).

A "common school" is a locally controlled and publicly funded school whose students come from the surrounding neighborhood. If the students come from differing family backgrounds—from poor families and rich, black families and white—then, Coleman et al. argue, the effect of the common school is to lessen the impact of family characteristics over time.

Low family income and the other family characteristics that are associated with low income (such as low parental education and a high proportion of single-parent families) are among the primary disadvantages that the "common school" hopes to overcome. If students from low-income families start out with lower cognitive skills, then the common school will have succeeded if those students learn more than their higher-income classmates. In the remaining sections, we use data from the High School and Beyond Survey (HS&B) to look not only at the differences between Catholic and public high schools in overall average performance, but also at differences across income classes within each sector to try to measure the extent to which such a common school effect exists.

Comparing the Effects of Public and Private Schools
Differences in High School Dropout Rates

The difference between high school dropout rates at public and Catholic high schools, unadjusted for differences in student characteristics, is quite striking. In the High School and Beyond survey, the overall sophomore-to-senior dropout rate for the public schools was 14.4 percent, while it was only 3.3 percent for the Catholic schools.

Table 3.2 shows the dropout rates for public and Catholic high schools broken down both by family income and by the HS&B socioeconomic status variable. Among public high school students, there is a clear pattern of declining dropout rates as socioeconomic status increases. Because of the small sample of Catholic high school dropouts, any conclusions about dropout rates by sector should be viewed with extreme caution.[6]

Multivariate analysis, summarized in the appendix to this chapter, shows that the overall difference between the Catholic and public school

6. Despite small sample sizes (there were only 54 Catholic high school dropouts), Coleman and Hoffer interpret the lower section of table 3.2 as showing that, in the Catholic sector, ". . . the relation of dropping out to SES is greater than in either of the other sectors" (Coleman and Hoffer 1987, 128). "Other sectors" refer to "other-private" schools that Coleman and Hoffer also analyzed. We do not analyze HS&B respondents from these schools because they represent an extremely small and unrepresentative sample (Goldberger and Cain 1982).

TABLE 3.2 High School Dropout Rates by Family Income
and Type of School, High School Class of 1982

Indicates percentage of 1980 sophomores who dropped out by the
spring of 1982; unweighted number of dropouts are shown in
parentheses.

	Public		Catholic	
Overall	14.4	(2,065)	3.3	(54)
ANNUAL FAMILY INCOME IN 1980				
Less than $7,000	24.6	(277)	3.4	(5)
$ 7,000–$11,999	18.8	(281)	9.2	(9)
$12,000–$15,999	12.4	(283)	1.7	(7)
$16,000–$19,999	11.8	(264)	0.2	(4)
$20,000–$24,999	11.1	(219)	5.6	(7)
$25,000–$37,999	9.3	(127)	0.2	(3)
$38,000 or more	9.5	(107)	1.1	(4)
Refused	18.0	(283)	6.0	(8)
Missing	24.2	(220)	12.7	(7)
SOCIOECONOMIC STATUS QUARTILE				
1 (low)	22.3	(857)	14.9	(23)
2	13.2	(470)	3.3	(14)
3	10.7	(331)	0.2	(5)
4 (high)	7.1	(186)	1.7	(8)
Missing	31.8	(221)	16.8	(4)

SOURCE: Calculations by the authors from the first followup of the
High School and Beyond Survey (U.S. Department of Education 1981).
All results are weighted by the HS&B variable PANELWT. The only ex-
cluded observations are those for which PANELWT = 0.

dropout rate is partly due to differences in background characteristics.
When we control for some of those differences in background, the seeming
11 percentage point difference—between 14.4 percent and 3.3 percent—
drops to about 5 percentage points. The multivariate analysis does *not*
support the hypothesis that the relationship between socioeconomic status
and dropping out is different for Catholic and public high school students.
In summary, Catholic-school students are less likely to drop out than
public-school students. In addition, students with high socioeconomic status are less likely to drop out than those with low socioeconomic status,
but the relationship between dropping out and socioeconomic status seems
to be no different for Catholic and public school students.

Differences in Gains in Cognitive Skills

The evidence pertaining to the relative ability of public and private schools to impart cognitive skills is controversial. The major source of that evidence is again the High School and Beyond survey. In the HS&B, "cognitive skills" were measured by seven achievement tests, administered to about twenty thousand sophomores in the spring of 1980. To measure "achievement again," the identical tests were readministered to the same individuals in 1982.

The raw differences between public and Catholic high school students in the level and growth of cognitive skills favor the Catholic sector. Even when researchers control for observable differences between the two groups of students, a "Catholic-school advantage" remains.[7] Using estimates generated by Hoffer, Greeley, and Coleman (1985), Jencks (1985, 133) calculated that public-school students gain, on average, about 0.15 of a standard deviation per year while Catholic-school students gain 0.18 to 0.19 of a standard deviation per year. Therefore, the Catholic-school "advantage," measured between the students' sophomore and senior years in high school, is 0.03 to 0.04 of a standard deviation per year.[8]

The average gains of 0.15 and 0.18 to 0.19 mean that students do not seem to "learn" very much between their sophomore and senior years in high school, at least as measured by the HS&B achievement tests. But because the average gain is so small, the seemingly minute Catholic-school "advantage" of 0.03 to 0.04 of a standard deviation per year looms large

7. In summarizing a set of articles on Catholic and public school differences, Jencks (1985, 128) wrote:

All three articles agree on the following points:

1. Sophomores scored higher in Catholic schools than in public schools on all the tests administered in 1980.

2. Between their sophomore and senior years, Catholic-school students' raw scores on all tests except civics increased more than public-school students' raw scores. On the civics test, both groups gained the same amount.

3. When other measured sophomore characteristics are controlled, Catholic-school students still show a larger gain on the reading, vocabulary, math and writing tests. On the science and civics tests the results are less clearcut, varying with the exact estimation procedure.

8. It is common to use the "standard deviation" of test scores as a measure of difference among students or groups of students. For example, suppose the average gain in test scores was three correct answers, with a standard deviation of 1.2 answers. If the average public-school student gained 2.8 answers and the average Catholic-school student gained 3.1 answers, the difference (0.3 answers) would be expressed as 0.25 (0.3/1.2) of a standard deviation.

when measured as a proportion of the average gain. For example, if the average student gains 0.15 of a standard deviation per year, the Catholic-school advantage translates into about one-third of a school year. Extrapolating to a four-year high school career, this method of measuring "gain" implies that a student receives an additional year of high school training by virtue of attending a Catholic high school.

Controversy continues to swirl about the importance of this Catholic-school advantage. Measured as a proportion of the variability within a school, the advantage is very small. But measured against how much students learn, on average, in their high school years, it can seem much larger.

Another strong and controversial claim by Coleman et al. (1982a, 1982b, and 1982c) was that the Catholic advantage was especially strong for low-income students. If Catholic schools are more like "common schools" than public schools, the relationship between income and achievement must be weaker in the Catholic schools. For example, if achievement rises quickly with family income in the public schools, it must rise more slowly in the Catholic schools, indicating that those with low family income have less of a disadvantage in the Catholic schools.

In their discussion of results based on the HS&B, both Noell (1982) and Goldberger and Cain (1982) argued, on statistical grounds, that the differences between Catholic and public schools, if any, were not related to income or any other background characteristic. That is, they argued that if achievement rose with family income, the rate of increase was the same in public and Catholic schools. Willms made the same argument (Willms 1985, 108). As a result of their statistical tests, these authors constrained the effect of income to be the same for Catholic and public school students.[9] These authors thus implicitly assert that the benefit of achievement gain is equally distributed across income classes. When the relationship between income and achievement growth is left unconstrained (despite the statistical tests), it appears that the Catholic-school advantage is greatest for those with lower socioeconomic status.[10]

9. Formally, Noell (1982), Willms (1985), and Goldberger and Cain (1982) argued that an "additive" regression model was appropriate for estimating differences in achievement. Such a model constrains the effect of income or socioeconomic status to be the same across the two sectors. In contrast, Coleman et al. (1982a, 1982b, and 1982c) have argued in favor of a "nonadditive" model, which allows the effect of income to be different across the two sectors. As a result, only Coleman et al. estimated different income effects for Catholic and public schools.

10. One set of such results (without controls for family background) is as follows (Hoffer, Greeley, and Coleman 1985, table 1.2, p. 77):

In reviewing the evidence concerning the differential benefits of Catholic schools for disadvantaged students, Jencks (1985, 131) wrote:

> All we can say is that although there is some evidence that Catholic schooling is especially effective for initially disadvantaged students, this evidence [of Hoffer et al.] should not be taken too seriously unless it is corroborated in other samples. The fact that Coleman, Hoffer and Kilgore (1982a, 1982b) found the same pattern among seniors in these schools in 1980 does, however, support their general argument.

The new longitudinal study being conducted by the Department of Education, the National Education Longitudinal Study (NELS), will soon yield "achievement gain" data for a nationally representative sample of students who were in the eighth grade in 1988. Analyses of NELS achievement gain, using techniques similar to those discussed here, will provide another look at the "common school" question.

Differences in Postsecondary Enrollment

Another potentially important difference between public and Catholic schools is in the percentage of students who enroll in postsecondary school. Again, the raw differences between Catholic and public school students are quite large. Table 3.3 shows that 51.7 percent of Catholic-school students enrolled in four-year colleges as compared to 28.7 percent of public-school students. The Catholic-school students maintain their advantage when we look at the percentage enrolled in *either* two-year or four-year schools—67.4 percent of all Catholic-school students were enrolled full time in two- or four-year schools as were 45.2 percent of public-school students.

When other background characteristics are statistically "held constant," the difference between the four-year college enrollment rates of Catholic and public-school students drops from 23 percentage points to about 12

Socioeconomic Status Quartile	Overall "Catholic Advantage" in Achievement Growth
1	2.37 items correct
2 & 3 combined	1.68 items correct
4 high	1.86 items correct

Here, the students from the lowest socioeconomic quartile gained more (on all tests combined) than students from the higher quartiles. The statistical significance of these results was not reported.

TABLE 3.3 College Enrollment Rates, by Family Income and Type of High School, High School Class of 1982

	Two-Year and Four-Year Institutions		Four-Year Institutions Only	
	Public	Catholic	Public	Catholic
Overall	45.2%	67.4%	28.7%	51.7%
ANNUAL FAMILY INCOME IN 1980				
Less than $7,000	26.1(%)	41.5(%)	14.4(%)	19.8(%)
$ 7,000–$11,999	35.2	57.5	19.2	36.2
$12,000–$15,999	40.1	67.7	23.7	54.5
$16,000–$19,999	44.9	60.6	27.0	40.3
$20,000–$24,999	48.6	67.5	31.2	49.5
$25,000–$37,999	56.2	76.1	39.2	62.2
$38,000 or more	59.9	72.5	44.1	60.3
SOCIOECONOMIC STATUS QUARTILE				
1 (low)	24.4(%)	42.0(%)	11.9(%)	25.6(%)
2	37.7	59.6	21.2	40.3
3	49.3	66.5	29.8	47.9
4 (high)	69.4	77.7	52.3	64.4

SOURCE: Calculations by the authors from the second followup of the High School and Beyond Survey (U.S. Department of Education 1981). All results are weighted by the HS&B variable TESTWT2.

percentage points. The public-Catholic difference in two- and four-year enrollment rates drops from 22 percentage points to 10. Table 3.3 also suggests a "common school" effect of Catholic schools—the relationship between income or socioeconomic status and enrollment seems weaker for the Catholic-school graduates. But when other variables are held constant, there is no evidence that the relationship between income and enrollment is any different for Catholic and public high school graduates. The details of these results are reported in the Appendix.

Discussion

The vast majority of American children attend public schools. Those who attend private schools have higher family incomes, on average, than those who attend public schools.

While questions of socialization are at the heart of the debate about the relative merits of public and private schools, empirical evidence is limited to objective indicators of school "success"—dropout rates, achievement growth, or college enrollment rates. "Better outcomes," on average, in one type of school versus the other, constitute one measure of success. Another is the extent to which one type of school succeeds more than the other in closing the gap between disadvantaged and advantaged students.

We have reviewed the evidence from the High School and Beyond longitudinal survey on the relative performance of public and Catholic schools. One of the outcomes—achievement growth—has been extensively analyzed by other researchers. It seems that the achievement scores of Catholic high school students do grow faster than those of public high school students (and start at a higher level as well). But the substantive importance of this "Catholic advantage" in achievement growth is not obvious. Evidence for greater "common-school" effect in Catholic schools—a greater advantage for low-income students—is "quite suggestive but not conclusive" (Jencks 1985, 134).

Dropout rates and the rate of enrollment in four-year colleges are significantly and substantively different in Catholic and public schools. After adjusting for differences in student background, Catholic school students are about 5 percentage points less likely to drop out of high school and about 12 percentage points more likely to enroll in a four-year college or university. In neither case is there any evidence that public or Catholic schools are "better" for low-income students.

While there has been considerably less research on dropout rates or enrollment rates using the HS&B, our results are consistent with those of Coleman and Hoffer (1987). But the small number of Catholic school students and the extremely small number of Catholic high school dropouts should lead readers to view all such analyses with extreme caution. Our analysis of college enrollment rates applies only to enrollment in the academic term following high school graduation. Further analysis of enrollment over longer time periods might lead to different results.

In closing, it is important to reiterate that the issue of whether public or Catholic schools are "better" is, in many ways, tangential to the important issue of "choice" among elementary or secondary schools. The range of alternative schools—public and private—is growing rapidly, especially in low-income areas. In coming years, we will be able to observe the relative performance of the children attending these new schools and we will be able to judge the relative effectiveness of these schools. If the public school/ Catholic school debate is any guide, however, the fact that parents *choose* to send their children to the new schools will create enough disagreement about the validity of statistical analysis to make any firm conclusion impossible.

II. The Distribution of the Benefits of Postsecondary Education

Public colleges and universities, heavily subsidized by public funds, make higher education accessible to virtually all high school graduates. The private nonprofit sector, consisting of about two thousand independent and church-affiliated institutions, furnishes another set of educational choices in addition to the already wide range of public colleges and universities. Because of the relatively high cost of private higher education, however, students from low- and moderate-income families may not be able to take advantage of these additional choices.

We begin this section by providing an overview of the distribution of family income among public and private college students. Next, we address the issue of whether the earnings of graduates of public institutions are different from the earnings of graduates of private institutions. We then examine the educational subsidies received by students with different family income levels.

The Clientele of Nonprofit Colleges and Universities

The relative size of the nonprofit sector has diminished over the last thirty years as the growth of community colleges has increased the proportion of students attending public institutions and as the proprietary sector has expanded. Table 3.4, adapted from Mortenson and Wu (1990), shows the proportion of unmarried students aged 18 to 24 attending private colleges and universities by family income quartiles. In 1971, the first year shown in table 3.4, the proportion of students enrolled in private institutions was 23 percent. The overall private sector share of enrollments rose somewhat in the late seventies and early eighties before dropping again toward the end of the decade.

Not surprisingly, the proportion of low-income students attending private institutions has been consistently lower than the proportion of high-income students attending private institutions. This "gap" ranged from 15 percentage points in 1977 to only 5 percentage points in 1979.

Another view of the relationship between private school enrollment and family income can be obtained using data from the National Postsecondary Student Aid Study (NPSAS), a national sample of students at all levels in all types of institutions in fall of 1986. The upper section of table 3.5 shows the percentage of dependent students attending public, private nonprofit, and for-profit proprietary institutions, by 1985 family income. The

TABLE 3.4 The Proportion of Students in the Nonprofit Sector:
Unmarried College Students, Ages 18–24, by Year and Family Income

		Family Income Quartile			
	Overall	1	2	3	4
Year	Proportion	(Low)			(High)
1971	22.9(%)	18.7(%)	19.4(%)	22.3(%)	28.2(%)
1972	24.0	16.2	21.0	25.0	30.2
1973	24.7	19.4	20.7	26.4	29.1
1974	24.3	16.5	22.0	24.2	30.4
1975	22.3	18.6	20.4	21.2	26.7
1976	22.6	16.4	21.3	22.5	27.1
1977	23.0	15.4	18.8	22.9	30.3
1978	26.0	21.3	23.8	26.5	30.1
1979	24.1	20.1	22.9	26.5	25.5
1980	NA	NA	NA	NA	NA
1981	25.8	17.5	22.1	29.4	30.2
1982	24.0	17.9	21.7	25.1	27.6
1983	24.5	21.6	21.0	25.1	27.5
1984	20.9	15.0	21.2	21.9	22.7
1985	22.9	17.5	19.8	23.1	27.7
1986	24.0	18.9	21.2	23.9	28.8
1987	NA	NA	NA	NA	NA
1988	NA	NA	NA	NA	NA
1989	21.3	17.9	20.2	18.7	25.9

SOURCE: Adapted from Mortenson and Wu (1990, table 27).

interesting point in that part of table 3.5 is the disproportionate percentage of students from upper-income families attending private colleges. Half of those with family incomes of more than $100,000 attend private colleges and universities. For those with family income below $75,000, only about one-fifth are in private colleges.

The lower section of table 3.5 organizes the same data in a slightly different way, showing the distribution of enrollment by family income in each of the three sectors. The fraction of students in private institutions coming from families with incomes of more than $75,000 is twice as large as the fraction of such students at public institutions. Still, about 20 percent of students in private institutions have family incomes below $20,000. These figures suggest that students in private institutions come disproportionately, but not exclusively, from wealthy families.

Yet another perspective on the incomes of students at different types of colleges and universities can be obtained from the data collected annually by the Cooperative Institutional Research Program (CIRP) through sur-

TABLE 3.5 Percentage of Students in the Nonprofit Sector by Family
Income and Type of Institution

PERCENTAGES OF STUDENTS ATTENDING PUBLIC, PRIVATE NONPROFIT, AND FOR-PROFIT
POSTSECONDARY INSTITUTIONS, BY FAMILY INCOME

Annual Family Income in 1985	Public	Private Nonprofit	For-Profit	Total
Less than $12,000	73.1(%)	18.8(%)	8.0(%)	100.0(%)
$12,000–$19,999	76.5	17.6	5.8	100.0
$20,000–$29,999	75.3	20.3	4.4	100.0
$30,000–$39,999	75.5	21.2	3.4	100.0
$40,000–$49,999	76.1	21.8	2.1	100.0
$50,000–$74,999	70.8	27.5	1.7	100.0
$75,000–$100,000	65.4	34.1	0.4	100.0
More than $100,000	49.3	49.8	0.7	100.0

DISTRIBUTION OF STUDENTS BY FAMILY INCOME, BY TYPE OF
POSTSECONDARY INSTITUTION

Annual Family Income in 1985	Public	Private Nonprofit	For-Profit
Less than $12,000	13.2(%)	10.6(%)	28.9(%)
$12,000–$19,999	12.2	8.8	18.3
$20,000–$29,999	17.0	14.2	19.6
$30,000–$39,999	18.2	16.0	15.7
$40,000–$49,999	15.3	13.8	8.1
$50,000–$74,999	17.1	20.8	8.0
$75,000–$100,000	4.1	6.8	0.5
More than $100,000	2.9	9.1	0.8
Total	100.0%	100.0%	100.0%

SOURCE: Calculations by the authors from the National Postsecondary Student Aid Study
(U.S. Department of Education 1987a).

veys of full-time, first-time, first-year students in public and private nonprofit colleges and universities. These data, shown for fall 1989 in table
3.6, reconfirm the disproportionate representation of higher-income students in nonprofit institutions. For example, 17.6 percent of first-year students at four-year private institutions come from families with income
greater than $100,000; the analogous percentage for first-year students at
four-year public institutions is 5.6 percent.

The socioeconomic imbalance differs somewhat by subcategories of
schools. The CIRP data break four-year private institutions into three categories: Protestant, Catholic, and private nonaffiliated. The distribution of
family income among Catholic and Protestant colleges is surprisingly sim-

TABLE 3.6 The Distribution by Family Income of Full-time College Freshmen, 1989

Family Income	All	Four-Year Public	Four-Year Private	Public University	Private University
Less than $10,000	5.8(%)	5.9(%)	4.5(%)	3.7(%)	2.5(%)
$10,000–$19,999	10.1	10.0	8.5	7.7	5.1
$20,000–$29,999	14.0	14.1	11.3	11.4	7.8
$30,000–$39,999	18.3	18.9	14.9	15.9	11.7
$40,000–$49,999	12.8	13.8	11.1	12.8	9.7
$50,000–$74,999	22.6	24.6	22.6	26.4	23.9
$75,000–$99,999	7.2	7.1	9.6	9.8	12.7
$100,000–$149,999	4.8	3.5	7.6	6.7	11.5
$150,000 or more	4.5	2.1	10.0	5.4	15.0
Total	100.0%	100.0%	100.0%	100.0%	100.0%
Unweighted Sample Size	216,362	32,108	77,846	59,021	31,482

NOTE: Two-year schools, with sample size of 15,905, are excluded from this table.

SOURCE: Cooperative Institutional Research Program, *The American Freshman: National Norms for Fall 1989*, December 1989. These data refer to full-time first-time freshmen; 22 percent of the surveyed schools are represented in these data.

ilar to the distribution of income at public four-year institutions.[11] Only in the "private university" category, where more than 25 percent of the students come from families with income greater than $100,000, is the distribution of income heavily weighted toward high-income families.

The important implication of these numbers is that the differential benefits from attending nonprofit institutions, if any, reach different income

11. The CIRP distribution for Protestant and Catholic schools is as follows:

Annual Family Income in 1985	Four-Year Protestant	Four-Year Catholic
Less than $10,000	6.2(%)	4.3(%)
$10,000–$19,999	10.5	8.0
$20,000–$29,999	14.7	11.4
$30,000–$39,999	17.7	16.9
$40,000–$49,999	11.8	12.1
$50,000–$74,999	21.0	24.0
$75,000–$99,999	7.2	8.8
$100,000–$149,999	5.2	6.8
$150,000 or more	6.0	7.6
Total	100.0%	100.0%
Unweighted Sample Size	22,621	13,856

groups, depending not only on type of control—public or private—but also on the type of public institution and the type of nonprofit institution.

Comparing the Effects of Public and Private Colleges
Differences in Earnings after Graduation

In assessing the quality of postsecondary institutions, we lack the achievement growth data that the High School and Beyond survey provides for secondary students. One way to assess the differential quality of public and private postsecondary institutions is to look at their differential effects on post-college earnings. While a number of attempts have been made to include measures of college quality in studies of the impact of education on earnings, the impact of institutional control has not been widely examined.[12] In principle, both detailed educational histories and lifetime earnings histories are required to assess the differential earnings impact of public and private colleges. Lacking such histories, the available options are limited.

The National Longitudinal Study of the Class of 1972 (NLS-72) provides some data appropriate for studying the different long-run outcomes generated by public and private colleges and universities. The best analysis of earnings using these data is James et al. (1989).

Using NLS-72 data on the 1985 earnings of male college graduates, James et al. looked at the influence of public versus private control, holding average scores on entrance examinations constant. The authors found that attending Eastern private colleges had a statistically significant impact on earnings, with graduates of these institutions having about a 5 percent earnings advantage over graduates of public institutions. Attending private institutions in other parts of the country, however, had a negative (but insignificant) impact on earnings. James et al. concluded that the characteristics of the college attended explain only about 1 to 2 percent of the variance in earnings among male college graduates. Variables such as college major and grade point average proved to have a much larger impact.

The most recent source of data on the differential impact of institutional control on post-college earnings is the High School and Beyond survey. We

---

12. A number of studies, using a variety of data sources, have found that college *quality* has a measurable impact on earnings. These studies include Reed and Miller (1970), Wales (1973), Solmon and Wachtel (1975), Trusheim and Crouse (1981), and Smart (1988). The consensus of this literature is consistent with the findings of James et al., in that college quality explains only a small part of the variation in earnings among graduates; other variables, including background differences, differences in motivation and area of study explain more of the variation in earnings.

have analyzed two groups of recent college graduates from the HS&B. One group had graduated from public colleges and universities by February, 1986, and the other had graduated from private nonprofit institutions. Using these data, we compared the postgraduation earnings of the two groups. We are interested in whether students from private nonprofit schools earn more, *ceteris paribus,* than students from public schools and in whether earnings differentials are similar for students at all income levels.

The latest available responses from the HS&B date from 1986, only six years after the students' high school graduation. At that time, many respondents had not yet finished their formal education. For example, based on the educational attainment of past cohorts, we expect that 25 percent of the HS&B respondents will eventually obtain a bachelor's degree. As of February, 1986, however, only about 19 percent of the HS&B class of 1980 respondents had obtained an undergraduate degree.

Furthermore, our analysis of earnings is complicated by the fact that those who are working in February of 1986 are a select subgroup of the college graduates. Over 11 percent of the sample were taking academic courses and about 4 percent were in graduate school. We exclude the workers who were simultaneously enrolled in school, but we do not attempt to adjust for the bias introduced by our sample selection.

For the sample as a whole, average hourly wages for public and private college graduates are approximately equal. However, public-college men earned about twenty cents more per hour than private-college men, while public-college women earned about twenty cents less per hour than private-college women. When we use regression analysis to control for other observable differences among graduates, these wage differences disappear. In addition, there are no statistically significant differences in earnings differentials across the different income groups.[13] The lack of any significant differences between the earnings of graduates of public and private institutions at such an early stage in their earnings history is not surprising. After all, as noted above, James et al. found few differences after many more years.

Differences in Subsidies while in School

Few college students pay the full cost of their education. Students and their families pay tuition, of course, but tuition normally covers only a part of

---

13. Detailed results of this analysis are shown in the Appendix.

the cost of education. The remaining educational costs are subsidized; that is, they are borne either by taxpayers in general or by colleges and universities themselves. If, as suggested in chapter 1 of this volume, we are attempting to approximate the benefits by the difference between the value of services received (or willingness to pay) and actual payment, these subsidies are related to benefits.[14]

The overall subsidy received by each college student is the difference between the cost of providing education and the amount of tuition and fees the student actually pays. The subsidy may come from either public or private (usually institutional) funds. If the money goes directly to the student to assist in paying tuition and fees, the subsidy is called a "direct" subsidy. Direct subsidies include federal dollars from student aid programs such as Stafford Loans (formerly Guaranteed Student Loans) and Pell Grants, as well as grants and loans from states, institutions, and other sources. Direct subsidies vary considerably from student to student; some students pay the full tuition, while others receive substantial amounts of direct aid.

An "indirect" subsidy is the difference between the cost of providing education and the tuition charged by the institution—the "sticker price" of education. Public funds provided to public colleges and universities and private contributions to private colleges and universities are the major sources of indirect subsidies.[15]

It is unclear whether subsidies should be defined as the difference between the sticker price of education (the maximum any individual student

14. By using subsidies as a measure of benefit, we are treating education as a consumption good rather than as an investment good that will yield a stream of future returns. This is not, of course, a complete view of education and our discussion of subsidies is meant only as a supplement to the incomplete information that we have on that stream of future returns. Subsidies would be a good proxy for the total benefits received from education only if the market worked so perfectly as to equate the resource cost of education (or the price charged to the highest-paying consumers) to the present value of the lifetime benefits generated.

15. Since we will be distinguishing between the various types of subsidies throughout the remainder of the chapter, it may be helpful to illustrate the four kinds of subsidy that we have defined. This list is not exhaustive.

	Public	Private
Direct	Pell Grant Stafford Loans	Institutional grants, loans, and tuition waivers
Indirect	Tax support for public colleges	Revenues from endowments

Aid in the form of "work-study" is not included since it is paid in return for productive services.

actually pays) and the amount paid by a student, or as the difference between the cost of producing education and the amount the student pays. Since neither of these is a precise measure of the benefit accruing to students, but both shed light on the issue, we examine the distribution of total subsidies, both direct and indirect.

The extent to which students are subsidized depends primarily on whether they attend public or private schools and on their family income. On average, tuition and fees constitute 55 percent of revenues at private higher education institutions, but only 18 percent at public colleges and universities (U.S. Department of Education 1987b, 117). Thus, students attending private colleges are subsidized at a lower rate than students attending public colleges. Direct subsidies depend both on income and on the type of institution attended. Among students at any individual institution, financial aid is greater for students from lower-income families because most financial aid to college students is need-based. Within any income group, financial aid is higher for those attending higher-cost institutions.[16]

The nature of the distribution of educational subsidies across income classes is not obvious.[17] Young people from low-income families are much less likely to be part of the postsecondary educational system than those from more affluent backgrounds, so educational subsidies are unlikely to be concentrated among people from families with very low incomes. But if they go to college, low-income students receive relatively high direct public subsidies from the need-based Pell and Stafford programs and from institutional funds at private colleges. This fact, plus the fact that low-income students are more likely to attend public institutions, where indirect subsidies are highest, contributes to the pro-poor character of subsidies. However, because low-income students are less likely to attend high-cost institutions, they may be receiving lower dollar subsidies than high-income students at high-cost private institutions.

The existing information on total subsidies received by college students is limited. Lee (1987) and Lee and Sango-Jordan (1988) used data on 1980

16. The extent of student subsidies also depends on the student's choice of major, but these subsidies are difficult to measure and we do not attempt to measure them here.

17. We examine only the incidence of subsidies across income classes, ignoring the taxes that individuals might have paid to fund the subsidy program. There is another line of research that tries to account for both subsidies and taxes. Leslie and Brinkman (1988) reviewed this literature, reanalyzing the data and standardizing methodology. They concluded that the public higher education financing system in the United States tends to be pro-poor, although the degree to which this is true varies considerably across states.

high school graduates from the High School and Beyond survey and institutional cost data from the Higher Education General Institutional Survey (HEGIS) for 1980 and 1983 to estimate average per student subsidies, including both direct and indirect subsidies for college students with different family incomes attending different types of institutions.

Lee found that while students from families with relatively low incomes received higher subsidies, on average, than those from more affluent families, the differences were not great.[18] The small advantage for the lower-income group was the result of two conflicting forces. The distribution of direct student aid, which was provided largely by public programs, was skewed in favor of the poor. But this advantage in student financial aid was offset, to some degree, by larger institutional subsidies received by the wealthier students.

Comparing the subsidies received by students at different types of institutions, Lee found that those in private four-year colleges received the largest average subsidy. For 1983, this figure of about $5,500 per student compared to about $5,000 for students in four-year public institutions and about $2,500 for those in two-year public institutions. Lee and Sango-Jordan found the type of institution attended, differentiated by length of program and tuition level as well as by type of institutional control, had a greater impact on the total subsidy a student received than did demographic variables, including family income. They did not calculate average subsidies by income separately for public and private institutions.

Following Lee's methodology, we have generated a somewhat different distribution of subsidies to postsecondary students.[19] The National Postsecondary Student Aid Study (NPSAS) provides information on all forms of aid received by a nationally representative sample of college students in fall of 1986. Merging these data with the institutional cost data provided by HEGIS allowed us to estimate average direct and indirect subsidies by income levels within each institutional type.[20]

18. In 1983, according to Lee, the average subsidy for students with family incomes below $12,000 was approximately $4,300. For those with family incomes between $25,000 and $38,000, it was $3,800, and for those with incomes above $38,000, it was $4,000. When the subsidy was broken down into its institutional and student aid components, the student aid component was pro-poor, while the institutional subsidy showed no clear pattern.

19. Lee and Sango-Jordan (1989) used NPSAS data to study direct aid to postsecondary students. They did not present results that allow examination of the distribution of direct subsidies by family income within institutional types.

20. Educational costs are defined in accordance with Lee's (1987) methodology. Because the HEGIS data are for the 1985–86 fiscal year, we adjusted for the change in the Consumer Price Index between 1985 and 1986. All expenditures reported as "education and general"

TABLE 3.7 Average Direct and Indirect Subsidies Received by Dependent Students by Type of Institution, Fall, 1986

Annual Family Income in 1986	Direct Subsidy		Indirect Subsidy		Total Subsidy	
	Public	Private	Public	Private	Public	Private
Less than $ 12,000	$1,393	$4,124	$5,183	$2,451	$6,576	$6,575
$12,000–$ 19,999	$1,255	$4,350	$5,092	$2,774	$6,347	$7,124
$20,000–$ 29,999	$ 786	$3,845	$5,286	$2,616	$6,072	$6,461
$30,000–$ 39,999	$ 515	$3,142	$5,414	$2,642	$5,929	$5,784
$40,000–$ 49,999	$ 410	$2,485	$5,474	$2,401	$5,884	$4,886
$50,000–$ 74,999	$ 282	$2,013	$5,953	$2,551	$6,235	$4,564
$75,000–$ 99,999	$ 243	$1,283	$6,084	$3,290	$6,327	$4,573
More than $100,000	$ 268	$ 542	$7,061	$3,380	$7,329	$3,922
Overall Average	$ 688	$2,770	$5,495	$2,660	$6,183	$3,430

NOTE: direct subsidies include grants, 30 percent of face value of loans, and other nonwork forms of aid to individual students. Indirect subsidies are calculated by subtracting tuition and fees from the institution's educational costs. Educational costs inlcude all expenditures reported as "education and general," except research and scholarship costs. Auxiliary costs, including dormitories and cafeterias, are not included. Average student costs are calculated by dividing costs by number of FTE's. For part-time students, this method will overestimate the indirect subsidy received.

SOURCE: Computations by the authors from the 1987 National Postsecondary Student Aid Study (U.S. Department of Education 1987) and the 1986 Higher Education General Information Survey.

Table 3.7 summarizes the results for dependent students at public and private colleges and universities.[21] The first two columns show the average direct subsidy received by students from families with different incomes at public and private institutions. These subsidies include publicly funded programs as well as funds provided by institutions to individual students. Following Lee, loan subsidies are assumed to be 30 percent of the face value of the loans received. The total amount of aid received by students in an income bracket is averaged over the total number of students in that bracket, including those who received no aid at all.

---

except research and scholarship costs are included. Clearly, this is a very rough approximation of the cost of educating students and alternative definitions might yield different results. We have assumed that the cost of education is the same for each student at a particular institution. In fact, the course of study has a significant impact on educational costs. In addition, the portion of faculty salaries which actually represents instructional costs rather than research subsidies differs widely across institutions.

21. All of our calculations from the NPSAS are based on data for *dependent* students only, both undergraduates and graduates. Dependent students (those, roughly speaking, who rely on their parents for financial support) make up approximately 55 percent of all undergraduate students; we exclude independent students because we have no information about the

The figures show that, on average, students in the nonprofit educational sector receive four times as much direct subsidy as do those in the public sector. Except in the two highest income brackets, the average subsidies to students in private colleges are larger than the average subsidy in the *lowest* income category in the public sector. Within the private sector, direct subsidies are pro-poor, with students from families with incomes below $30,000 receiving about $4,000, those from families with incomes between $30,000 and $75,000 receiving between $2,000 and $3,000, and those with incomes over $100,000 receiving an average of about $500.

As the third and fourth columns indicate, the indirect subsidy received by students attending public colleges and universities is about twice as high as that received by private sector students. In both the public and private sectors, indirect subsidies are relatively flat across income categories, although there is some increase at the top of the distribution.

Because the indirect subsidies tend to be evenly distributed, the distribution of total subsidies (shown in the last two columns) must be less pro-poor than the distribution of direct subsidies. If we define lower-income as less than $12,000, middle-income as $30,000–$39,999 and upper income as $75,000–$99,999, the average total subsidy of $6,575 to lower-income students in private institutions is about 1.4 times the $4,573 subsidy to upper-income students. The $5,784 total subsidy to middle-income students is about 1.3 times that received by upper-income students. These ratios for direct subsidies in the private sector are 3.2 and 2.4, respectively. Still, these total subsidies appear to be significantly more pro-poor than are those in the public sector, where evenly distributed indirect subsidies

---

income of the family in which they grew up. The results are not significantly different when only undergraduates are considered.

The unweighted NPSAS sample sizes used to construct tables 3.6 and 3.7 are as follows:

Annual Family Income in 1985	Public	Private
Less than $ 12,000	1,535	1,145
$12,000–$ 19,999	1,405	1,000
$20,000–$ 29,999	2,060	1,541
$30,000–$ 39,999	2,260	1,756
$40,000–$ 49,999	1,934	1,525
$50,000–$ 74,999	2,315	2,297
$75,000–$100,000	583	744
More than $100,000	482	1,016
Overall	12,574	11,024

dominate need-based direct subsidies and the highest total subsidies actually accrue to those in the highest income bracket.

In sum, if benefits are defined as the difference between full tuition and actual tuition paid (a difference we have called the direct subsidy), subsidies to students in the nonprofit sector are clearly pro-poor. At the same time, they are much higher than those received by the somewhat less well-off students in the public sector. If benefits are defined as the difference between the cost of producing education and the price paid by individual students (the total subsidy), the subsidies in the nonprofit sector, while less pro-poor than direct subsidies, are definitely more heavily weighted toward the poor than are those in the public sector. But, in contrast to direct subsidies, they are lower, on average, than those received by public-sector students. Low-income students receive similar total subsidies, regardless of the type of school they attend, but higher-income students are much more heavily subsidized in the public sector.

Table 3.8 shows the percentage of all subsidies received by students in various income categories. The upper section pertains to private institutions, while the lower section contains the same information for public institutions. The first column in each panel shows the income distribution of the student bodies, reproduced from table 3.1. The remaining columns show the percentages of the direct, indirect, and total subsidies that accrue to students in each income category. In private colleges, 30 percent of the direct subsidies and 24 percent of the total subsidies go to the 19 percent of students who are in the two lowest income brackets. The 44 percent of students in the $20,000 to $50,000 income range get 50 percent of the direct subsidies and 46 percent of the total subsidies, while the 37 percent of students in the three upper-income categories share 20 percent of the direct subsidies and 30 percent of the indirect subsidies.

The distribution of direct subsidies in the public sector is much more heavily weighted toward the lower-income brackets, with 48 percent going to the 25 percent of students in the two lower brackets and only 10 percent going to the 24 percent of students from families with incomes of $50,000 or higher. But the distribution of total subsidies is quite similar to that in the private sector, with just under half going to the thee middle-income brackets and the rest almost equally divided between the top and the bottom of the distribution. In the private sector, more of the subsidy goes to the upper brackets, which include a significantly larger portion of the student body than in the public sector.

College students tend to come from families with relatively high income.

TABLE 3.8 Distribution of Total Direct and Indirect
Subsidies to Dependent Students in Private and Public
Postsecondary Institutions by Income Bracket

Annual Family Income in 1985	Percent of all Students	Percent of Subsidy Received by Students		
		Direct	Indirect	Total
PRIVATE NONPROFIT SECTOR				
Less than $12,000	11(%)	16(%)	10(%)	13(%)
$ 12,000–$19,999	9	14	9	11
$ 20,000–$29,999	14	20	14	17
$ 30,000–$39,999	16	18	16	17
$ 40,000–$49,999	14	12	12	12
$ 50,000–$74,999	21	15	20	18
$ 75,000–$99,999	7	3	8	6
$100,000 or more	9	2	11	6
Total	100%	100%	100%	100%
PUBLIC SECTOR				
Less than $12,000	13(%)	26(%)	12(%)	14(%)
$ 12,000–$19,999	12	22	11	12
$ 20,000–$29,999	17	19	16	17
$ 30,000–$39,999	18	14	18	17
$ 40,000–$49,999	15	9	15	15
$ 50,000–$74,999	17	7	19	17
$ 75,000–$99,999	4	2	5	4
$100,000 or more	3	1	4	4
Total	100%	100%	100%	100%

SOURCE: National Postsecondary Student Aid Study, 1987; U.S. Bureau of
the Census (1985); computations by the authors.

That is, subsidies to postsecondary students are unlikely to be concentrated on the poor since college attendance is positively correlated with income. Thus, when we look at average subsidies from the perspective of the population of 18–24-year-olds as a whole, their distribution is dramatically altered.[22] Columns (1) and (2) of table 3.9 show the total subsidies received by college students in both the public and the nonprofit sectors,

22. These data on 18–24-year-olds are based on Census data for 1985, which provide income distributions for families with one child between the ages of 18 and 24 and for families with two or more children in this age range. The approximations we have used do not account for the fact that some families have more than two children in this age bracket.

TABLE 3.9 Distribution of Total Subsidies by Family Income for All Dependent Students and for All Youth Aged 18–24

Annual Family Income in 1985	Total Subsidy ($billions)		Population Aged 18–24 (3)	Number of Students	
	Private (1)	Public (2)		Private (4)	Public (5)
Less than $12,000	$1.67	$4.48	3,201	254	682
$12,000–$19,999	1.53	4.01	2,407	215	632
$20,000–$29,999	2.24	5.42	2,629	347	893
$30,000–$39,999	2.24	5.65	2,660	388	953
$40,000–$49,999	1.65	4.80	1,581	337	815
$50,000 and over	3.96	8.21	2,705	898	1,286
Total	$13.29	$32.57	15,183	2,439	5,261

Annual Family Income in 1985	Average Subsidy per Student		Average Subsidy per Person, 18–24	
	Private (6)	Public (7)	Private (8)	Public (9)
Less than $12,000	$6,575	$6,576	$ 522	$1,401
$12,000–$19,999	7,124	6,347	636	1,667
$20,000–$29,999	6,461	6,072	853	2,062
$30,000–$39,999	5,784	5,929	844	2,124
$40,000–$49,999	4,886	5,884	1,041	3,033
$50,000 and over	4,408	6,383	1,463	3,034
Total	$5,430	$6,183	$ 875	$2,145

SOURCE: National Postsecondary Student Aid Study, 1987; U.S. Bureau of the Census (1985, 35); computations by the authors.

broken down by family income.[23] Those columns illustrate that the total amount of subsidy rises with income class. This pattern is the result of both larger numbers of students in the higher-income classes and the relatively flat pattern of average total per-student subsidies across income classes.

Columns (3)–(5) show the number of 18–24-year-olds in the U.S. population and the number of (dependent) students in the public and nonprofit sectors. When we calculate the distribution of average total subsidies *per student*, as in columns (6) and (7), we note again the pro-poor appearance of average total subsidies observed in table 3.7. But when we use the same

23. Recall that our calculations are based in NPSAS data for dependent students only, a group constituting only slightly more than 50 percent of overall college enrollment. Because of this, the total dollar values of subsidies reported in columns (1) and (2) of table 3.9 are smaller than the usual aggregates.

subsidy estimates to calculate the average total subsidy per *young adult,* we observe a pro-rich distribution.

Using all young people as the base group, the total subsidies in the private sector are concentrated in the higher-income brackets.[24] On average, young people in families with incomes below $12,000 received $522 of total subsidy for study in a private college. This compares to $1,463 for those whose family incomes are $50,000 or higher. In the public sector, total subsidies are also pro-rich, ranging from $1,401 in the lowest income bracket to $3,034 in the highest.

As we noted above, the distribution of subsidies is broadly pro-poor when we look at the income distribution of students receiving those subsidies. But table 3.9 should drive home the point that the pro-poor nature of that distribution quickly turns around if we account for the observed fact that students come disproportionately from high-income families.

Implications of Subsidy Levels

Suppose the nonprofit sector were to shrink, marginally, because of higher relative tuition increases in that sector. How would the distribution of educational subsidies change?

Previous research suggests that increases in the public-private price differential between the two sectors will cause some shifting but that the shifting will be limited. We assume that it would be middle-class students who shift, continuing a pattern suggested by Mortenson and Wu (1990) and Schapiro, O'Malley, and Litten (1990). Need tends to be met by aid for low-income students, and high-income students tend to be less sensitive to price changes.

Based on the above discussion, it is clear that middle-income students transferring from the private sector to the public sector would receive higher indirect public subsidies. They would, however, receive lower

24. The distribution of direct aid is as follows:

Annual Family Income in 1985	Average Direct Subsidy per Young Person, 18–24	
	Private	Public
Less than $12,000	$327	$297
$12,000–$19,999	389	330
$20,000–$29,999	507	267
$30,000–$39,999	458	185
$40,000–$49,999	530	211
$50,000 and over	505	130

amounts of need-based direct federal aid and give up the subsidies they receive from private institutional and philanthropic sources.

Using the average subsidy levels reported in tables 3.6–3.8, we see that the average student in a private college transferring to a public college would receive a higher total subsidy—an increase from $5,430 to $6,183. The decline in direct subsidy from $2,770 to $688 would be more than offset by an increase in indirect subsidy from $2,660 to $5,495. The $753 net increase in subsidy would be the result of a loss of $4,013 in privately funded subsidy and an increase of $4,766 in publicly funded subsidy.

On the one hand, if public funding for higher education remained constant, the transfer of middle-income students from private to public sectors would leave less public money to support the education of low-income students. On the other hand, these students would be receiving lower direct public subsidies, which are federally funded. So more federal funding might be available for lower-income students.

Discussion

While it is impossible to measure the benefits accruing to participants in higher education precisely, the available evidence indicates that the benefits accrue to a student body that has higher family incomes than the student body at public postsecondary institutions and higher family incomes than the population at large. However, a significant number of lower- and middle-income students attend nonprofit postsecondary institutions.

The limited available evidence does not show any earnings advantage for private college graduates relative to public college graduates. As more evidence becomes available from longitudinal studies of earnings, researchers will be able to address this issue more completely.

Students in private colleges receive significantly higher levels of direct financial aid than do those in public colleges and the distribution of this aid is distinctly pro-poor. But students in private colleges receive, on average, slightly *lower* total educational subsidies than do those in public colleges. These total subsidies, while less pro-poor than the direct subsidies, are weighted more heavily toward the low end of the income distribution than are total subsidies in the public higher education sector. This difference is largely the result of large publicly provided tuition subsidies available to all students in public institutions, regardless of their family income.

The fact that subsidies are distributed more heavily in favor of the poor in the private sector than in the public sector is reflected in the comparisons of subsidies received by students at particular income levels in the different sectors. While low-income students receive similar total educational subsidies whether they study in the private sector or the public sector, high-income students are much more heavily subsidized in the public sector.

III. Conclusion

Students from high-income families are more likely than students from low-income families to attend secondary and postsecondary schools in the private nonprofit sector. Measuring the benefits received by students in the public and private sectors, however, remains a difficult undertaking.

Whether a private education is better than a public one is a subject of ongoing debate. Without adjusting for differences in the kind of students who attend, students at Catholic high schools have higher average achievement test scores, lower high school dropout rates, and higher rates of postsecondary enrollment than public high school students. But the apparent superiority of the Catholic high schools is considerably reduced, though not eliminated, when differences among students who attend the different types of schools are taken into account.

Definitive statements about the distribution of the benefits of private schools across income classes are not possible. At the elementary/secondary level, the question arises of whether the "common-school" effect leads those low-income students who do attend private schools to benefit more from the experience than their wealthier classmates. The answer seems to be "no" with respect to dropping out and postsecondary enrollment and "maybe" with respect to achievement gain.

The relative benefits of private higher education are similarly debatable. Just as "private school" at the secondary level is sometimes taken to mean the few elite preparatory schools rather than the more prevalent parochial schools, "private college" frequently conjures up the image of the small number of highly selective institutions concentrated in the Northeast. Because the students attending these schools are only a fraction of those in the nonprofit sector, it is not surprising that statistical evidence for superior outcomes of private education is weak. The analyses discussed here suggest that recent graduates of private colleges do not have any earnings advantage over similar graduates of public colleges.

Because of the high cost of private colleges and universities and the resulting higher "need" of those paying that cost, students attending private colleges and universities receive much larger direct subsidies than do students in the public sector. But the indirect subsidies received by all students at public colleges and universities are larger than the public subsidies received by most students in the private sector. Unlike direct subsidies, the indirect subsidies are unrelated to financial need. As a result, the distribution of total educational subsidies is clearly more pro-poor in the private sector than in the public sector, even though the level of subsidy is higher in the public sector.

When the focus shifts from average subsidies *per student* to average subsidies per *young person*, the distribution of average subsidies becomes markedly pro-rich instead of mildly pro-poor. This is a result of a system in which young people from upper-income families are considerably more likely to go to college than young people from lower-income families.

If the private sector were to shrink slightly, it is likely that it would be middle-income students who would shift from private to public schools. Were this to happen, the amount of public funds going to these students would probably rise, since these middle-income students would now receive the large indirect tuition subsidies provided to all students at public universities. That increase would be offset somewhat by a reduction in the direct subsidies now provided to private college students through the student aid programs.

APPENDIX
REGRESSION ANALYSIS OF DIFFERENTIAL EFFECTS OF CATHOLIC SCHOOLS
High School Dropout Rates

The results pertaining to differences in the sophomore-to-senior high school dropout rate are based on the following analysis of the HS&B. We estimated a regression in which the dependent variable took the value 1 if the student had dropped out between 1980 and 1982 and 0 otherwise. The independent variables included only a 0–1 Catholic-school variable (CATHOLIC), base year achievement (the HS&B variable BYTEST), and 0–1 variables indicating students' base year socioeconomic status quartile (SESQ2, SESQ3, and SESQ4, based on the HS&B variable BYSESQ). The results were as follows:

Independent Variable	Unrestricted Model (t-statistic) (1)	Restricted Model (t-statistic) (2)
Intercept	0.525 (41.5)	0.526 (41.7)
BYTEST	−0.007 (26.6)	−0.007 (26.2)
CATHOLIC (1 = Yes)	−0.024 (1.0)	−0.051 (6.0)
SES2	−0.058 (9.4)	−0.059 (9.8)
SES3	−0.072 (11.5)	−0.075 (12.1)
SES4	−0.077 (11.5)	−0.077 (11.7)
SES2*CATHOLIC	−0.037 (1.2)	—

Independent Variable	Unrestricted Model (*t*-statistic) (1)	Restricted Model (*t*-statistic) (2)
SES3*CATHOLIC	−0.050 (1.7)	—
SES4*CATHOLIC	−0.013 (0.5)	—
R^2	0.0623	0.0621
Sample Size	22,211	22,211

These results suggest that the single most important correlate of high school dropout is ability. Once ability is held constant, the relationship between income (or socioeconomic status) and dropping out becomes much less marked. For students with average ability, those in the lowest socioeconomic status quartile are about 6 percentage points more likely to drop out than those in the next highest quartile; those in the upper two quartiles are only 1 to 2 percentage points less likely to drop out than those in the second quartile.

The regression in column (1) is "unrestricted" in the sense that the effect of socioeconomic status is allowed to be different for the public and Catholic schools. The regression in column (2) restricts the effect of socioeconomic status to be the same across sectors by omitting the SES/Catholic schools interactions. The result that the relationship between socioeconomic status and dropping out is "no different" for Catholic and public school students is based on a test of the hypothesis that all of the coefficients on the SES/CATHOLIC interactions are zero.

Because the mean of the dependent variable is close to zero, it would be better to use limited dependent variable techniques, but we have not done this as yet. A longer list of independent variables does not change the basic result reported here, and, because the number of Catholic dropouts is so low, produces some implausible coefficient estimates.

Postsecondary Enrollment

The interpretations in the text are based on the following analysis of the HS&B. For those who graduated in 1982, we estimated a regression in which the dependent variable took the value 1 if the student had reported being enrolled in a four-year college, public or private, in October, 1982. This information was drawn from the High School and Beyond second followup variable PSESOC82. The independent variables included a 0–1 Catholic-school variable (CATHOLIC), base year achievement (the HS&B variable BYTEST), and 0–1 variables indicating students' base year socioeconomic status quartile (SESQ2, SESQ3, and SESQ4, based on the HS&B variable BYSESQ). Dummy variables for gender, race, ethnicity and handicap status were also included. The results were as follows:

Independent Variable	Unrestricted Model (*t*-statistic) (1)	Restricted Model (*t*-statistic) (2)
Intercept	−0.838 (24.7)	−3.839 (24.8)
BYTEST	0.019 (31.1)	0.019 (31.1)
CATHOLIC (1 = Yes)	0.049 (0.8)	0.111 (5.9)

Independent Variable	Unrestricted Model (*t*-statistic) (1)	Restricted Model (*t*-statistic) (2)
FEMALE	0.031 (3.3)	0.031 (3.3)
BLACK	0.134 (8.1)	0.134 (8.1)
HISPANIC	0.040 (2.6)	0.040 (2.6)
BOTH PARENTS	0.018 (1.5)	0.017 (1.5)
HANDICAP	−0.012 (0.7)	−0.012 (0.6)
SES2	0.038 (2.6)	0.040 (2.8)
SES3	0.075 (5.1)	0.079 (5.6)
SES4	0.246 (15.8)	0.246 (16.3)
SES2*CATHOLIC	0.066 (0.9)	—
SES3*CATHOLIC	0.098 (1.4)	—
SES4*CATHOLIC	0.050 (0.7)	—
R^2	0.2245	0.2243
Sample Size	7,405	7,405

The result that the Catholic school advantage drops from 23 percentage points to about 12 percentage points is based on the coefficients in column (2) (where the Catholic advantage is 11 percentage points) and on another regression (not shown), using income categories instead of SES quartiles, in which the Catholic advantage was 13 percentage points.

The result that the relationship between income and four-year enrollment is no different for Catholic- and public-school graduates is based on a test of the hypothesis that the coefficients on the interaction terms in column (1) are all zero. The relevant test statistic is 0.63 with a critical value of 2.6.

If we take the point estimates at face value, the four-year enrollment rate grows faster for Catholic graduates of increasing socioeconomic status, as indicated by the positive coefficients on the interaction terms.

We also estimated regressions with a dependent variable that indicated whether or not the respondents were enrolled in either a two-year or a four-year school. Those regressions were similar in that we could reject the hypothesis that the relationship between enrollment and socioeconomic status quartile is the same for both public-school and private-school students.

Earnings after College

We report only the regressions using socioeconomic status as the measure of "income." The regression results using family income lead to similar conclusions.

For men:

Independent Variable	(1)	(2)
Intercept	1.65 (5.0)	1.72 (5.2)
Base Year Achievement	0.01 (1.4)	0.01 (1.3)

Independent Variable	(1)	(2)
Black? (1 = Yes)	0.10 (1.0)	0.09 (0.9)
Hispanic? (1 = Yes)	−0.10 (0.9)	−0.11 (1.0)
Catholic High School? (1 = Yes)	0.04 (0.6)	0.03 (0.5)
Residence in Northeast? (1 = Yes)	−0.13 (2.1)	−0.15 (2.2)
Residence in North Central? (1 = Yes)	−0.10 (1.7)	−0.11 (1.8)
Residence in the South? (1 = Yes)	−0.12 (1.6)	−0.12 (1.7)
Quartile #3	−0.02 (0.2)	−0.09 (1.0)
Quartile #4	−0.07 (0.5)	−0.08 (0.6)
Private Nonprofit School? (1 = Yes)	0.15 (1.0)	—
Quartile #3*Nonprofit School	−0.30 (1.7)	—
Quartile #4*Nonprofit School	−0.15 (1.0)	—
R^2	0.0492	0.0357
Mean of Log Earnings	2.06	2.06
Sample Size	302	302

For women:

Independent Variable	(1)	(2)
Intercept	1.37 (4.6)	1.43 (4.8)
Base Year Achievement	0.01 (1.8)	0.01 (1.6)
Black? (1 = Yes)	−0.09 (1.2)	−0.09 (1.1)
Hispanic? (1 = Yes)	0.06 (0.5)	0.04 (0.4)
Catholic High School? (1 = Yes)	0.08 (1.3)	0.10 (1.6)
Residence in Northeast? (1 = Yes)	−0.08 (1.6)	−0.07 (1.4)
Residence in North Central? (1 = Yes)	−0.07 (1.5)	−0.06 (1.3)
Residence in the South? (1 = Yes)	0.06 (1.1)	0.06 (1.1)
Quartile #3	−0.06 (0.9)	−0.08 (1.1)
Quartile #4	−0.05 (0.4)	−0.06 (0.5)
Private Nonprofit School? (1 = Yes)	0.14 (1.6)	—
Quartile #3*Nonprofit School	−0.10 (0.8)	—
Quartile #4*Nonprofit School	−0.10 (1.0)	—
R^2	.0525	0.0455
Mean of Log Earnings	1.94	1.94
Sample Size	443	443

The conclusion that there are no differences in earnings between public school graduates and private nonprofit school graduates is based on the test of the hypothesis that the three coefficients involving the nonprofit school indicator (the last three in the table) are simultaneously zero. The relevant test statistic is a function of the R^2 values reported above in columns (1) and (2). The value of the test statistic is 2.0 for men and 1.6 for women; these values are well below the critical values for rejecting the hypothesis that the nonprofit coefficients are zero.

4

Religious Organizations

Jeff E. Biddle

There are over 300,000 religious congregations across America. Together they collect and spend more than 50 billion dollars each year, with the bulk of their income being in the form of charitable contributions. In addition, their activities annually absorb millions of hours of volunteer labor.[1] As a result of this rather substantial expenditure of time and money, buildings are built, furnished, and heated; hymns are sung, sermons are preached, religious doctrines are disseminated; the hungry are fed, the poor are provided for, and the troubled are comforted; and opportunities are created for people to socialize. The purpose of this chapter is to give some idea regarding how the benefits generated by the multifaceted activities of America's religious congregations are distributed across income classes.

I have restricted my attention to the activities organized and implemented by local congregations as well as any additional activities funded by money contributed to local congregations. The regional and national offices of the various denominations derive a considerable portion of their income from money originally collected by local congregations, so the activities of these bodies are considered.[2] However, many organizations regarded by some as part of the religious segment of the nonprofit sector fall outside the focus of this study, including, for example, the Catholic Chari-

The author would like to acknowledge the comments and suggestions of Frank Stafford, Larry Martin, and participants in the conference on the beneficiaries of the nonprofit sector sponsored by the Duke University Center for the Study of Philanthropy and Voluntarism. Thanks are also due to F. Marvin Myers of the National Association of Church Business Administration for the data on church staff salaries, to David Zin and Nils Bjorksten for research assistance, and especially to the numerous scholars and church officials who shared information with me and patiently answered my questions.

1. The 300,000 figure is from Independent Sector (1988a) based on a survey of telephone listings in the forty-eight contiguous states. Independent Sector also estimated congregational income in 1986 to be about $50 billion and the number of hours volunteered each month to be over 100 million.

2. See Interfaith Research Committee (1977), tables 14, 16; pp. 388–95.

ties and hospitals, the regional and national Jewish Federations, and various philanthropic bodies nominally associated with Protestant denominations. These organizations receive only a small fraction of their income through the conduit of the local religious congregation, relying mainly on direct gifts from individuals and corporations, government funds, and service fees.[3]

In one sense, America's religious congregations are mutual benefit organizations, similar in some respects to country clubs or other social clubs. Between 85 and 90 percent of their financial income comes directly from the membership in the form of charitable contributions and bequests, while almost none comes from explicit service fees or government funds.[4] These monetary contributions and members' contributions of time are in turn used to produce collective services, or what economists call "club goods," that are made available to the membership on a nondiscriminatory basis—for example, worship services, educational programs, and social or recreational activities. However, religious congregations are also philanthropic organizations, using member contributions of time and money to provide or support the provision of goods and services that fill the individual needs of people who may have no formal association with the congregation.

My attempt to identify the beneficiaries of the activities of religious congregations will hinge on this distinction between the congregations' mutual benefit activities and their philanthropic activities, and on the idea that each of these two types of activity benefits a different set of people and thus has different distributional consequences. I will first estimate the share of total congregational activity that is mutual benefit in nature versus the share that is philanthropic and then treat the distributional consequences of each class of activity separately.

Section I details my procedure for determining the share of congregational activities that are mutual benefit versus philanthropic in nature. The procedure makes use mainly of data relating to the flow of funds through local congregations, as this is the sort of data that is most available and least ambiguous, and I conclude that about 70 percent of aggregate congregational expenditure supports mutual benefit activities. However, be-

3. See Interfaith Research Committee (1977, 371–72, table 1). MacDonald (1985) also investigates the activities and finances of these organizations.

4. Charitable contributions alone account for more than 80 percent of congregational income. See Interfaith Research Committee (1977, tables 9, 40) and Independent Sector (1988a, table 4.22).

cause existing financial data have, for the most part, been collected for reasons other than answering the questions with which this chapter is concerned, this conclusion is subject to numerous caveats and qualifications, some of which are described in section II. Also, in recognition of the importance of volunteer labor as an input into the activities of local congregations, section II includes information on contributions of time to congregations for readers to consider alongside the conclusions drawn from the financial data.

Section III looks at who consumes the club goods produced by religious congregations, with the main focus being on differences across income classes in levels of participation in congregational activities. The main sources of data used in this section are comprehensive studies of household time-use patterns conducted by the University of Michigan Survey Research Center in 1975–76 and in 1981 (see Juster et al. 1979 and 1983), which include information on household income and on time spent in church and church-related activities.[5] Section IV is an attempt to identify the beneficiaries of the 30 percent of congregational spending that is devoted to philanthropy. This proves difficult to do with any precision, but the findings of other researchers (particularly the other contributors to this volume) provide a basis for some generalizations regarding the distributional impact of this spending.

Section V presents evidence regarding possible positive or negative externalities associated with the mutual benefit activities of religious congregations, and section VI involves speculation on the impact on the activities of religious congregations of marginal changes in the level of charitable giving to religion. A final section summarizes the findings of the paper.

It is worth noting at the outset that the available data on the finances and activities of religious congregations are often highly aggregated, and the conclusions presented here will accordingly be stated in terms of estimated national averages and aggregate totals. It is occasionally possible to break down the data on the basis of congregation size or broad religious tradition (Catholic, Protestant, Jewish), but even this involves aggregation over a heterogeneous group of units. Denominations differ with respect to polity, and there are often considerable differences of opinion from denomination to denomination and from church to church within a denomination regarding the activities in which the congregation should be engaged

---

5. Throughout, I will use the term "church" as a shorthand for "church, temple, synagogue, or mosque."

and the ends to be promoted by those activities. Thus, in many cases, what holds true in the aggregate may not even come close to holding true for many individual congregations, and extrapolation from the experience of one or a few units is hazardous.[6]

I. CLASSIFYING THE CONGREGATIONS' ACTIVITIES
Previous Studies, Primary Data Sources, and Basic Concepts

In 1974, the Interfaith Research Committee of the Filer Commission (The Commission on Private Philanthropy and Public Needs) conducted a study of the financial activity of America's religious organizations (Interfaith Research Committee 1977). The basic goals of the study were to determine the sources and magnitude of the income of religious organizations, the fraction of that income expended on "sacramental" activity (religious services and exclusively religious education) and the distribution of the remaining expenditures across several broad categories of nonsacramental spending. Officials of two hundred Protestant congregations and fifty Catholic parishes were surveyed regarding the incomes and expenditures of their congregations during 1972. In addition, twelve Protestant denominations submitted financial reports, and two national Jewish organizations provided statistics on temple and synagogue finances. In 1985, Independent Sector commissioned the Gallup organization to conduct a survey of the characteristics, activities, and finances of America's religious congregations (Independent Sector 1988a). As part of the survey, over thirteen hundred randomly selected congregations provided detailed information on finances and activities for 1986.

I have relied heavily on these two studies in attempting to allocate congregational spending into the mutual benefit and philanthropic categories, but their application to this purpose is not unproblematic. Fourteen years separate the two studies, with the Filer Commission data now being almost two decades old. Fortunately, comparison of the two data sets suggests some stability over time in the fiscal behavior of the congregations.[7] The Filer Commission was unable to obtain data from the Mormons or from

6. The extent of heterogeneity among religious congregations can be overstated—for example, when it comes to matters of staffing, raising and handling money, or the day-to-day operations of the church, most congregations of similar size look surprisingly alike, regardless of denomination.

7. For example, the two studies basically concur on the share of congregational income coming from charitable contributions and the shares of expenditures going to operating expenditures, capital improvements, and higher levels of the denomination.

the major black denominations, groups which at the time of the study constituted about 16 percent of the churchgoing population.[8] The Independent Sector survey promised confidentiality regarding denominational affiliation to all participants, so it is difficult to know if it is representative along denominational lines.[9]

The Independent Sector study followed the Filer Commission study in asking respondents to classify activities or expenditures as sacramental and nonsacramental, with the nonsacramental category further broken down into the subcategories of education, human services/welfare, health, societal benefit, arts and culture, international, and environmental.[10] Unfortunately, the sacramental/nonsacramental dichotomy does not fit exactly with the mutual benefit/philanthropic dichotomy used here. Many nonsacramental activities of congregations are, for all practical purposes, mutual benefit or club-type activities. For example, participants in many church-sponsored recreational activities and youth programs, programs which would be placed in the nonsacramental human services category, come overwhelmingly from the church membership even though the programs may be nominally open to all.

The sacramental category is less problematic. It is probably safe to assume that a congregation's sacramental activities (church services, Sunday school classes) are consumed by members. Even those nonmembers who attend services are expected to contribute as members would in exchange for their consumption of the collective good. One possibly important exception to the assignment of all sacramental activities to the mutual benefit category is missionary activity. The Filer Commission asked that all spending on overseas missions programs be separately identified, whether it supported sacramental or nonsacramental activity, while the Independent Sec-

8. See Interfaith Research Committee (1977, 367, 382).

9. It does seem to be the case that the construction of the Independent Sector sample from telephone directories led to an underrepresentation of small congregations in the survey. For example, storefront churches, congregations that used the facilities of another church, and congregations without telephones or with telephones listed under the pastor's name could not appear in the sample. Black congregations are also underrepresented in the sample, in part perhaps because of the omission of congregations without telephone listings. These two matters are discussed at more length in section II of the text.

10. The sacramental/nonsacramental dichotomy employed by the Filer Commission invited some ambiguity, as many churches regarded all their activities as an aspect of their sacred mission or ministry (Interfaith Research Committee 1977, 371). Independent Sector wisely avoided altogether the use of the term sacramental, employing instead a category titled "Religious Ministry and Education." Independent Sector also defined more carefully the sorts of activities belonging in each of their categories.

tor survey did not. Neither requested that domestic missionary activities of a sacramental nature be separately identified. In the subsections that follow, the obvious incompatibilities between the sacramental/nonsacramental and mutual benefit/philanthropic dichotomies have been resolved sometimes by use of auxiliary data, sometimes by appeal to assumptions that it is hoped the reader will accept as reasonable.

Another important data source for this study is the University of Michigan Survey Research Center's study of time use. During 1975–76, members of a nationally representative sample of 1,500 households participated in the study, providing demographic and socioeconomic information as well as information on patterns of time use. The survey was repeated in 1981 on a subset of these households. From these data, it is possible to estimate the amount of time the respondent and his or her spouse spent in church or at church-related meetings during an average week. Also, because the sample was representative, sample information can be used to project aggregate totals for time spent in worship services or church-related activities nationwide. Further details on these data and the variables constructed from them for this study are in Appendix A.

Categorizing Congregational Expenditures

Table 4.1 breaks down the expenditures of America's religious congregations into several functional categories. There is a breakdown for all congregations, then separate breakdowns for small congregations (fewer than 100 members), medium congregations (between 100 and 400 members) and large congregation (more than 400 members). Table 4.2 breaks down the expenditures on wages, salaries, fringes, and supplies not associated with occupancy into sacramental and nonsacramental expenditures and further disaggregates the nonsacramental expenditures into the subdivisions employed by Independent Sector. This breakdown is based on three types of information. Information on the size and composition of church staffs and the ratio of clergy to nonclergy on the staff was obtained by surveying 108 churches. The average share of total payroll (wages, salaries, and fringes) going to clergy versus nonclergy in small, medium, and large congregations was estimated using this information in conjunction with a salary survey conducted by the National Association of Church Business Administration (1990). The share of payroll going to clergy was then allocated to sacramental versus nonsacramental spending on the basis of Independent Sector's estimates of how clergy allocated their time between sacramental and the various nonsacramental activities. (Indepen-

TABLE 4.1 Congregational Expenditures Breakdown

	All Congregations	Small	Medium	Large
Total Expenditures[a] (millions of dollars)	49,327.5	3,342.5	11,582.7	34,402.3
Expenditures in Congregations of this Size as % of Total	100.0	6.8	23.5	69.7

PERCENTAGE OF CONGREGATIONAL EXPENDITURES DEVOTED TO

Wages and Salaries	30.1	30.0	32.4	29.4
Fringe Benefits	8.5	13.3	9.5	7.6
Supplies and Services	15.9	11.1	10.0	18.4
Construction, Capital Improvements, Acquisition of Property	8.4	6.3	7.6	8.9
Costs Associated with Occupancy	19.7	17.9	20.0	19.7
Payments to Denominational Bodies	11.4	10.6	13.0	10.9
Donations to Other Organizations	3.9	5.1	4.5	3.6
Direct Assistance to Individuals	2.1	5.8	2.7	1.5
Total[b]	100.0	100.1	99.7	100.0

SOURCE: Independent Sector (1988a, table 4.25).
[a]Total expenditures figures multiplied by 1.026, as per note [a] in Independent Sector (1988a), table 4.25.
[b]Column totals reflect rounding error.

TABLE 4.2 Assignment of Payroll, Supplies, and Services Expenditures to Sacramental and Nonsacramental Categories

Category	All	Small	Medium	Large
Sacramental	60.6(%)	68.0(%)	64.6(%)	58.8(%)
Nonsacramental	39.4	32.0	35.4	41.2
Education	15.3	—	—	—
Human Services	9.2	—	—	—
Health	5.5	—	—	—
Public Benefit	3.0	—	—	—
Arts and Culture	2.1	—	—	—
International	2.6	—	—	—
Environmental	1.7	—	—	—
All Expenditures	100.0	100.0	100.0	100.0

SOURCES: Author's calculations based on NACBA salary survey and Independent Sector (1988a) tables 4.18 and 4.19. See text.
NOTE: The expenditures allocated in this table represent 54.5 percent of total expenditures.

dent Sector 1988a, tables 4.18, 4.19). The same procedure was used to allocate the nonclergy payroll between sacramental and nonsacramental activities. The distribution between sacramental and nonsacramental uses of the budget for supplies not associated with occupancy was assumed to be the same as for the payroll. The data and process used to derive the figures in table 4.2 are described in more detail in Appendix B.

The expenditure categories "Supplies, services and other costs associated with occupancy" and "Construction, capital improvements, and acquisition of real property" are associated with the construction, operation, and maintenance of church facilities. Classification of these expenditures as mutual benefit or philanthropic should thus be based on information regarding who uses church facilities. Section A of table 4.3 reports information from the Independent Sector survey on the average number of days per week that congregational facilities are open for worship services, for other use by congregational members, and for use by groups outside the congregation. This information is used to allocate facilities-related spending into the mutual benefit and philanthropic categories with the help of three assumptions: first, that facilities uses in the first two categories represent mutual benefit activity, while uses in the third category represent philanthropic activity;[11] second, that on the average day in which facilities are open for congregational activities other than worship, these activities involve the same number of person-hours of facilities utilization as the activities of noncongregational groups on the average day that congregational facilities are open to them; third, on the average day that congregational facilities are used for worship services, these services involve about twice as many person-hours of facility utilization as the congregation's nonworship activities on the average day on which these take place.[12] Using these three assumptions leads to the breakdown of total person hours of congregational facilities use reported in table 4.3, sections B and C.

11. Outside groups are seldom charged more than a nominal clean-up fee for the use of church facilities. Current tax laws tend to dissuade congregations from attempting to derive significant rental revenue from their physical facilities.

12. The first assumption is based on information from the University of Michigan time-use study that less than 1 percent of the time spent in meetings and activities of church groups is "helping oriented." It should be remembered that time spent in these activities does not encompass all time spent providing volunteer services to one's congregation. Realistically, however, the first assumption probably leads to overstatement of the extent to which facilities are used for mutual benefit purposes. The assumption that worship services provide, on average, twice as many hours of facility utilization as nonworship uses is also based on information from the time-use data that the ratio of time spent in church to time spent in other meetings

TABLE 4.3 Assignment of Expenditures Related to Physical
Facilities to Mutual Benefit and Philanthropic Categories

| | A. AVERAGE NUMBER OF DAYS PER WEEK THAT CONGREGATIONAL FACILITIES ARE OPEN | | |
	Worship Services	Other Congregational Activities	Use by Other Groups
Small	3.56	3.50	1.49
Medium	3.71	4.38	2.31
Large	4.42	5.60	3.20
All	3.93	4.63	2.46

| | B. SHARE OF PERSON-HOURS OF FACILITIES UTILIZATION FOR MUTUAL BENEFIT VERSUS PHILANTHROPIC PURPOSES, BY CONGREGATION SIZE | | |
	Mutual Benefit	Philanthropic	Total
Small	87.6	12.4	100.0
Medium	83.5	16.5	100.0
Large	81.8	18.2	100.0

| C. AGGREGATE DIVISION OF PHYSICAL FACILITIES—RELATED EXPENDITURE BETWEEN MUTUAL BENEFIT AND PHILANTHROPIC USES | | |
Mutual Benefit	Philanthropic	Total
82.5	17.5	100.0

NOTE: Expenditures in these categories represent 28.1 percent of total congregational expenditures.
SOURCE: Section A is based on Independent Sector (1988a), tables 3.9–3.11. The Mutual Benefit share in section B is calculated from section A by expressing 1.98 times the column one figure plus the column two figure as a percentage of the row total (see text). In section C, aggregate share is an average of the shares reported in section B for small, medium, and large congregations, each weighted by the fraction of total facilities-related spending done by congregations in that size category (small—.058, medium—.231; large—.711).

Independent Sector (1988a) reported that the nation's congregations devoted 11.4 percent of their budgets to the support of regional and national denominational organizations, while my own survey of Catholic dioceses indicates that Catholic parishes send, on average, 8.8 percent of their income to the diocese.[13] These figures are fairly consistent with the Filer Commission estimate that in 1972, 11 percent of Protestant congrega-

and activities of church groups is 1.68:1 (see Appendix A), combined with the information that the average congregation is open 3.93 days a week for services and 4.63 days a week for other congregational meetings (1.68 divided by (3.93/4.63) equals 1.98). It must be further assumed that all church meetings make use of church facilities and that the 1.98 weighting factor for worship-related facilities use holds within each congregational size category.
13. I sent questionnaires concerning diocesan income and expenditure to a randomly selected twenty-two of America's 188 dioceses, and eleven responded. The relevant question on

tional expenditures went to denominational organizations while 9 percent of Catholic parish expenditures went to the dioceses (Interfaith Research Committee 1977, tables 11, 43). The estimated ratio of Protestant to Catholic congregational expenditures in 1972 was 3.4:1. If this ratio has remained constant (as has the ratio of Catholic to Protestant churchgoers [Gallup Organization 1987]), we can conclude that 82.5 percent of the total money sent to denominational organizations originates in the Protestant sector and the remainder in the Catholic parishes.[14]

Table 4.4 breaks down the money flow from congregations to denominational organizations into sacramental and nonsacramental categories. The Protestant breakdown is based on the Filer Commission data (Interfaith Research Committee 1977, tables 14–18, pp. 389–97). The Catholic breakdown is based on my own survey of dioceses.[15]

The remaining expenditure categories in table 4.1 deal with money donated by the congregation to outside organizations and to individuals. Donations to outside organizations clearly fall in the philanthropic category. I also place all donations to individuals in the philanthropic rather than the mutual benefit category. Such money often is meant to benefit congregation members, but on an individual basis and in response to an individual-

diocesan income was, "What percentage of parish income, on average, is sent to the diocese to support its programs?" Respondents were asked to, and did, provide detailed explanations if a single percentage figure would be misleading.

14. Most Jewish congregations pay affiliation fees to one of three synagogue movements. Discussions with representatives of these movements indicated that the portion of a typical synagogue's income going to affiliation fees is less than 10 percent by a comfortable margin, while the Filer Commission data indicates that less than 2 percent of total congregational income flows through Jewish congregations. Thus, the amount of money going from Jewish congregations to the synagogue movements is small enough to be ignored. It is worth noting at this point that over 97 percent of the spending of the Jewish congregations is of a mutual benefit character, with nonsacramental spending going mainly to support schools for Jewish children and cultural activities of particular significance to the Jewish community (Interfaith Research Committee 1977, 434–35). The movements with which the congregations affiliate exist mainly to assist congregations in the provision of education. The philanthropic activity of the American Jewish community is carried out almost entirely by Jewish charitable Federations, which receive contributions directly from individuals rather than through congregations. It is partly because the Jewish congregations have divested themselves of the philanthropic functions that are still being carried out by the Christian congregations directly and through their denominational organizations that Jewish congregational spending makes up a relatively small share of total congregational spending.

15. Half of the respondents gave less detailed information on expenditure patterns than I requested or sent raw material on their expenditures which I then attempted to fit into the categories used in this chapter. As a result, the figures in section B of table 4.4 should be regarded as rather rough estimates.

TABLE 4.4 Expenditure Patterns of
Denominational Organizations[a]

A. PROTESTANT (RECEIVING 82.5 PERCENT OF TOTAL
FINANCIAL FLOW FROM CONGREGATIONS TO
DENOMINATIONS)[b]

	Share of Expenditures
Sacramental	74.3(%)
International	4.7
Nonsacramental	21.0
Health	.6
Social Welfare	2.2
Education	16.8
Arts/Culture	.1
Other	1.3
Total	100%

B. CATHOLIC (RECEIVING 17.5 PERCENT OF TOTAL FINANCIAL
FLOW FROM CONGREGATIONS TO DENOMINATIONS)[c]

	Share of Expenditures
Education	21.6(%)
Mutual Benefit, Sacramental	14.3
Mutual Benefit, Nonsacramental	36.3
Philanthropic	27.8
Total	100.0%

[a]Denominational organizations receive 11.4 percent of congregational expenditures.
[b]Source: Interfaith Research Committee (1977), tables 15, 18.
[c]Based on survey responses from dioceses (see text).

specific need, rather than through the provision of collective goods made available to the entire congregation on a nondiscriminatory basis.

The remaining task of this section is to divide the nonsacramental expenditures of tables 4.2 and 4.4 into mutual benefit and philanthropic categories. Independent Sector's descriptions of the activities belonging in the international, public benefit, health, and environment categories suggest that classifying as philanthropy all expenditures associated with these activities would contribute only slightly to the overestimation of that category. The same can be said for the Filer Commission's categories of health, public affairs, community-wide activities, international, environment, and science. The education, arts/culture, and human services categories are not so easily handled. Human services include recreational and youth camp programs, family counseling, and preschool day care, the first two being the most frequently reported activities in this category (Independent Sector 1988a, table 3.1). As mentioned earlier, however, recreational, camp, and other youth programs often have a mutual benefit aspect, involving almost exclusively members of a particular congregation or denomination. The same can be said for certain programs coming under the heading of arts or culture, for example, music or dance groups linked to the ethnic heritage of the congregation. These groups typically perform for outside audiences, but they also represent a satisfying leisure activity for their participants. Most important quantitatively is the education category. Jewish synagogue schools and day schools serve the members of Jewish congregations and are supported by tuition fees, general contributions to the synagogue, and special levies on congregational members with school-age children. In the Catholic school system, congregational support of parish and diocesan schools typically translates into tuition subsidies for parish or diocese members. The situation in the Protestant community is too varied to allow easy generalization, but denomination-specific schools and subsidies in exchange for congregational support are not unknown. Of course, much congregational support of education is philanthropic—scholarship funds for needy or meritorious individuals, grants to Christian schools or church-affiliated colleges that are not associated with any tuition subsidy, etc.

Lacking a more reliable basis for handling the expenditures in the ambiguous nonsacramental categories, I have simply classified half of these expenditures as mutual benefit. Given the prevalence of church youth and recreational programs and the magnitude of the Catholic education system, this arbitrary decision probably underestimates mutual benefit spending.[16] In an equally arbitrary fashion, I have divided the share of facilities-related expenditures in the "other congregational activities" column of

16. One source of information on the nature and extent of congregationally supported education programs is found in the American Association for the Advancement of Science report on the nonreligious educational programs of black congregations. With regard to the division of the benefits of educational expenditures between those inside the congregation and those outside it, the report indicates that there is usually little or no tuition charge associated with the programs offered by these congregations and that, on average, 58 percent of the participants in a congregation's program are members of the congregation (George et al. 1989, 14, fig. 10).

The education and human services spending that I split evenly between the mutual benefit and philanthropic categories makes up 16 percent of total congregational spending, so that different assumptions about how to handle this spending could raise or lower the estimated share of congregational spending supporting mutual benefit activities by as much as eight percentage points.

table 4.3 and the gifts to other organizations evenly between sacramental and nonsacramental uses. Applying this classificatory process to the information found in tables 4.1–4.4 leads to the conclusion that America's congregations spend 71 percent of their income on mutual benefit activities and 29 percent on philanthropic activities, with 59 percent of the total spending supporting sacramental activities. The breakdowns within each size category of congregation are virtually the same.

The reader could be forgiven at this point for having doubts about the reliability of estimates produced by the process of assuming and approximating described above, despite the fact that in the course of so much guessing some errors have no doubt been canceled out by others. Fortunately there are previous studies containing results that can be used as a check on the estimating process; these studies are discussed in Appendix C.

II. Possible Problems and Shortcomings of the Financial Data
Underrepresentation of Small Congregations and Black Congregations

The Independent Sector sample was drawn from a population of almost 300,000 congregations listed in the nation's telephone directories, and Independent Sector's (1988a) projections of aggregate income and expenditures, which form the basis of the previous section's estimates, are meant to be valid for that population. However, as mentioned earlier, there are many congregations that are not listed in telephone directories for various reasons. The number of excluded congregations may be substantial—estimates based on statistics reported annually in *The Yearbook of American and Canadian Churches* place the number of congregations in the United States at around 340,000. If most of the 40,000 congregations left out of Independent Sector's sampling universe were small, the effect of their exclusion on the estimates of the previous section would not be too severe.[17] However, there is reason to believe that Independent Sector undersampled not only small congregations but also black congregations. About 6 percent of the churches in the Independent Sector sample reported that their

17. The money flowing through the small congregations in the Independent Sector sample represents only about 7 percent of total congregational expenditures. If the number of small congregations in the sample had been increased by two-thirds to adjust for the exclusion from telephone directories of 40,000 small congregations, total expenditures would increase by only 4.7 percent. Further, small congregations tend to spend about the same fraction of their funds on nonsacramental and philanthropic activity as do other congregations.

membership was over 20 percent black, while 8.4 percent gave no response to questions regarding congregational ethnicity. Under the generous assumption that one quarter of the nonresponding congregations were primarily black, one can conclude that there were about 24,000 black congregations in the population sampled for Independent Sector. Recent estimates from other sources place the number of black congregations at somewhere between 65,000 and 75,000, leaving over 40,000 congregations unaccounted for in the Independent Sector study.[18]

All this implies that Independent Sector's (1988a) estimate of 50 billion dollars of aggregate congregational spending in 1986 undershoots the true mark by a nontrivial amount.[19] The estimated percentage of congregational spending going to philanthropic activities is potentially biased also, but only to the extent that black congregations differ from others along this dimension. Carson (1990) presents evidence, based on people's perceptions of their congregations' activities, that in general black congregations devote more of their funds than do white congregations to programs benefiting people outside the congregation.[20] There is currently little information beyond this on the spending practices of black congregations.[21]

Possible Omission of Special Collections

Many churches occasionally take up, in addition to their regular weekly collections, special collections for the support of a particular cause or program. These collections are usually philanthropic in nature. In many congregation the special collections do not show up on the regular church budget, and it is possible that the officials answering questionnaires about church finances would fail to include information on special collections.

18. George et al. (1989, 2); these estimates suggest that the statistics reported in *The Yearbook of American and Canadian Churches* also exclude many black congregations.

19. For example, if 50,000 congregations are unrepresented for reasons related to their ethnicity or size, with half being small and half being medium-sized, the Independent Sector projection of total congregational expenditure is low by about 7.5 percent.

20. One of Carson's specific conclusions, that rural black congregations spend a smaller share of their income on philanthropy than other black or white churches, is supported by evidence presented in Lincoln and Mamiya's (1988) profile of rural black congregations.

21. There are at least two projects underway that will (upon their completion) provide a much clearer picture of the finances and activities of black congregations. Lincoln and Mamiya's (1988) study of rural black congregations is part of a larger study of all black congregations, the results of which are to be reported in a forthcoming book. The Black Church Family Project, now ongoing under the direction of Andrew Billingsly at the University of Maryland, includes an empirical study of black congregations as social service institutions.

There is no way of knowing how many of those responding to the Independent Sector survey failed to include such information. To get a sense of the potential magnitude of the problem, I checked the records of a church that takes a special collection every week as part of its commitment to outreach activities. In 1989, the sum contributed to special collections by members of this congregation, in which the median income is above the national average, was one-ninth the size of the regular annual budget. This should be regarded as an upper bound. A more typical situation might be that of the Catholic Diocese of Nashville, where special collections in the fifty-two parishes for charitable and missionary activity raised funds equaling 3 percent of aggregate parish income (Comptroller, Diocese of Nashville to author, 8 October 1990). Given that some congregations probably did include their special collections when responding to the Independent Sector survey, it is probably safe to assume that accounting for all special collections would increase the philanthropic category at most by two or three percentage points.

In light of the above described problems with the financial data, I would suggest that a better estimate of aggregate congregational expenditures in 1986 would be about 54 billion dollars and that a reasonable estimate for 1989 would be 68 billion.[22] This latter figure is the one I work with for the remainder of the chapter, and I will assume that 70 percent of this spending (about 48 billion dollars) supported mutual benefit activities and 30 percent (24 billion dollars) supported philanthropic activities.

Nonfinancial Contributions
Volunteer Labor

Virtually all congregations rely on volunteer labor as an input in their production of both mutual benefit and philanthropic services; indeed, it is not uncommon for small congregations to be run completely by volunteers. Independent Sector (1988a) estimates that over 10 million people donate volunteer services to their congregations each month, with the average volunteer working over ten hours per month. Given the importance of volunteers to the operation of the congregations, using congregations' expendi-

---

22. The $54 billion figure is arrived at by adding 2 percent to Independent Sector's estimate to account for special collections, and 7.5 percent to account for the exclusion of small and black congregations. The projection for 1989 congregational income is based on the assumption that, since 1986, total congregational income has grown at an annual rate of 8 percent per year, which is the annual rate of growth of charitable giving to religious causes from 1984 to 1988 (as reported in *Giving USA* 1990).

tures on inputs as a rough proxy of the value of the services they produce results in a considerable underestimation of the latter.

Ideally, one would want to place a financial value on the services donated by volunteers, and previous studies have attempted to do this. Independent Sector (1988a), for example, multiplies the number of donated hours by the average wage rate, and then adds this amount to church income (or expenditures). However, such a procedure is misleading, as it ignores certain conceptual and practical difficulties associated with any attempt to value volunteer labor services.

In standard economic models of volunteering, the donor of a volunteer hour is seen as receiving a benefit in the form of utility and/or human capital equal to the opportunity cost of his time. The value of this benefit may be proxied by the volunteer's wage rate (see, for example, Menchik and Weisbrod 1987). By this logic the congregations, in facilitating the contribution of volunteer labor, are creating benefits for their members beyond those associated with the services produced by the volunteer labor.[23] I think it best for the purposes of this study, however, to set aside the benefits enjoyed by volunteers as a result of the act of volunteering and focus only on the value of the volunteers' marginal product in the production of mutual benefit and philanthropic services.

The economists' theorem that in a competitive economy a worker's value of marginal product will equal his or her wage cannot be used as a basis for valuing the marginal product of the church volunteer. The church does not pay for volunteer labor, so it has little incentive to adopt an efficient mix of inputs or to assign volunteers to the tasks in which they would be most productive. In addition, the volunteers themselves are receiving benefits from their donation and may be as much concerned with enhancing those benefits as with seeking an assignment in which the value of their marginal product is maximized. Thus we have engineers delivering meals to shut-ins, two volunteers minding the thrift shop and enjoying each other's company when one would suffice to get the job done, and so on.

All this implies that the use of the volunteer's wage rate as a measure of the value of the services he or she produces results in a gross overstatement of that value. A more theoretically satisfying measure of the value of the marginal product of volunteer labor in producing a service for the congre-

23. Technically, the volunteer's opportunity cost of time will equal the value of marginal product of the last hour volunteered in the production of congregational services to be consumed by the donor plus the monetary value of any psychic or human capital benefits that come from the act of volunteering that hour.

gation would be the difference between the cost to the congregation of providing the service with the aid of volunteers and the cost of hiring a private sector firm to provide the service. Unfortunately, such a measure would be extremely difficult to construct, given available data.

As I do not believe that I can provide a reliable estimate of the value of volunteer hours, I will conclude this section simply by presenting Independent Sector's (1988a) findings on the volume of hours contributed to congregations and their distribution across various activities, to be considered alongside the financial information presented earlier. As mentioned above, Independent Sector (1988a) estimates that over 10.5 million people donate time to religious congregations in an average month and that the average volunteer gives 10.3 hours per month to the congregation.[24] Further, it is estimated that 52.3 percent of these volunteer hours support sacramental activities and 47.7 percent support nonsacramental activities. Assuming again that activities related to arts and culture, education, and human services should be split evenly between mutual benefit and philanthropic categories, one can conclude that 70 percent of volunteer time supports the congregations' mutual benefit activities (Independent Sector 1988a, table 4.20).

In-Kind Contributions

At least 60 percent of all congregations reported that they played some role in directing in-kind contributions from members to others (Independent Sector 1988a, 29), most of it presumably in the form of food and clothing and none of it reflected in the financial statistics discussed earlier.[25] Although it is possible that some in-kind contributions made to congregations help to support mutual benefit activities, as when such contributions

24. The estimate of 10.5 million volunteers, which is based on figures provided by church officials filling out a questionnaire, is much lower than estimates that follow from recent surveys asking people about their own volunteering. For example, in a 1985 Gallup survey, 16 percent of a sample of adults reported donating time to a religious congregation in the previous month. If this percentage holds for the entire adult population, it implies that well over 20 million people serve as congregational volunteers each month. An earlier Gallup survey yields comparable figures (see Independent Sector 1989, table 4.3). Independent Sector's (1988a) estimate that the average volunteer gives 10.3 hours a month to the congregation is more consistent with recent Gallup Surveys—for example, Independent Sector (1986) reports that teaching Sunday school involves, on average, eight hours per month, choir membership 9.7 hours per month, and assisting the pastor 8.3 hours per month. Given these figures and the fact that it is not uncommon for volunteers to serve the church in more than one capacity, the 10.3 hours per month figure seems reasonable.

25. See Salamon and Teitelbaum (1984, 63) for a similar estimate.

are sold in bazaars or rummage sales to augment the church's income, the vast majority of these contributions are destined to benefit needy individuals. A congregation may serve merely as a collection point for in-kind donations that are then distributed by some other agency, or the congregation may itself run a thrift shop, food bank, etc., but in either case it is performing a redistributive function.

According to a recent Gallup survey, 13.2 percent of households contributed some form of property (such as food, clothing, furniture, or real estate) to a religious congregation in 1989. The average contributing household placed the value of their in-kind contributions at $584 (Independent Sector 1990, table 1.4). These figures would indicate an aggregate level of in-kind giving to congregations in excess of $7 billion. It seems probable that many contributors of property overestimated the actual value of their contribution, but even if it is assumed that the average respondent reported his or her gift to be worth twice as much as it actually was, we are left with evidence of an appreciable flow of in-kind giving passing through the congregations.[26]

III. The Distribution of the Congregations' Club-Type Benefits Across Income Classes

In this section, I use the relative amounts of time spent by people in church and church-related activities as a proxy for benefits those people receive as a result of congregations' provision of collective services and examine the distribution of this type of time use across income classes. This method of measuring the relative benefits accruing to different income classes is not without problems. It assumes, for example, that high-income and low-income churchgoers receive the same benefit from an hour spent in their churches. However, American congregations tend to be segregated on the basis of income, making it likely that more money has been spent to produce the hour-long worship service enjoyed by the average high-income churchgoer than has been spent to produce the hour-long worship service

---

26. A check on the Gallup estimates of in-kind giving is provided by IRS statistics on deductions claimed for noncash charitable gifts, a category including the types of property gifts Gallup asked about, but also gifts of stocks and bonds. In 1986, $10.5 billion of noncash gifts were claimed by itemizers, although over $4 billion of this was accounted for by the gifts of those with adjusted gross incomes of over 1 million dollars, a large proportion of which are likely to be stocks or other financial assets (Internal Revenue Service 1989, 65). By comparison, Gallup's estimate that 26.7 percent of American households gave property to a charitable organization in 1989, with the average gift being valued at $582, implies a total of 15 billion dollars' worth of in-kind giving in 1989 (Independent Sector 1990, table 1.4).

enjoyed by the average low-income churchgoer. This suggests, on the one hand, that the benefit associated with attending church for an hour may be greater for those with larger incomes. On the other hand, there may be systematic differences in tastes between the wealthy and the poor, such that the typical poor person would derive greater pleasure than his wealthy counterpart from the same hour-long worship service.

The University of Michigan time-use data provide one possible means for assessing the relative amounts of pleasure members of each income class receive from an hour of church-related activities, for all respondents were asked to rate their enjoyment of church attendance on a scale from one to ten. Interestingly, there is a statistically significant negative correlation between this subjective enjoyment measure and household income in both waves of the data. The first column of table 4.5 shows the average of the enjoyment measure for each income quintile.

The remaining columns of table 4.5 show how the total amounts of time spent per week nationwide in various church-related activities, as projected on the basis of the time-use data (see Appendix A), break down according to the household incomes of those who spent the time. The top section of the table is derived from the 1975–76 data, and the bottom section from the 1981 data. The second column looks at time spent by adults in worship services, and the third breaks down the projected amount of time spent by both adults and children in worship services. This column is included because it seems probable that households consisting of adults and children derive more total benefit from an hour at church than households with the same number of adults but no children, even if one considers only the benefits enjoyed by the adults. The fourth column deals with the time spent in church meetings and related church group activities. The fifth and sixth columns deal with variables created when household time spent in church and household time spent in religious group activities are summed.

The important conclusion to be drawn from table 4.5 is that the time spent in church-related activities is distributed fairly evenly across the income quintiles. There is no evidence that participation in the activities of religious congregations rises or declines monotonically with household income, and there are only a few instances in which an income class contributes more than 25 percent or less than 15 percent of the total for any of the variables in the table.[27] If the proper measure of the benefit associated with

27. One measure of religiously oriented time use that is strongly correlated with household income is time spent in individual or informal religious observance (that is, prayer, medita-

TABLE 4.5 Enjoyment of and Time Spent in Church-related Activities, by Income Quintile

		Share of Total Time Spent by				
Income Quintile[a]	Average Subjective Rating of Enjoyment of Church Attendance	Adults in Worship Services	Adults and Children in Worship Services[b]	Adults in Religious Group Activities	Adults in Worship Services and Other Religious Group Activities	Children in Worship Services and by Adults in Other Activities
A. ESTIMATES FROM 1975–76 UNIVERSITY OF MICHIGAN TIME-USE DATA (975 HOUSEHOLDS)						
Lowest	7.6	19.1(%)	19.2(%)	23.3(%)	20.6(%)	20.2(%)
Second	7.3	19.1	19.4	13.8	17.3	18.8
Third	7.0	21.9	21.4	24.5	22.8	22.1
Fourth	6.7	17.6	19.1	14.4	16.4	17.9
Highest	6.5	22.3	20.9	24.0	22.9	21.0
Total	—	100.0%	100.0%	100.0%	100.0%	100.0%
B. ESTIMATES FROM 1981 UNIVERSITY OF MICHIGAN TIME-USE DATA (480 HOUSEHOLDS)						
Lowest	7.7	21.1(%)	14.6(%)	22.7(%)	21.9(%)	17.8(%)
Second	6.8	20.3	26.9	7.3	13.5	19.2
Third	7.2	17.6	18.5	14.6	16.0	16.9
Fourth	6.9	24.9	23.6	32.5	29.0	27.2
Highest	6.5	16.1	16.4	22.9	19.6	18.9
Total	—	100.0%	100.0%	100.0%	100.0%	100.0%

[a] 1975 household income (for section A of table only).
[b] The 1975–76 data combined worship services and informal religious observances into one category called "religious practices." The figures in this column are calculated under the assumption that in each quintile the share of religious practices taken up by worship services is the same in 1975–76 as in 1981.

consumption of an hour's worth of congregational collective services is deemed to be the amount of expenditure associated with the production of that hour, then the time in the upper quintiles should probably be weighted more heavily. If people's subjective assessments of the pleasure they receive from churchgoing are seen as more appropriate weights to be used for converting time into benefits, then the time in the lower quintiles should be weighted more heavily.

One concern with using these time-use data to identify beneficiaries of congregations' mutual benefit activities is the age of the data set. Its reliability as an indicator of the current state of affairs depends on the stability over the past fifteen years of patterns of church attendance and involvement and of relationships between economic status and religious behavior. Opinion polls collected over the past twenty years show considerable stability in national rates of church membership and attendance. The share of churchgoers identifying with each of America's three major religious traditions has been similarly stable (Gallup Organization 1987). The lack of correlation in table 4.5 between income and time spent in congregational activities is due in part to the lack of a correlation in the time-use data between income and the probability of reporting participation in congregational activities, and similar findings show up in more recent surveys. A Gallup poll conducted in 1986 showed that the percentage of the respondents that did not attend worship services was constant across income classes,[28] while a Gallup poll conducted in 1989 showed frequency of attendance to be unrelated to income (Independent Sector 1990, table 4.1). One contrary piece of evidence is found in Independent Sector (1988b, table 3.4), where it is reported that the average income of nonattenders is some 30 percent higher than that of frequent attenders.

Another concern is the accuracy of the religious group activities variable as a measure of benefits received from congregational activities. A first possible source of error in this variable arises because much of the time spent in this category may represent contributions to the church rather than ben-

---

tion, Bible reading, etc.). In 1981, those in the lowest quintile accounted for 32 percent of the total time spent at this activity, while those in the fourth and highest quintiles contributed 11 percent and 5 percent of the total, respectively. Of course, time spent in this manner does not make use of the resources of a religious congregation.

One also finds no significant relationship between income and the various measures of time spent in church and church-related activity discussed in table 4.5 when the effect of the respondent's age is controlled for using multivariate regression analysis.

28. Reported in *Emerging Trends,* March 1987, p. 5.

efits received from it. Such would be the case, for instance, with time spent in choir practices or teaching Sunday school. (Participation as an usher or a choir member during a religious service is less problematic, because such duty to the congregation does not detract seriously from the individual's ability to enjoy the worship service.) A second reason the variable may not be accurate is that time spent in many church-sponsored activities, such as recreational athletic leagues or scout troops, is not likely to be included in this variable. More importantly, time spent in elementary or secondary education by students whose tuition is subsidized by the church is not measured.

The first source of error in the religious group activities variable biases the distributional conclusions drawn from table 4.5 only if those who participate in activities that represent gifts of time to the church differ with regard to income from those who participate in church activities as consumers. The second source of error causes bias only if those who participate in the congregationally sponsored activities falling outside the religious group activities category differ with regard to income from those who participate in the activities falling within the scope of the category. I have no evidence on these matters, but my guess is that only the exclusion of time spent in education from religious group activities represents a potentially serious source of bias.

Do Richer Congregation Members Subsidize Poorer Ones?

The analogy between a church and a social club has its limitations, even when one is considering only the church's provision of services to its members. In particular, most congregations allow members to decide for themselves how much to contribute to support the organization and consider it perfectly reasonable that members' financial support be based on ability to pay. For this reason, it is possible that within congregations the distribution of collective benefits does not match the (before tax) distribution of contributions and that wealthier members of a congregation subsidize the less wealthy members' consumption of the congregation's collective services.[29]

Survey evidence suggests that this takes place. The time-use data reviewed above implies that all income classes share roughly equally in the consumption of congregational services. Data from a Gallup poll pre-

---

29. It is well known that religious giving as a percentage of income falls as income rises, but this does not rule out the possibility that levels of religious giving rise with income.

sented in Jencks (1987) shows that contributions to religious congregations rise with household income. Econometric studies of charitable giving to religious organizations that separate the effect of rising income from that of rising tax rates produce statistically significant estimates of the income elasticity of such giving in the .4 to .6 range (Clotfelter 1985, table 2.14). Sullivan (1985) estimates a simultaneous model of church attendance and religious contributions using a sample of 2,300 Protestant church members interviewed in 1963 and finds a positive and statistically significant effect of income on contributions, holding constant attendance. (The income elasticity is around .3.)

This evidence supports but does not establish the proposition that rich parishioners subsidize poorer ones; such evidence could be a reflection of the above-mentioned segregation of congregations on the basis of income, with members of wealthy congregations contributing more to their churches and in turn enjoying more richly appointed worship services and facilities. Information on the relationship between giving and income at the congregational level would be required to establish more conclusively that congregations' wealthier members tend to contribute more per unit of collective congregational services consumed. Some Protestant denominations, such as the Mormons and the Seventh-Day Adventists, stress or require tithing, and many Jewish congregations levy membership fees on the basis of ability to pay. In these instances, richer parishioners clearly subsidize poorer ones. I have been unable to turn up any hard data on giving and income at the congregational level in the mainstream denominations; churches in general know who gives how much, but an organized attempt to link giving information with income information would not go over very well in most congregations for understandable reasons.

There is evidence on the concentration of giving within congregations. The Filer Commission reported that in the average Protestant congregation, 52 percent of total financial support came from the top 20 percent of givers, while in the average Catholic parish 45 percent of total support came from the top 20 percent of givers (Interfaith Research Committee 1977, tables 26, 43). These figures suggest that wealthier members of a congregation tended to give more than poor ones, although they probably also reflect differences in contributions among those at the same income level.

I suspect that there is a strong positive correlation between income and giving within the typical religious congregation. I also suspect that the correlation between giving and permanent or average lifetime income would be noticeably weaker. More to the point, I believe that the religious congregation has historically been an environment in which intergenerational transfers take place, with older adults accepting the responsibility of providing those in their childrearing years with a materially adequate spiritual home. This conjecture represents an alternative to the "closeness of death" explanation of why religious giving increases with age, holding income constant.[30]

IV. The Distribution of Benefits of Congregations' Philanthropic Spending across Income Classes

The estimates of previous sections imply that congregations spend around $20 billion in the promotion of philanthropic activities. One should probably add two or three billion dollars' worth of in-kind giving, if not more. In considering the distribution across income classes of the benefits created by congregational philanthropic activity, it should be remembered that America's major religious traditions stress the importance of meeting the spiritual as well as the material needs of God's people. Because the spiritually needy are found in abundance in all income classes, we should not consider anything to be amiss if congregational outreach programs are found to be serving those in the middle- and upper-income quintiles. Churches may offer programs, such as divorce recovery workshops, singles groups, or elderly visitation, which serve people of all income classes and for which secular and even private sector substitutes exist, because churches feel their own programs will include an important spiritual component missing from programs organized by secular agencies.

It is not possible for me to construct a table paralleling table 4.5 that assigns the benefits of congregational philanthropy to the various income quintiles. I can, however, report on the extent of congregational support for various types of philanthropic activities and, with the help of some assumptions, make a few generalizations regarding the distributional impact of such support.

As reported in table 4.1, 2.1 percent of congregational expenditure ($1.43 billion) represents assistance to individuals. It is probably safe to assume that the bulk of this benefits those in the lowest-income quintile. It is also likely that the majority of in-kind giving to congregations is made up of gifts of food, clothing, and furniture that ultimately benefit low-income individuals.

30. Reece (1979) and Sullivan (1985) present evidence on the relationship between age and giving to religion.

Congregational "public benefit" spending, which basically involves spending on politically oriented activities (such as lobbying and other activities related to abortion laws), combined with congregational expenditure on environmental improvement, amounts to $1.74 billion. This can be regarded as spending on the "public goods" of environmental quality and political dialogue. Economists have argued at some length over the proper procedure for allocating the benefits of such spending, and I will not try to resolve the debate here.[31]

I have been able to identify $1.26 billion in expenditures that benefit persons overseas. This is certainly an underestimate of the total, as some overseas spending for both sacramental and nonsacramental purposes is undoubtedly included in the congregations' donations to other organizations and in both the sacramental and the philanthropic spending of the Catholic dioceses. A substantial amount of missionary spending also takes place under the auspices of those religious bodies falling outside the scope of this paper.

The estimates of section I indicate that $7 billion in payroll and diocesan or denominational spending supports education in some way. A certain amount beyond this is also flowing from congregations to educational institutions in the donations to other organizations category. Congregational support of nonreligious education can take various forms, including the direct provision of after-school tutoring or adult literacy instruction, the financial support of parochial schools and religious colleges, or the provision of scholarships to individual students.[32] As mentioned earlier, there are both mutual benefit and philanthropic aspects to this sort of spending, and different sorts of church-sponsored educational programs are likely to have very different distributional implications.

The financial support of secondary schools, colleges, and universities, and the provision of scholarships to students attending such schools, are among the most visible and quantitatively important ways in which congregations and denominational organizations support education. It is possible to at least get a sense of how the benefits of this spending are distributed across income classes from figures found in Schwartz and Baum's chapter in this volume. Table 4.6 reproduces information presented in that

31. For example Aaron and McGuire (1970) argue for a procedure that assigns a greater share of the benefits of public goods spending to households with higher incomes, while Brennan (1976) would allocate the benefits of such spending equally across households.

32. See George et al. (1989) for an indication of the variety of educational programs that congregations support.

study. The top section contains information on the household incomes of students enrolled in Catholic and public high schools in 1980, showing that the Catholic high schools serve a more affluent clientele than the public high schools. In assessing these figures, however, it should be recognized that some of the Catholic school students pay a full tuition rate, some receive parish or diocesan subsidies, and some receive scholarships granted on the basis of need. Common sense and economic theory would suggest that the share of the cost of education borne by the student's family will tend to rise as household income rises, making the distribution of benefits from parish support of Catholic secondary schools less skewed toward higher-income families than the figures in section A of table 4.6 would indicate.

Section B of table 4.6 gives figures on family income of the dependent freshman attending four-year Catholic colleges and four-year Protestant colleges in 1989. Schwartz and Baum (chapter 3) present evidence that at private colleges and universities, the share of a student's educational costs covered either by the institution or through scholarships and other grants-in-aid rises as parental income falls. Their discussion of this point suggests that it would hold true for the strictly religious private colleges, implying that the figures in part B of table 4.6 also understate the extent to which lower-income families benefit from congregational support of education.

Payroll and denominational spending to support the provision of health and human services amounts to almost $4 billion, some of which is mutual benefit spending. The activities falling in this category are the same sorts of activities engaged in by the agencies discussed in Salamon's study in chapter 5 of this volume of the beneficiaries of the nonprofit sector's provision of social services. Salamon reports that among social service agencies with a religious affiliation (and these are the ones most likely to be receiving support from congregations), 25 percent report serving mostly poor people, and another 17 percent report that they serve some poor people. It is difficult to say whether congregations, in their direct provision of (nonmutual benefit) social services, are more or less likely to focus on serving the poor than the religiously affiliated agencies, but Salamon does find that agencies with smaller paid staffs and a larger ratio of volunteer to paid staff are less likely to have low-income clients, and congregationally run social service programs tend to have these characteristics.

There is little I can say about the distributional impact of the congregational philanthropic spending that is related to cultural activities or the use of congregational facilities by noncongregational groups, and I am uncer-

TABLE 4.6

A. THE DISTRIBUTION OF FAMILY INCOME AMONG STUDENTS
IN CATHOLIC AND PUBLIC HIGH SCHOOLS, 1980

Annual Family Income	Percentage of Students	
	Catholic	Public
$ 7,000 or less	2(%)	8(%)
$ 7,000–$11,999	7	13
$12,000–$15,999	15	18
$16,000–$19,999	18	20
$20,000–$24,999	21	18
$25,000–$37,999	18	13
$38,000 or more	19	10
All Families	100%	100%

NOTE: Median household income in 1980 for all households
was approximately $21,000.
SOURCE: Schwartz and Baum, chapter 3 of this volume.

B. THE DISTRIBUTION OF FAMILY INCOME AMONG COLLEGE
FRESHMEN AT FOUR-YEAR RELIGIOUSLY AFFILIATED
COLLEGES, 1989

Annual Family Income	Percentage of Students	
	Catholic	Protestant
$ 10,000 or less	4.3(%)	6.2(%)
$ 10,000–$ 19,999	8.0	10.5
$ 20,000–$ 29,999	11.4	14.7
$ 30,000–$ 39,999	16.9	17.7
$ 40,000–$ 49,999	12.1	11.8
$ 50,000–$ 74,999	24.0	21.0
$ 75,000–$ 99,999	8.8	7.2
$100,000–$149,999	6.8	5.2
$150,000 or more	7.6	6.0
All Families[a]	99.9%	100.3%

[a]Totals reflect rounding error.
NOTE: Median household income in 1989 for all households
was approximately $35,000.
SOURCE: Schwartz and Baum, chapter 3 of this volume.

tain about the ultimate destination of the $2.6 billion that congregations
donate to organization outside their denomination. Thus, I have no broad
distributional conclusion to draw concerning the philanthropic activities
of congregations. It is clear, however, that an appreciable share of the philanthropic activities supported by the congregations do benefit the lower-
income quintiles. Reasonable assumptions about the spending on educa-

tion, health and human services, environmental and public improvement, and aid to individuals discussed above allow one to conclude that over 20 percent of this spending goes to members of households in the lowest income quintile—and this does not include the in-kind giving flowing through congregations.[33]

No discussion of the beneficiaries of congregations' philanthropic spending would be complete without mention of the traditional role of congregations in providing disaster relief. Time and again religious congregations have served as dispensers of aid to the victims of floods, hurricanes, tornadoes, droughts, and other natural disasters. In and around the community actually hit by the disaster, religious congregations represent established and trusted institutions to which people feel comfortable turning for help and are seen by their members as the natural organizational vehicle through which aid can be provided both immediately after the disaster and in the rebuilding period. Religious congregations around the country serve as locations in which sympathy for the victims of disaster can be focused and translated into financial support for those victims. Associated with most any major natural disaster are stories of the aid rendered to victims by people acting through their religious congregations; a recent example is Goss's (1990) account of congregational activity following hurricane Hugo.

The victims of natural disasters come from all income classes. The poor victim probably loses less in financial terms than the rich one, but the poor are more likely than the rich to turn to or be sought out by charitable agencies (in part because they are less likely to be adequately insured), so that, on the balance, the lower-income classes probably benefit disproportionately from church-provided disaster relief. The amount of money devoted to disaster relief by the congregations in an average year is difficult to ascertain from data I have seen; most of it probably takes the form of donations to individuals, to established relief organizations, or to denomination-wide appeals.

V. Do the Mutual Benefit Activities of Religious Congregations Generate Externalities?

If religious congregations were to vanish, along with peoples' desire for and memory of them, what would be the result? What would happen to the more than 50 billion dollars in charitable contributions currently flow-

---

33. Assuming, for example, that 100 percent of congregational giving to individuals, 25 percent of spending on health and human services, 10 percent of spending on the environment

ing through the religious congregations? I think it rather unlikely that all this money would be donated to secular philanthropies. The reason that churchgoers currently permit 70 percent of the money they donate to congregations to be used in the production of sacramental and other mutual benefit services is that churchgoers feel a personal need or desire for these services. If the need or desire for the services now provided by religious congregations were to vanish, chances are that the myriad other personal needs and desires possessed by human beings would absorb most of the freed-up dollars. What of the thirty cents of each dollar donated to congregations now spent philanthropically? Would the population's philanthropic impulse be unchanged in our hypothetical world without organized religion, so that the money would find its way into the hands of secular charities and government agencies that would take over the philanthropic functions once handled by congregations? Or would the silencing of the message to care for the needy preached in all of America's religious traditions lead to an erosion of altruism? More generally, in the absence of the moral teaching currently provided by organized religion, would there be a decay of moral standards and a subsequent decline in the quality of life? Or is it the case, as some argue, that organized religion encourages an undue concern with matters of the hereafter, so that a disappearance of religion would lead to increased attention and resources being devoted to the problems of this world?

Contemplating this counterfactual scenario is a way of considering the question of whether there are externalities associated with the sacramental and mutual benefit activities of America's religious congregations; that is, whether an individual's participation in such activities has positive or negative repercussions for other individuals. And while the questions asked above are quite speculative, there are more concrete questions relating to this matter that social scientists have tried to answer. For example, does participation in the activities of a religious congregation diminish a person's tendency to engage in antisocial behavior? Does it increase one's tendency toward altruism and philanthropy? Does church attendance make one a better neighbor or citizen?

In this section, I review some of the quantitative social science literature that explores the relationship between certain behaviors—crime, drug use, philanthropy, etc.—and church attendance or some other measure of par-

---

and political action, and 5 percent of educational spending benefits members of households in the lowest income quintile.

ticipation in congregational activities. All the studies imply cross-section data, so one must be careful in making causal statements about the correlations uncovered. The interrelationships between religiosity and other personality characteristics that lead people to behave as they do are potentially complex, and it is always worth asking whether something like church attendance should be regarded as the cause of a behavior or a joint effect along with that behavior of a more fundamental personality trait.

It is a widely though not universally held belief that commitment to the doctrines of organized religion, such as would be evidenced if not engendered by active participation in a religious congregation, tends to foster moral development and socially desirable conduct. In recent decades, social scientists have subjected this common sense to test by constructing a variety of measures of both religiosity and moral development and exploring the covariances between such measures. This research program has been unable to produce a consensus, however, and is currently marked by disagreements over matters of conceptualization and measurement (Sapp and Jones 1986, 208–9).

More clear-cut results have emerged from studies that attempt to link specific externality-generating behaviors to measures of religious commitment. There is, for example, strong evidence that adherents to creeds that emphasize abstinence from alcohol, tobacco, and other drugs are less likely to use those substances, and several studies show that, in general, church attendance is negatively correlated with use of drugs, alcohol, and tobacco among adolescents.[34] Church attendance has also been found to be negatively related to teenagers' likelihood of being involved in property crime or interpersonal violence (Sloane and Potvin 1986). Studies such as these that focus on the behavior of adolescents are of particular interest, for they give some insight into the socialization function of the religious congregation both as a provider of instruction for youths and as an institution influencing the childrearing practices of parents. Participation in the activities of organized religion has been tied to antisocial behaviors as well. There is an extensive literature linking prejudice and intolerance of various sorts to measures of religiosity, including church attendance (for example, Allport 1966; Beatty and Walter 1984).

Of particular interest for this study is the question of whether there is a link between church attendance and philanthropy. Many have noted the existence of a positive relationship between church attendance or religious

---

34. See Dudley, Mutch, and Cruise (1987) and references cited therein.

giving and total charitable giving as a percentage of income. However, neither this relationship nor the parallel relationship between church attendance and donations of time demonstrates a greater tendency toward philanthropy on the part of churchgoers. Participation in a religious congregation essentially requires a certain nontrivial amount of giving to the congregation that is technically classified as charitable giving, but which is more of the nature of payment for services received. The positive relationship between giving to religious congregations and total giving is analogous to the relationship that would exist between union membership and the percentage of an individual's income going to political lobbying organizations in a study that defined labor unions as political lobbying organizations.

Some recent public opinion polls, however, imply that participation in the activities of a religious congregation tends to be associated with greater amounts of charitable giving aside from that which supports congregational mutual benefit activities. In a 1988 survey of over 2,700 adult Americans, 57 percent of church members reported giving to nonreligious charities, while 48 percent of nonmembers reported giving to nonreligious charities. A similar result emerged from a 1990 survey, in which the relevant percentages were 66 percent for church members and 58 percent for nonmembers (Independent Sector 1990, table 1.15). A survey of 502 teenagers found that among those who attended church regularly, 31 percent were involved in activities that helped the poor, the sick, or the elderly, while the percentage among those who did not attend church regularly was 16 percent.[35]

VI. Possible Causes and Effects of the Expansion or Contraction of Congregations' Activities

Congregations receive well over 80 percent of their income from their members in the form of charitable contributions and bequests, and it is unlikely that this situation will change in the near future. Thus, a discussion of possible causes of expansion or contraction of the income and expenditures of American congregations is essentially a discussion of the causes of increases or decreases in real levels of charitable giving to religion.[36] Events that could plausibly lead to such increases or decreases

35. Reported in *Emerging Trends,* May 1988, p. 1.
36. An exception to this generalization concerns the tax treatment of the congregations' activities, for example, property tax exemptions, changes in which would have a considerable effect on the scale of congregational activities.

would include changes in the tax treatment of charitable contributions, macroeconomic upturns or downturns, changes in the age composition of the population, or wide-ranging changes in Americans' attitudes toward organized religion.[37]

In order to get a feel for the impact that a substantial change in religious giving would have on congregational activities, I interviewed about a dozen people, including congregational financial officers, professional financial consultants to congregations, and denominational officials whose work had given them a familiarity with congregational finances. I asked them to generalize to the extent that they could concerning how congregations reacted to long-term changes in per member giving, such as might be caused by substantial changes in local economic conditions. I asked in particular about the relative impact of such changes on the congregation's mutual benefit versus philanthropic activity. Most respondents were reluctant to generalize and stressed the peculiarity of each congregation, but certain themes emerged from the discussions.

A common reaction of congregations to flush times is the expansion of programs for the young and elderly of the congregation, which generally means expansion of staff. Beyond that, churches go in two separate directions, with some investing heavily in building or improving the congregation's physical facilities and others expanding outreach programs. One respondent expressed dismay at the fact that prosperous churches would often expand their physical facilities and then fail to take advantage of the outreach opportunities represented by those facilities.

Not surprisingly, the congregational response to hard times was to curtail programs or replace paid staff with volunteers if possible. Some mentioned neglect of routine maintenance of the physical plant as a strategy for making ends meet; others noted that contributions to outside organizations and to the denomination were common targets of budget cutters. One interesting theme emerged from the discussions of the hypothetical congregation facing hard times, and it related to the interrelationship between the congregation's mutual benefit activities and its ability to support philanthropic programs. It appears that an important variable affecting

37. The growth rate of real charitable giving to religion was only slightly slowed by the recessions of the 1970s and 1980s, suggesting that aggregate congregational income is relatively stable in the face of economic fluctuations (see *Giving USA* 1990, 94). Recent demographic and attitudinal changes that might have an impact upon Americans' support of organized religion (such as the return of the baby boomers to churches or growing disgust with corrupt televangelists) are much discussed, but have yet to affect overall membership or attendance rates.

congregational giving is member satisfaction with the mutual benefit and especially sacramental programs of the church. A healthy, vigorous sacramental program leads to a congregation more willing to support any project the church leadership might recommend, while members often express dissatisfaction with the church's mutual benefit programs by cutting back on contributions. This leads to a dilemma when exogenous forces cause a fall in church revenues, for cuts made in mutual benefit programs in response to such a downturn may generate member dissatisfaction that exacerbates the congregation's financial problems. All respondents agreed that sacramental programs were the last to be touched during hard times, an understandable fact given that the provision of sacramental services is the religious congregation's reason for existence. One told a cautionary tale of a congregation that had attempted to save outreach programs by cutting mutual benefit programs, a tactic that led to a disgruntled membership and a deeper financial crisis. Others agreed that this tale illustrated a basic truth.

In light of these interviews, I am unable to predict whether an expansion of congregational revenues and expenditures would result in philanthropic activities making up a greater or lesser share of congregational expenditures. It does seem fairly clear, however, that if a widespread contraction were to hit the congregations, the cuts in philanthropic spending would be disproportionately large.

There is a considerable body of anecdotal evidence suggesting that congregations step up their philanthropic activities when economic downturns and cutbacks in government services bring hardship to their community. This evidence would seem to run counter to the conclusion that congregational financial problems are likely to bring a contraction of philanthropic spending. This apparent contradiction disappears, however, if it is the case that the expansion of philanthropic services in response to negative economic shocks is a response mainly of those congregations whose members have been relatively unaffected by the shock to the emergent needs of the primary victims of the shock. Such a situation, which clearly represents a redistribution of income toward the economically less fortunate, apparently shows up in the data of Salamon and Teitelbaum (1984, 63).

VII. Summary and Conclusions

An estimated 68 billion dollars flowed through America's religious congregations in 1989. Congregations exist primarily to meet the spiritual needs of their membership, which they do through the provision of sacramental or spiritually oriented services that tend to have the character of what economists call "club goods." This activity consumes about 60 percent of congregational expenditures, and there are essentially no other institutions in this country besides the congregations that perform this activity. The government cannot provide or support the provision of sacramental services, while any nongovernmental agency that began to provide such services would likely soon become a religious congregation in the eyes of the law. The congregations also serve their membership in the same way that many secular clubs and organizations do, providing opportunities for socializing, recreation, organizational involvement, and so on. I have estimated that the provision of services for members consumes about 70 percent of congregational expenditure.

People from all income classes join and take advantage of the services offered by America's religious congregations. Data on time-use patterns of American households give no indication that the amount of time spent in worship services and other church-related activities is related to household income. The evidence on religious giving indicates that more affluent households contribute more to congregations per hour spent participating in congregational activities, and there is reason to believe that this occurs within individual congregations, so that wealthy members subsidize the spiritual consumption of less wealthy members.

Close to 30 percent of congregational expenditure (some 20 billion dollars in 1989) is philanthropic in nature, including that which addresses the specific material needs of individual members of the congregation and that which supports the provision of services to people regardless of their affiliation with the congregation. Congregational philanthropic expenditure often supports congregationally administered programs, but also takes the form of donations to outside philanthropic agencies. Because most of America's religious bodies see their mission as the alleviation of spiritual as well as material deprivation, there is no reason to presume that congregational philanthropic spending should be concentrated exclusively on those in the lower-income brackets. In fact an appreciable share of that spending does benefit the poor; and the incomplete evidence I have been able to gather does not seem to indicate any pronounced pro-rich tilt in the distribution of benefits of congregational philanthropy taken as a whole.

As providers and supporters of philanthropic services, the congregations are operating on the same turf as secular philanthropic agencies and the government. While the congregations' 20 billion dollars of philanthropic spending appears rather substantial when looked at in the context of total nonprofit philanthropy, it is worth reiterating the conclusion of Salamon and Teitelbaum (1984) that when it comes to the support or provision of education, health services, and social services, the financial contribution of the congregations is dwarfed by that of the government.[38] The extent to which the nature and scope of congregational philanthropic activity has historically responded to changes in the scale and focus of government social service activity is a subject I have not taken up here, but it is certainly one worthy of investigation.[39]

APPENDIX A
THE UNIVERSITY OF MICHIGAN TIME-USE STUDY

The University of Michigan Survey Research Center conducted a national survey of time use in 1975–76 and again in 1981. The 1975–76 survey involved a nationally representative sample of households, while the 1981 survey involved a non-representative subset of the 1975–76 participants. Respondents (and their spouses, if present) were asked standard demographic and socioeconomic questions. They were also asked to describe, in sequence, their activities of the previous day, with attention to the time that each activity began and ended. More information on this "recall diary" method of ascertaining time use information and its reliability can be found in Juster and Stafford (1985). In particular, the recall diary method is more reliable than methods that inquire about typical time commitments to specific activities.

Respondents were contacted four times over a twelve-month period in such a way that each respondent described two weekdays, a Saturday, and a Sunday. The activities described in the time diaries were coded into eighty-seven categories in the 1975–76 survey and 223 categories in the 1981 survey. The amount of time spent by a respondent on a given type of activity during a week was estimated by multiplying the minutes spent on that activity during each of the two described weekdays by 2.5, and adding to that the minutes spent on the activity during the two described weekend days.

The 1975–76 data included for each respondent and spouse a measure of weekly time spent in "religious practices" (attending or participating in organized worship services; or prayer, meditation, or Bible study outside the setting of a church service or organized class) an din religious group activities (meetings and other activities of "church groups"). For the 1981 study, each of these variables

---

38. For example, in 1989 the government spent about 90 billion dollars on education, training, social services, community development, and health (not including Medicare). Medicare, Social Security, and other income support programs involved an additional 453 billion dollars (U.S. Council of Economic Advisers 1990, table C-77).

39. An interesting paper by Wuthnow and Nass (1988) attempts to test the thesis that the expansion of governmental activity undermines the vitality of voluntary collective action. The authors find in the U.S. data a negative correlation, both cross-sectionally and across time periods, between the size of government and the level of voluntary affiliation with religious congregations.

was split in two, with time in worship services being separated from informal religious practices, and with religious group activities being divided into activities of "religious helping groups" and activities of all other church groups. Religious group activities were not classified as sacramental and nonsacramental.

It is worth noting that 36.4 percent of those interviewed in 1975–76 and 33.7 percent of those interviewed in 1981 reported attending a worship service. In Gallup polls conducted in 1976 and in 1981, 42 percent and 43 percent, respectively, reported that they had attended church in the previous week (Benson 1981). Based on what is known about the behavior of survey respondents, one would expect the Gallup poll to overestimate the rate of church attendance. Those who reported spending time in organized worship services in 1981 spent an average of ninety minutes a week in those activities, a figure that seems reasonable.

To estimate the time spent each week in an activity by all adult members of a household, I multiplied the number of adults in the household by the mean of the respondent's and spouse's time use, if the spouse was present, and by the respondent's time use if no spouse was present. This procedure is sensible in light of the fact that the respondent was selected randomly from each household in the sample. In the case of church attendance, I also created a variable that measured the time spent by all members of the household, including children. The idea here is that attending church services tends to be a family activity, with children accompanying their parents or participating in religiously oriented classes that run concurrently with services.

In computing means for these household variables and in projecting aggregate amounts of time spent in the various activities, I made use of weights designed to make the sample representative of the national population of households. The weights used with the 1975–76 data were calculated by the Survey Research Center, and I constructed a set of weights for the 1981 data based on Census information on household composition and income.

The weighted means for the household time use variables and for household income are reported in table 4.A1. The mean values for the variables in 1975–76 are similar to those in 1981, with one exception: the mean number of minutes spent in church meetings is nearly twice as large in 1981 as in 1975–76. A higher percentage of the 1981 sample reported attending a church meeting, and the average length of time spent in church meetings by those who attended was also greater in 1981 than in 1975. Because the reliability of the results of this study depend in part on the stability over time of religious behavior, I attempted to uncover the reason for the large increase in the mean of the meetings variable. The increase shows up whether the means are calculated with or without weights, and the outliers in the 1981 sample are not extreme enough to have caused the increase. The households appearing in both samples have a mean for the meetings variable in 1975 that is within three minutes of the mean for the 1975 sample as a whole, so that nonrandom sample attrition between 1975 and 19081 cannot explain the change. A cross-section regression of time spent in meetings on age using the 1975 sample does not support the hypothesis that the aging of the sample between 1975 and 1981 led to the increase in meeting attendance. I have thus concluded that the increase in the mean of the meetings variable represents a

TABLE 4.A1 Weighted Means of Household Time-use Variables (Standard errors in parentheses under estimates)

	1975–76	1981
Number of Households	975	480
MINUTES PER WEEK OF:		
Religious practices (adults)	118.7	104.0
	(8.3)	(8.1)
Individual or informal religious practices (adults)	—	24.4
		(3.8)
Organized religious services (adults)	—	79.6
		(6.5)
Religious practices (adults and minors)	187.6	172.3
	(15.1)	(19.4)
Organized religious services (adults and minors)	—	134.3
		(14.6)
Other religious group activities (adults)	47.7	88.1
	(5.8)	(13.2)
Religious groups, not helping oriented (adults)	—	0.5
		(0.6)
Household income in dollars	13,328.3	26,249.6
	(538.0)	(2,410.7)

SOURCE: Author's calculations based on survey described in Juster et al. (1979).

change in peoples' behavior and that the 1981 religious group activities variable is probably more reliable than the 1975–76 version as an indicator of current behavior.

Why people spent more time in religious group activities in 1981 than in 1975–76 is not clear. There was much written around the time of the 1980 presidential election of a new religious revival in America, but doubt is cast on the importance of this phenomenon by the evidence from public opinion polls described by Benson (1981), as well as the fact that the time-use data shows little change in actual church attendance between 1976 and 1981. A more likely explanation of the increase might be the vigor during the 1970s and 1980s of the "Church Growth" movement. Those associated with this movement (mainly Protestant churchmen) emphasize the importance of membership growth to a congregation's health and attempt to discover and disseminate reliable techniques for achieving such growth. Among other things, the consulting organizations and publications that carry the Church Growth message recommend that churches establish an extensive structure of lay committees in order to involve parishioners more in the administration of church affairs. This, of course, leads to more time being spent in committee meetings.

Appendix B
Allocating Payroll Expenditures

To determine the share of payroll expenditures that should be considered nonsacramental spending, I used the following procedure: for each congregation size (small, medium, and large), I multiplied the estimated share of time that the clergy employed by congregations of that size spent in nonsacramental activity by the estimated share of payroll going to clergy in congregations of that size, and added to it the estimated share of time that paid nonclergy employees spent in nonsacramental activities multiplied by the share of payroll going to nonclergy employees in congregations of that size. The three resulting sums were each multiplied by the share of total payroll expenditures originating in their size category, then summed to get an overall estimate of the share of congregations' payrolls devoted to nonsacramental spending. A similar procedure was used to divide the nonsacramental payroll into the several nonsacramental spending categories.

Estimates of the share of time spent in each of the nonsacramental activities by clergy and nonclergy employees of the congregations come from Independent Sector (1988a), as do estimates of the share of total congregational expenditures associated with each size category (see table 4.A2). The average division of payroll between clergy and nonclergy for each size of congregation was estimated using two data sources. The first was a survey I conducted during the summer of 1990 of 108 churches listed in the phone books of Lansing, Michigan, Charleston, West Virginia, and Topeka, Kansas. Churches were selected randomly, contacted by telephone, and asked the size of their paid staff, the titles or job descriptions of each employee, and whether the employee worked part time or full time. Nominally paid employees, such as an organist working two hours a week, were ignored. Table 4.A3 compares summary statistics fro this sample to comparable ones reported for the Independent Sector sample and shows the two data sets to be fairly consistent with one another.

The second data source used in estimating the payroll split between clergy and nonclergy employees was a survey of church employee compensation compiled by the National Association of Church Business Administration. This survey, based on information supplied by 727 churches in 1989, reports the average compensation (including benefits such as housing and travel allowances, insurance and retirement plans, etc.) for twenty-six positions commonly offered by congregations. Averages are also reported for subsets of the sample based on congregation size and broad denominational groupings. The survey is not representative—the 727 respondents were only a tiny fraction of the number of churches contacted, and the average salaries are noticeably higher than one would expect based on other sources. However, the relative pay levels for various positions calculated from these data correspond closely to information reported in Judy (1969), and it is pay ratios, not pay levels, that are important here.

The information from this salary survey was used to construct a hypothetical payroll for each of the 108 churches that described their staffs, based on the size of the church and whether it was Catholic or Protestant. (There are considerable

TABLE 4.A2 Time Use of Congregational Employees

	Congregation Size			
	Small	Medium	Large	All
Share of total payroll and supplies paid by congregations of this size	6.7(%)	22.4(%)	70.8(%)	100(%)
CLERGY TIME USE				
Total	100.0	100.0	100.0	100.0
Sacramental	74.4	71.9	62.9	68.3
Nonsacramental[a]	25.6	28.1	37.1	31.7[b]
Education	7.2	7.9	10.4	8.9
Human Services	5.5	6.0	7.9	6.8
Health	5.3	5.8	7.6	6.5
Public Benefit	2.8	3.1	4.1	3.5
Arts and Culture	1.1	1.2	1.6	1.4
International	2.2	2.4	3.2	2.7
Environmental	1.5	1.7	2.2	1.9
NONCLERGY TIME USE				
Total	100.0	100.0	100.0	100.0
Sacramental	38.2	51.6	52.9	51.7
Nonsacramental	61.8	48.4	47.1	48.3
Education	31.8	24.9	24.3	24.9
Human Services	15.8	12.4	12.1	12.4
Health	4.0	3.1	3.0	3.1
Public Benefit	2.2	1.7	1.6	1.7
Arts and Culture	4.0	3.1	3.0	3.1
International	2.5	2.0	1.9	2.0
Environmental	1.4	1.1	1.1	1.1

NOTE: Nonsacramental subcategories may not add up to total nonsacramental share due to rounding.

[a]Independent Sector (1988a) does not report a breakdown of non-sacramental time by congregation size. I have assumed that the overall pattern of nonsacramental spending prevails within each congregation size category.

[b]The "error of closure" reported in Independent Sector (1988a) has been allocated into the six categories on a prorated basis.

SOURCE: Independent Sector (1988a), tables 4.19, 4.20, 4.25.

TABLE 4.A3 Congregational Hiring and Pay Practices

	Congregation Size		
	Small	Medium	Large
Proportion of congregations this size in IS sample[a]	21%	43%	36%
Proportion of congregations this size in Biddle sample[a]	22%	45%	33%
Average number of clergy employed, IS sample	.96	1.39	2.00
Average number of clergy employed, Biddle sample	1.00	1.63	2.63
(standard error)	(.06)	(.12)	(.27)
Average size of full-time nonclergy staff, IS sample	.36	.63	2.45
Average size of full-time nonclergy staff, Biddle sample (standard	.08	.83	2.34
error)	(.06)	(.14)	(.26)
Average size of part-time nonclergy staff, IS sample	.65	1.61	2.54
Average size of part-time nonclergy staff, Biddle sample (standard	.63	1.87	2.48
error)	(.23)	(.18)	(.37)
Average share of payroll going to clergy[b]	82%	64%	59%

[a]Independent Sector sample size is 1,862; Biddle sample size is 108.
[b]Calculated using Biddle sample, NACBA salary survey (see text).
SOURCE: Independent Sector (1988a), table 4.7; survey conducted by author (see text).

differences between Catholic and Protestant practices regarding remuneration of clergy.) The split of this hypothetical payroll between clergy and nonclergy employees was then calculated for each congregation and averaged within each size class of congregation. These averages are reported in table 4.A3.

APPENDIX C
THE SECTION I ESTIMATES AND FINDINGS OF EARLIER STUDIES

The purpose of this appendix is to examine the extent to which both the results and certain elements of the process used to estimate the pattern of allocation of congregational spending are consistent with the findings of previous studies.

Taken alone, the evidence gathered by the Filer Commission suggests that about 80 percent of congregational expenditure ultimately supports sacramental activity, a figure considerably higher than the one reported in section I. One probable reason for the discrepancy is the fact that the Filer Commission's questionnaire allowed respondents considerable latitude in deciding what constituted a sacramental activity, creating a tendency toward the overestimation of this category. Also, the Filer Commission investigators made no attempt to assign payroll expenditures into the nonsacramental category on the basis of the nonsacramental activities of clergy and other employees in nominally sacramental posts (Interfaith Research Committee 1977, 370). If all the payroll and expenditures that I associated with clergy's nonsacramental activities were put into the sacramental category, my estimate of that category would rise by ten percentage points. Finally, there is no indication that the use of church facilities by outside groups was taken into consideration by the Filer Commission.

A study of the philanthropic activities of religious congregations undertaken by the Urban Institute in 1982 concluded that about 7 percent of the congregations' religious contributions (about 6 percent of total congregational income) went toward the provision of human services (Salamon and Teitelbaum 1984), with the term "human services" corresponding roughly to the activities in the education and human services categories of the Independent Sector study. By contrast, the analysis of section I indicated that at least 16 percent of congregational spending could be classified as education or human services spending. This suggests that if the Urban Institute figures are correct, I have overestimated the share of congregational expenditures going for nonsacramental and philanthropic purposes. I have been unable to determine what differences in methodology might have led to the differences between the estimates of this study and those of Salamon and Teitelbaum (1984). A reasonable inference from the text of that paper is that the 6 percent figure refers only to direct expenditures of congregations on human service programs, plus donations to organizations explicitly concerned with the provision of human services, and does not include money sent to the denomination or overhead related to facilities and administrative activities. This may explain some of the difference.

The estimates of the previous section depend heavily on data reported in Independent Sector (1988a) concerning the allocation of church employees' hours between various activities. It is important to know how accurate these data are, as they are used as a basis for classifying over half of the congregations' expenditures. Also, my use of such data in an attempt to assign payroll expenditures into the sacramental and nonsacramental categories represents a major methodological difference between my study and previous studies, a difference that leads my estimate of the extent of congregations' nonsacramental activities to be relatively large. A partial check on the reliability of these data is provided by Douglass and McNally's (1980) study of the time-use patterns of seventeen Protestant ministers from small- and medium-sized congregations. The ministers kept detailed records of their time use for a week, using a fifteen-category classification system that can be matched fairly well with the sacramental/nonsacramental, philanthropic/mutual benefit distinctions used here. The resulting data indicated that about 80 percent of the ministers' time was spent in activities that supported the mutual benefit functions of the congregation, while between 50 percent and 60 percent of their time was devoted to sacramental activity. By comparison, the Independent Sector's data on clergy time use led me to classify 77.5 percent of clergy time as mutual benefit and 68 percent as sacramental. Thus, the Douglass-MacNally study suggests that if my estimate of the size of the nonsacramental category is too large, it is not because of the overestimation of the extent of ministers' nonsacramental activities.

5

Social Services

Lester M. Salamon

Of all the components of the nonprofit or charitable sector, none might be expected to adhere more closely to the dictionary definition of "charity" as "generosity to the poor" (Random House Dictionary 1978, 154) than the social service or human service component. Nonprofit human service organizations owe their origins to the efforts to cope with the poverty and want that accompanied the massive influx of immigrants into American cities in the latter nineteenth and early twentieth centuries. Though often combining their efforts to relieve material distress with efforts to instill various religious and moral values, these organizations clearly took the problems of the poor as their principal focus of activity.

Although the development of government social welfare programs in the 1930s brought new resources into the field, it hardly eliminated the need for significant private action. America has long been at best a "reluctant" welfare state, restricting public aid to narrow categories of people and, even then, keeping benefits at minimal levels. The "rediscovery of poverty" in the 1960s provided clear evidence, if any were needed, that the public assistance system created by the New Deal hardly eliminated the need for aggressive, private voluntary action.

At the same time, the needs of the poor have not been the only ones competing for the attention of nonprofit human service organizations. Developments in the social work field were already creating tensions between service to the poor and service to a broader client population during the 1940s and 1950s (Cloward and Epstein 1965). Despite the spurt of interest in the problems of the poor in the 1960s, moreover, a "profound reorientation of purposes" (Gilbert and Sprecht 1981, 1) took place in the social services field in the 1970s and 1980s as a "new social service system" took

The author wishes to express his appreciation to Dr. Jaana Myllyluoma for invaluable assistance in developing the data reported here.

shape. The principal feature of this reorientation was a shift in focus away from the narrow goal of reducing poverty and economic dependency toward the broader goal of enhancing human development (Kamerman and Kahn 1976, 3). Under the new approach, social services of the sort provided by nonprofit human service agencies came to be viewed as something appropriate not simply for the poor, but for a broad cross section of the population as well.

How have nonprofit human service agencies coped with the pressures that have resulted from this broadening of the human service client base? To what extent have they remained true to their historic missions? To what extent have they shifted their attention from the poor to broader segments of the population? To the extent such a shift has occurred, what accounts for it? Who, in fact, is served by nonprofit social service agencies and who foots the bill?

The purpose of this chapter is to answer these questions. In the process, however, the chapter seeks to explore a number of more basic theoretical issues about the character of nonprofit organizations, issues that an analysis of client focus throws into bold relief. In particular, by examining who nonprofit social service agencies serve it is possible to shed interesting empirical light on the relative explanatory power of four alternative theories that have been advanced to explain the existence or behavior of the nonprofit sector: the market failure/government failure theory, the voluntary failure theory, the supply of charitable entrepreneurs theory, and organization theory.

To carry out these objectives, the discussion here falls into four major sections. Section I, which follows, defines what we mean by the nonprofit social service sector and provides some basic background information on its scope and scale. Section II then reviews what is known about the client focus of this set of organizations, drawing particularly on an extensive survey that the author carried out in 1983 and repeated in 1985–86. In section III, attention turns to the alternative theoretical concepts that can help explain the pattern of client focus that exists and to a test of these concepts using the empirical evidence from the survey. Section IV then reviews the central conclusions and implications that flow from this work.

I. HUMAN SERVICE NONPROFITS: AN OVERVIEW

"Social services" or "human services" are inherently amorphous terms. In the British context, these terms are used to refer to the entire range of people-oriented services and benefits, including basic income support for the elderly and the unemployed (Brenton 1985). In the United States, this broad array of services and benefits is more commonly referred to as "social welfare,"[1] and the term "social services" is used slightly more narrowly. Thus, under the basic federal program that funds such services—originally known as the Title XX program and now broadened and renamed the Social Services Block Grant Program—social services were defined as any activities that helped to support five broad goals: (1) economic self-support; (2) self-sufficiency; (3) protective care for children or adults; (4) prevention of institutionalization; or (5) provision of services to help people in institutions (Wickenden 1976, 572). In the first year of implementation of this program, states specified 1,313 different services that fell within these five broad goals. These were subsequently grouped into no fewer than forty-one different Title XX service categories, including adoption assistance, case management, chore services, counseling, day dare, education and training services, family planning, foster care, information and referral, legal services, protective services, provision of meals, recreational services, residential care, special services for the handicapped or disadvantaged, sheltered workshops, and vocational rehabilitation (Gilbert and Specht 1981, 4).

While this definition is quite broad, it nevertheless excludes some activities that fall within the domain of nonprofit organizations active in the human services field. Accordingly, we will adopt a usage that is closer to the U.S. Census of Service Industries' concept of "social and legal services." In particular, we exclude hospitals, schools, and arts, culture, and recreation institutions, but include agencies that provide direct income and other material support, individual and family services, day care, residential care (except for nursing homes), job training, mental health and addiction services, nonhospital health care, as well as agencies that engage in community organizing, advocacy, or community development, including research and public education. We will refer to the organizations that fall within this field as the "nonprofit human service sector."

Scale of the Nonprofit Human Service Sector

Perhaps reflecting the diversity of the field, human service nonprofit organizations constitute the largest single component of the charitable non-

1. Thus, the annual *Social Security Bulletin* series on "public social welfare services" defines such services as "the cash benefits, services, and administrative costs of public programs that directly benefit individuals and families" (Bixby 1990, 11). Included are social security, un-

profit service sector[2] in terms of numbers of organizations. According to the 1987 *Census of Service Industries,* which provides the most recent available data, 75,612 organizations fall within the nonprofit human service sector as we have defined it here. This represented an estimated 52 percent of all charitable nonprofit organizations, as shown in table 5.1.

Of the various types of human service nonprofits, the most numerous were individual and family service agencies, as table 5.1 shows. These organizations represented nearly 30 percent of the human service agencies and 15 percent of all nonprofit organizations as of 1982. This was followed by child day care, representing 18 percent of human service agencies and 9 percent of all agencies.

While they represent the largest single component of the charitable nonprofit service sector in terms of numbers of organizations, however, human service agencies do not constitute the largest component in terms of expenditures. Rather, as shown in table 5.2, such organizations account for only 15 percent of the total expenditures of charitable nonprofit service organizations. Of this, assorted "other" social service agencies account for 7 percent of the total, and residential care facilities and individual and family service agencies account for 3 percent each. Clearly, the typical nonprofit human service agency is quite a bit smaller than the typical higher education institution or hospital, even though many are still quite substantial and the subsector as a whole represented a $37 billion "industry."

This picture of the nonprofit human service sector is somewhat incomplete, moreover because social services are delivered by many other types of organizations as well. Thus, counseling is often provided directly by hospitals, which have also recently moved into the field of home health. Employment and training, considered a form of social service, is also provided by training institutes and community colleges. Similarly, numerous

---

employment insurance, Medicare, Medicaid, welfare assistance, education, veterans' programs, and related assistance.

2. The term "charitable nonprofit service sector" is issued here to refer to organizations exempt from taxation under section 501(c) (3) of the Internal Revenue Code that are engaged in the provision of services to people other than religious services. These organizations are not only themselves exempt from taxation but are also eligible to receive tax-exempt gifts from individuals and corporations to pursue "charitable, educational, scientific" and related purposes. Not included are business and professional associations or membership associations. Also excluded are nonservice-providing 501(c) (3) organizations such as foundations (which provide financial support to other nonprofits) and sacramental religious congregations and churches.

TABLE 5.1 Nonprofit Human Service Agencies in Relation to Other Charitable Nonprofit Organizations

	Number	% of Total	% of Human Service Organizations
Human Services	75,612	52(%)	100(%)
Legal services	1,439	1	2
Child day care	13,822	9	18
Individual and family services	21,862	15	29
Job training and vocational rehab.	5,005	4	7
Residential care	10,474	7	14
Civic[a]	2,021	1	3
Other[b]	20,989	14	27
Other "Charitable" Nonprofits	70,276	48	
Health and hospitals	12,370	8	
Education	6,350	5	
Arts, culture, recreation	13,162	9	
Other civic, social	38,394	26	
Total	145,888	100%	

[a]Includes 5 percent of all civic, social, and fraternal associations based on survey results indicating this proportion is engaged in community organizing and advocacy.
[b]Includes 2,414 noncommercial research organizations and 6,736 home health providers and outpatient clinics.
SOURCES: Higher education data from U.S. Department of Education, (1991, 229); remaining data from U.S. Bureau of the Census (1989, 13–14).

churches operate day care centers that do not show up as separately incorporated nonprofits. The $37 billion is estimated human service agency expenditures thus probably understates the size of the nonprofit human service industry.

Not all of the revenue to support the estimated $37 billion in nonprofit human service agency expenditures in 1987 came from private charitable giving, however. To the contrary, private donations to human service agencies as of 1987 amounted to just under $10 billion, or about one-fourth of human service agency revenues. What is more, this represented only about 10 percent of all private charitable contributions, down from 14 percent in 1970. While charitable giving grew during this period, in other words, the growth was more substantial outside the human service field than inside. In fact, adjusted for inflation, private giving to human service activities increased by only 6 percent over the entire seventeen-year period between 1970 and 1987, though this was due principally to the sharp decline in real growth of such giving during the early 1970s.

TABLE 5.2 Operating Expenditures of Nonprofit
Human Service Organizations in Relation to
Other Charitable Nonprofits
(in billions of dollars)

Type	Amount	% of Total
Human Services	36.6	15(%)
Legal services	0.4	—
Child day care	2.9	1
Individual and family services	7.5	3
Job training and vocational rehab.	2.8	1
Residential care	6.0	3
Civic[a]	0.4	—
Other[b]	16.6	7
Other "Charitable" Nonprofits	202.1	85
Health services	134.2	56
Education	54.5	23
Arts, culture, recreation	5.2	2
Other civic, social	8.2	4
Total	$238.7	100%

[a]Includes 5 percent of civic, social, and fraternal associations engaged in community organizing and advocacy according to survey results.
[b]Includes 1,946 noncommercial research organizations.
SOURCE: Adapted from Hodgkinson and Weitzman (1989, 183).

Human Service Nonprofits versus Government Expenditures

Compared to the $10 billion in private contributions to the support of human service activies, and the $37 billion in total nonprofit human service agency expenditures, government spending on social welfare activities in 1987 totaled $834 billion (Bixby 1990, 18–19). Included in this total, however, is spending on social security, health, veterans benefits, and education in addition to the more narrow "human service" activities of principal concern to us here. If we define the latter to include needs-tested cash and direct material assistance (for example, food assistance), housing, and other social and human services such as day care and services for the elderly, then total government spending on just these human service activities amounted to $87.1 billion as of 1987, of which 71 percent came from federal sources and the remaining 29 percent from state and local governments (see table 5.4).

Government spending even on human services thus outdistances private

TABLE 5.3 Private Contributions to Human Services in
Relation to Total Contributions, 1970–87
(constant 1987 $, billions)

Year	Contributions to Human Services	Total Contributions	Human Service as % of Total
1970	$8.18	$58.91	13.9(%)
1980	6.74	66.93	10.1
1987	9.84	95.15	10.3
Change, 1970–87	+20%	+62%	

SOURCE: American Association of Fund-Raising Counsel (1990, 14–15).

TABLE 5.4 Government Spending versus Private Giving and Nonprofit
Expenditures for Human Services and Other Social Welfare, 1987
($ billions)

	Government Spending	Private Giving[a]	Nonprofit Expenditures[a]
Human Services	$ 87.1	$ 9.8	$ 36.6
Need-based income support[b]	48.5	NA	NA
Housing	13.2	NA	NA
Other social services[c]	25.4	NA	NA
Other Social Welfare	$747.3	$ 37.1[d]	$196.6[e]
Social insurance/veterans	349.9	NA	
Health	192.2	9.2	134.2
Education	205.2	9.8	54.5
Total Social Welfare	$834.4	$ 46.9	$233.2

[a]Excludes religion, arts and culture.
[b]Includes public aid except for social services, vendor medical payments, and employment assistance.
[c]Includes maternal and child health, social services under public assistance, and other social welfare.
[d]Includes $18.1 billion in giving for "public/society benefit" and "other" not separately reported.
[e]Includes $8.2 billion in spending by other civic and social organizations.
SOURCE: Government spending data from Bixby (1990, 18); private giving data from AAFRC (1990, 14–15); nonprofit expenditure data from table 5.2.

philanthropic support for these same activities by a factor of 9 to 1 ($87.1 billion versus $9.8 billion), as table 5.4 shows. When total nonprofit expenditures are included, however, the disparity narrows considerably. Thus, for the "human service" activities of principal concern to us here, government spending outdistances the spending of nonprofit organizations by a factor of only about 2½ to 1. In other words, despite the extensive expansion of government human service activities over the past several decades, the nonprofit sector remains a significant presence in the field.[3]

Sources of Income

One reason for this is that government spending and nonprofit activity have gone hand in hand. Far from displacing nonprofit organizations, government agencies have often enlisted them in the operation of government programs. The result is an extensive pattern of government-nonprofit cooperation in the delivery of human services, with government functioning as the financier and the nonprofit sector as the deliverers of the services (Salamon and Abramson 1982).

Reflecting this, government has emerged as a major—indeed *the* major—source of revenue of nonprofit human service agencies. This is apparent in table 5.5, which records the sources of income of a cross section of human service nonprofit agencies surveyed by the present author in 1985. As detailed more fully below, this survey covered close to 2,300 agencies in sixteen jurisdictions throughout the United States. What it revealed is that close to 40 percent of the income of these nonprofit human service agencies came from government as of the mid-1980s. By contrast, private giving accounts for just over 30 percent of total income and fees and service charges for close to 25 percent.[4]

II. Whom Does the Nonprofit Human Service Sector Serve?

What role does this nonprofit human service sector play in the overall social welfare system? Do these organizations supplement the public system,

---

3. Which items to include as part of government spending on human services is, of course, open to debate. A strong case could be made, for example, for inclusion of a significant portion of social security spending on grounds that such spending plays a significant role in reducing poverty among the elderly. Similarly, the distinction between income transfers and services is somewhat arbitrary since income transfers can be used to purchase services. Thus a portion of the expenditures under the Aid to Families with Dependent Children (AFDC) program—an income transfer—is earmarked for day care; while day care is also supported by the Social Services Block Grant Program, a service program. The figures reported here under Human Services thus probably give a conservative picture of the extent of government spending in fields where nonprofit human service agencies are active.

4. Data presented by Hodgkinson and Weitzman (1989, 177) provide a similar picture, but for a slightly different set of agencies. Using Hodgkinson and Weitzman's data, government accounts for 41 percent of the income of nonprofit social and legal service agencies, private

TABLE 5.5
Estimated Sources of Income of
Nonprofit Human Service Agencies, 1987
(by percent)

Private giving	31
Government	38
Fees	23
Other	8
Total	100

SOURCE: Salamon/Urban Institute Nonprofit Sector Project Survey, rounds 1 and 2, 1982 and 1985.

filling in significant gaps in public provision? Or have nonprofits carved out a particular "market niche"? Who benefits from the activities of the nonprofit human service sector? What distributional consequences does it have?

Conceptual and Empirical Challenges

Unfortunately, the answer to these questions is far from straightforward. For one thing, the benefits that result from the activities of nonprofit human service agencies are varied. In addition to the *direct benefits* that accrue to the immediate recipients of services, there are a variety of *indirect or community benefits* that accrue to a wide assortment of other people— family members, acquaintances, neighbors, the general public. A drug addiction center may provide direct benefits to poor, inner-city drug addicts, for example, but its chief beneficiaries may be middle-class suburbanites whose neighborhoods become more safe as a consequence. Difficult decisions consequently have to be made about whether it is the direct or the indirect benefits that should be included, and if the latter, which ones.

Beyond this, there are problems in deciding who even the direct beneficiaries are. For example, is the principal beneficiary of an adoption service the natural mother, the adopted child, the new parents, or all of the above? If there are differences in the income levels of these various parties, the

giving for 38 percent, and fees and service charges for 14 percent. The rank order of funding sources thus remains the same, but private giving is somewhat larger and fees somewhat lower.

distributional consequences of the service will vary depending on the definition of the beneficiary used. What is more, some services involve multiple "treatments" whereas others involve far fewer contacts. This poses thorny empirical problems about whether to count the number of "clients" or the amount of contact time with the human service provider in calculating the distributional effects of agency activity. If the typical poor client absorbs far less of an agency's resources than the typical nonpoor client, which method is chosen can have significant implications for the outcome.

Finally, the great diversity in the human service field poses further problems in reaching aggregate judgments about the distributional consequences of the services that are provided. Even when it becomes possible to settle on an appropriate measure of who is being served and by how much in one service field, it is rare to be able to compare another service field in the same terms. Developing a client count for a day care center, for example, is a far different thing from assessing the number of people served by a disaster assistance program. The former may involve daily contact stretching over many months while the latter may involve one night on a cot in a church social hall during a tornado. Adding together the number of clients in the latter with the number in the former to measure the overall clientele of the nonprofit human service sector and the distribution of the sector's efforts among income groups can therefore be very misleading.

Perhaps because of these difficulties, few analyses of the client base of the nonprofit human service sector exist, and almost none treats the potential distributional consequences. Thus, the United Way of America regularly solicits information on the clientele served by the agencies to which its local chapters provide support, but information is collected on only three client characteristics—age, sex, and race. Data on client *income* are not solicited. What is more, the data collected apply to "programs," not to actual recipients of services. In other words, United Way asks what the primary client focus is of the various programs its local affiliates are funding in terms of these three client characteristics, but it does *not* ask who is *actually served*. Since many programs do not have a primary client focus, however, the results turn out to be fairly ambiguous even in these limited terms. Thus, in the 1988 *Funds Distribution Profile* (United Way 1990, 66, 69, 72), we learn that 10 percent of United Way service dollars went to support programs specially targeted on the aged, but 57 percent went for programs open to all age groups. What we do not learn is how many aged people were actually served by these latter programs. Similarly, we learn that 11 percent of all dollars went for programs targeted to blacks, but 53 percent went for programs open to persons of all races with no indication of how many blacks are served by these latter programs.

Similar problems exist with the client surveys regularly conducted by Catholic Charities USA, another large federation of human service agencies. For example, the *1989 Annual Survey Report* (Catholic Charities USA 1990) reports that Catholic Charities agencies throughout the United States provided eleven different types of services that touched 9,123,337 persons in 1989, including 2.4 million children, 5.4 million adults, and 1.3 million aging persons. While it is possible to infer from the services they received what income level at least some of these individuals were in, income data were not collected on the clients. Nor is any attempt made to assess the different service efforts represented by the different agency activities—for example, the provision of food to 3,895,340 persons compared to the provision of counseling to 599,374 persons. While it is possible to assess the number of people touched by the Catholic Charities network, therefore, it is extremely difficult to work out the distributional consequences of the network's activities.

A far more useful picture of the client base of at least a portion of the nonprofit human service sector emerges from a series of surveys conducted by Family Services of America, a network of some two hundred family service agencies throughout the United States. Unfortunately, however, the most recent FSA client data that are available cover only 1970. Nevertheless, they are quite revealing. As shown in table 5.6, FSA reported that in 1970 only 10 percent of the white clients, and 35 percent of the nonwhite clients, of FSA's local affiliates had incomes below the official poverty line (Beck and Jones 1973, 29). This was somewhat higher than for the population at large (7 percent and 25 percent respectively), but not overwhelmingly so. More generally, after combining measures of income, education, and occupational status, FSA found that only 20 percent of the clients of its member agencies fell in the bottom third of the socioeconomic status index (see table 5.6). Although it covers only a small portion of the human service field, this information suggests quite strongly that the nonprofit human service sector is by no means targeted primarily on the poor. For better or worse, many of the agencies in the sector devote a considerable portion of their time and resources to other segments of the population.

The Salamon/Urban Institute Nonprofit Sector Survey

This tentative conclusion finds confirmation in a broader survey of nonprofit human service agencies conducted in the early and mid-1980s as

TABLE 5.6 Clientele of Family Service
Association of America Member Agencies,
by Socioeconomic Status, 1970

Socioeconomic Status	Percentage of Families
Upper (75–100)	16(%)
Middle (50–74)	33
Low-Middle (30–49)	30
Lower (0–29)	21
Total	100%

NOTE: Numbers in parentheses are index scores for an index embracing measures of income, education, and occupational status.
SOURCE: Beck and Jones (1973, 33).

part of the Urban Institute Nonprofit Sector Project, which the present author directed. In many respects, this survey provides the most complete and current data available on the distributional consequences of the nonprofit human service sector, and the balance of this chapter will consequently draw primarily on it.

The Urban Institute Nonprofit Sector Project surveyed a broad array of nonprofit human service agencies in sixteen communities throughout the United States—a large metropolitan area, a medium-sized metropolitan area, a small metropolitan area, and a rural county in each of the four major Census regions of the country. The survey covered all public-benefit, nonprofit service agencies except hospitals and higher education institutions. Agencies were identified for inclusion in the study by cross-checking Internal Revenue Service lists against local directories, umbrella groups, and other listings. All together, 6,868 agencies were targeted for inclusion. Of these 3,411 responded to a first-wave survey in 1982. A second round survey was then conducted with the same agencies in 1984–85 in order to chart changes over time. A total of 2,308 agencies responded to this second-round survey, and the responses from the two rounds were merged into a "matched" data set. The result is an extraordinary body of data about the structure and finances of the nonprofit human service sector and the early impact on these agencies of the significant shifts in national policy enacted in the early 1980s. Among other things, agencies were asked in the first-round survey to indicate what percentage of their clients were poor, defined as below the official poverty line.[5] While this is admittedly still a

5. The actual question reads as follows: "Please estimate the percentage of your clients who fall into the following major target groups:

crude measure for the reasons noted above, it provides at least a partial picture of the distributional impact of these agencies.

For the purposes of this chapter, we focus on a subset of this "matched" round 1/round 2 data set. In particular, we exclude from the analysis the agencies primarily engaged in arts, culture, and recreation since these agencies typically provide services that lie outside the human service field of principal concern to us here.[6] In addition, we focus here only on those respondents to both rounds of our survey that actually responded to the question about the percentage of their clientele who are poor. These two exclusions leave us with a sample of 1,474 agencies.[7] Excluding agencies that failed to indicate what proportion of their clients are poor probably overstates somewhat the extent of poverty focus within the nonprofit human service sector since the agencies that failed to respond to this question are most likely to have few poor clients. Had these agencies been included in the analysis, therefore, it would have reduced considerably the percentage of agencies with significant proportions of low-income clients. But it seemed safest to err, if at all, in the opposite direction rather than assume that agencies that failed to respond to this particular question had no poor clients.

Client Focus: An Overview

Perhaps the central conclusion that emerges from our survey, as from the other studies of the clientele of nonprofit human service agencies, is that these agencies focus far less heavily on the poor than is sometimes imagined. Thus, of the 1,474 nonprofit human service agencies for which we were able to compile complete round 1 and round 2 data, only 27 percent indicated that most of their clients were poor (that is, had incomes below the poverty line), as shown in table 5.7. Another 20 percent reported some

---

____ % working class	____ % single parents
____ % income below poverty	____ % disabled
____ % women	____ % unemployed
	____ % ex-offenders"

The "% income below poverty" is the variable used here. Throughout this chapter, we use the terms "poor" and "low-income" to refer to the clients with "income below poverty."

6. Some arts, culture, and recreation agencies do, of course, provide social services. This is true of YMCA's, for example. We assume, however, that most of the recreation-oriented agencies that function as social service providers would have classified themselves in one of the social service and human service fields for the purpose of our survey.

7. Response rates for some individual questions naturally vary from this total slightly, as noted in individual tables.

TABLE 5.7 Poverty Focus of Nonprofit Human
Service Agencies

Focus	% of Agencies ($n = 1,474$)
Client focus	
Mostly poor (> 50% of clients)	27(%)
Some poor (21–50% of clients)	20
Few or no poor (20% of clients or less)	53
Total	100%
Provide Material Assistance	
Yes	16(%)
No	84
Total	100%

NOTE: The sample consists of 1,474 nonprofit human service agencies in twelve metropolitan areas and four rural counties throughout the United States surveyed by mail in 1982, with a follow-up survey in 1984–85.

SOURCE: Salamon/Urban Institute Nonprofit Sector Project Survey, rounds 1 and 2, (1982 and 1985.)

poor clients (that is, between 21 percent and 50 percent of the agency's clientele). Significantly, over half (53 percent) of the agencies reported "few" (that is, 20 percent or less) or no low-income clients.[8]

A similar picture emerges from an examination of the service offerings of these agencies. Although the poor have many needs, it seems reasonable to conclude that basic material needs—food, shelter, and financial assistance—would be particularly prominent. Agencies serving the poor could therefore be expected to offer many of these basic material resources. Yet, as table 5.7 also shows, the proportion of agencies providing material assistance was quite small. In particular, only 16 percent of all human service agencies we surveyed indicated that they provided any direct material assistance of this sort. Quite clearly, the nonprofit human service sector does not appear to be primarily engaged either in providing the kind of material assistance most needed by the poor or in serving the poor in other ways.

As noted earlier, this general conclusion is consistent with the results of the Family Service Association of America's surveys (Beck and Jones 1973). It is also consistent with the results of a study of the service offerings of over 1,000 private social welfare agencies conducted by Michael Sosin in twelve communities in the early 1980s. Sosin (1986) too found that rel-

8. These figures are virtually identical to those that emerged from the round 1 sample alone. Thus, of the 3,411 round 1 respondents, 2,526 answered the clientele question, and only 29 percent of these indicated that most of their clients had incomes below the poverty line.

atively few human service nonprofits focused on the most pressing needs of the poor. In particular, only 13.5 percent of the agencies offered material assistance, compared to 34 percent that offered individual or family counseling, 22 percent that offered recreation, and 20 percent that offered information and referral.

Variations among Types of Agencies

Not all types of agencies performed the same in terms of their extent of focus on the poor, however. To the contrary, some types focused more heavily on the poor than others. In particular, as shown in table 5.8, agencies specializing in employment and training and legal rights and advocacy were far more likely to focus primarily on the poor than agencies specializing in education and research, outpatient health care, or social services. One reason for the latter finding may be that substantial numbers of day care centers are included among the social service agencies, and these centers tend to have a broader clientele than human service agencies generally. Thus only 24 percent of the day care providers focus primarily on the poor compared to 27 percent of all agencies.

Extent of Human Service Agency Expenditures Focused on the Poor

The fact that only 27 percent of the human service *agencies* focus primarily on the poor still does not tell us precisely what share of the *resources* of the human service sector goes to support the poor since agencies differ markedly in size. The share of resources going to the poor may therefore be greater or less than 27 percent depending on whether the primarily poor-serving agencies are on average larger or smaller than other agencies.

To take account of agency size, we attempted to estimate the actual resources devoted to the poor among the agencies surveyed. To do so, we assumed that agency expenditures were split among agency clientele roughly equally so that the proportion of expenditures going to the poor were roughly equivalent to the proportion of poor people among the agency's clientele. For example, if an agency reported that 50 percent of its clients were poor, then we assumed that 50 percent of its expenditures were allocated to poor clients. This approach probably overstates the share of resources going to the poor since prior research has shown that poor clients of human service agencies tend to receive less personalized and intensive forms of treatment (Hollingshead and Redlich 1965; Cloward and Epstein 1965), but there was no reliable basis for any alternative assumption. Furthermore, as noted above, we excluded from the analysis any

148

TABLE 5.8 Agency Field of Service and Client Focus

	% of Agencies Whose Clientele Include			
Principal Field of Service	Mostly Poor[a]	Some Poor[b]	Few or No Poor[c]	Total
Employment, training, income support	53(%)	10(%)	37(%)	100(%)
Legal rights and advocacy	43	19	38	100
Institutional/residential care	31	19	50	100
Mental health	30	25	45	100
Housing, environment	29	24	47	100
Multiservice	29	25	46	100
Social services	26	19	56	100
Health (excluding hospitals)	23	30	47	100
Education, research	10	12	78	100
All	27	20	53	100

[a]Over 50 percent of clients poor.
[b]20–50 percent of clients poor.
[c]Fewer than 20 percent of clients poor.
NOTE: The chi-square test yields a probability of 0.000.
SOURCE: Salamon/Urban Institute Nonprofit Sector Project Survey, rounds 1 and 2.

agencies that failed to specify the proportion of poor people among their clients, even though it is likely that these agencies serve very few poor people. Once again, therefore, our analysis probably overstates somewhat the share of all resources going to support services for the poor.

The results of this analysis are reflected in table 5.9. As this table shows, even with the rather generous assumptions detailed above, we estimate that only about 40 percent of the expenditures of the agencies we surveyed went to support services targeted to the poor and that 60 percent went for services to other income groups. Among some types of agencies, however, the proportion of total expenditures devoted to poor people was higher than this—72 percent for legal service and advocacy agencies and 55 percent for employment and training agencies. Interestingly, social service agencies, which ranked well below average in terms of the proportion of agencies focusing primarily on the poor nevertheless rank slightly above average (44 percent) in terms of the proportion of all *expenditures* targeted to the poor. This likely reflects the generally larger size of the primarily poor-serving social service agencies.

Summary

In short, only about a quarter of the nonprofit human service agencies we surveyed focus primarily on service to the poor, although another 20 per-

TABLE 5.9 Estimated Share of Nonprofit
Human Service Agency Expenditures
Devoted to the Poor, by Type of
Agency, 1982
($n = 1,399$)

Type of Agency (Sample sizes in parentheses)	% of Total Expenditures
Legal, advocacy (55)	71.8(%)
Employment and training (84)	55.4
Social services (462)	43.9
Multiservice (244)	42.1
Health (145)	36.6
Mental health (52)	36.3
Housing (58)	32.6
Institutional care (130)	30.9
Education/research (148)	16.2
All (1,399)	39.5

SOURCE: Salamon/Urban Institute Nonprofit Sector Project Survey.

cent of the agencies reported some (that is, between 21 percent and 50 percent) poor clients. In terms of total expenditures, approximately 40 percent of the expenditures of these agencies goes to service to the poor, though this figure may be somewhat exaggerated since it allocates expenditures in proportion to numbers of clients and excludes agencies that failed to report their client focus. Compared to other segments of the nonprofit sector, such as health or higher education, the human service agencies seem to focus more heavily on the poor, but it is still the case that most agencies focus primarily on the nonpoor, and most of the resources go to persons other than the poor.

III. EXPLAINING CLIENT FOCUS

How can we explain this pattern of client focus among nonprofit human service agencies? Why is it that so few of these agencies focus primarily on the poor despite a rhetoric of charitable intent? And what light does this shed on the character of the nonprofit human service sector and the theories available to understand it?

Theoretical Perspectives

To answer these questions, it is useful to examine the characteristics of the poor-serving agencies in our sample in the light of a number of theories that have been developed to explain the role, character, and scale of the nonprofit sector. Properly speaking, such an analysis does not constitute a "test" of these theories since the theories were not explicitly designed to explain this particular facet of nonprofit operations. Nevertheless, given the importance of this "charitable" dimension in the public's understanding of the nonprofit sector and in the shaping of government policy toward it, it is still useful to determine what light these theories can shed on the pattern of client focus that is evident, and, in turn, what light the evidence of client focus can shed on the explanatory power of the theories.

Four such theories or theoretical perspectives are especially deserving of attention in this regard. Three of these are theories of the nonprofit sector and one reflects organizational theory more broadly.

Market Failure/Government Failure Theory

Perhaps the dominant theoretical perspective for interpreting the character and role of the nonprofit sector grows out of classical economics, with its emphasis on the inherent limitations of the private market in producing collective goods. The central thesis of this theory is that both the market and government have limitations in producing collective goods—the former because of the "free rider" problem that allows consumers to benefit from collective goods without having to pay for them and the latter because of the need to generate majority support in order to get the government to meet the resulting unmet need. The nonprofit sector, according to this theory, exists as an alternative provider of collective goods, satisfying the demands for such goods that are left unmet by both government and the market (Weisbrod 1978).

A relatively low level of nonprofit activity focused on the poor is perfectly consistent with this theory. Since nonprofits come into existence in this view to meet demands for collective goods that are not met by government, it is reasonable to expect that the demands that will be met by the sector will be those of the people with the resources to pay for them. To the extent that the unmet demands that these people have are "charitable" in character and focus on helping the disadvantaged, however, this theory would lead us to expect the most extensive nonprofit attention to the poor where government involvement is lowest. In this view, charitably oriented individuals desiring a level of care for the poor that the general political system has not been willing to support can be expected to utilize the non-profit sector to help fill the resulting gaps. Other things being equal, the greater the level of private support, therefore, the greater the level of private-agency attention to the poor that this theory would lead us to expect. Otherwise the public sector could be expected to be involved. Conversely, the greater the level of *government* support, the *lower* the level of private-agency attention to the poor that would be expected.

Voluntary Failure Theory

A second body of theory posits a somewhat different dynamic at work between government support and nonprofit service to the poor. In this view, the same "free rider" problem that inhibits the market in providing collective goods also inhibits the voluntary sector in generating private support, particularly for aid to the poor (Salamon 1987). In addition, the nonprofit sector also has other inherent limitations as a mechanism for meeting human needs, such as its frequent paternalism and its particularism, namely, the tendency of agencies to restrict aid to narrow groups of people defined along religious, ethnic, or racial lines. Left to their own devices, therefore, nonprofit organizations can be expected to provide only limited aid to the poor. To expand on their efforts, they need access to broader sources of funds of the sort that government can provide. In this view, nonprofit service to the poor and government support for service to the poor spring from essentially the same social and economic dynamics. But for nonprofits to be able to act on this impulse, outside support from government is crucial. Far from expecting nonprofits to operate where government does not, therefore, this theory would lead us to find both sectors working in tandem. Far from decreasing as government support increases, nonprofit service to the poor would thus be expected to *increase* as government support increases.

Supply-side Theory

A third body of theory views the activities of the nonprofit sector as a response not simply to eternal "need" or demand, but also to the supply of entrepreneurs who choose to meet that demand through the creation of charitable institutions (James 1987a). Historically, religious institutions have been among the most prominent sources of such charitably inclined "entrepreneurs." The common assumption is that sponsorship of nonprofit organizations by religious organizations reflect the altruistic values that religions typically espouse (Wuthnow 1990, 7–9). According to this theory, therefore, nonprofit service to the poor will be closely related to the availability of a pool of religiously inspired individuals who create a set of religiously oriented nonprofit organizations. As a consequence, the more closely a nonprofit is associated with religious activity or religious organizations, the more likely it should be to focus on the poor. An alternative version of this theory, associated with the work of Estelle James (1987a), argues that the formation of nonprofit organizations by religious groups has less to do with altruistic sentiments toward the poor than with the desire to retain and attract members by offering them tangible services. Since such groups probably prefer to attract middle- and upper-income adherents, this version of the supply-side theory would lead us to expect a negative relationship between religious affiliation and service to the poor, other things being equal.

Organization Theory

This alternative form of the supply-side theory brings us to a final set of theoretical perspectives on the client focus of nonprofit organizations, which flows from organization theory. Rather than viewing the operation of nonprofit and other organizations as a product simply of the external environment and consumer demand, these theories find the explanation for organizational behavior within the organizations themselves—in the maintenance and enhancement needs of agency staff, in the missions and patterns of task accomplishment that are chosen, and in the operating style that agency managers adopt. In this view, organizations have significant latitude in their choice of client focus, and they choose the one that best meets the professional and organizational goals of the agency (Etzioni 1964; Scott 1974; Dess and Beard 1984). Among the factors likely to explain variations in agency focus on the poor, therefore, are the service focus of the agency (which relates to the professional training and preferences of staff members), the degree of professionalization within the agency, the initial focus of agency efforts (since organizations often find it difficult to change in response to external pressures), and the size and consequent degree of bureaucratization within the agency. Some analysts (Cloward and Epstein 1965; Riley 1981) thus argue that the efforts of social workers to acquire professional status in the 1940s and 1950s led to the adoption of a preferred style of task accomplishment that was rooted in psychological conceptions of family problems, and that led private agencies dominated by social work professionals to turn away from advocacy for improvement in the social environment of the poor toward a much more intensive, interpersonal, therapeutic model of treatment that was more suitable for a middle-class clientele. Similarly, Hollingshead and Redlich (1965) found that professional treatment of neurotics varied widely by social class and economic status. Not only were lower-class neurotics much more likely to be referred to public hospitals instead of private clinics or private practitioners, but they were also far more likely to receive organic forms of treatment, such as shock therapy, drugs, and lobotomies. These findings suggest that an agency's focus on social work and social services and its degree of professionalization will be negatively related to its propensity to focus on the poor. In a similar vein, Scott (1974, 495) found in a study of agencies serving the blind that the services these agencies offered "are often more responsive to the organizational needs of agencies through which services are offered than they are to the needs of blind persons." This suggests that the larger and more bureaucratized the agency, the less likely it is to focus on the needs of the poor, other things being equal.

Empirical Results

To what extent do these various theoretical perspectives find support in the data on nonprofit client focus available through our survey?

The answer to this question, not surprisingly, is somewhat complex since some of the theories are difficult to translate into operational form and not all the variables that might be useful to test the theories are available in the survey. What is more, the survey treats the agency as the unit of analysis rather than the individual program within an agency. It is therefore quite possible that a set of relationships that might operate at the program level—for example, between funding source and client focus—might be obscured, particularly in large agencies, by data that apply to the agency as a whole.[9]

While it is important to recognize these potential limitations, however, the data we have collected still make it possible to shed some valuable empirical light on the causes of the patterns of client focus and distributional effects that are apparent. In this section we examine these data. The discussion first examines the effects of a number of the individual factors that the prevailing theories suggest may be important. Because many of these factors are interrelated, however, we then present the results of a multiple regression analysis intended to sort out the independent effects of the various factors while holding constant the effects of the others.

9. This is similar to the so-called "ecological fallacy" in social or political research, in which characteristics of individuals are erroneously attributed to the social units (neighborhoods, voting districts, counties, etc.) of which they are a part.

TABLE 5.10 Client Focus of Urban and Rural Nonprofit
Human Service Agencies
($n = 1,474$)

| | % of Agencies | | |
Client Focus	Urban Agencies	Rural Agencies	All Agencies
Mostly poor	27(%)	27(%)	27(%)
Some poor	20	23	20
Few or no poor	53	50	53
Total	100%	100%	100%

NOTE: Chi-square probability = 0.173.
SOURCE: Salamon/Urban Institute Nonprofit Sector Project Survey, rounds 1 and 2. See tables 5.7 and 5.8 for sample and definitions.

Social and Economic Context

According to the "market failure/government failure theory" of the non-profit sector, nonprofits should be expected to focus more heavily on the poor in circumstances where existing government programs for the poor are least effecting or adequate. This is so because the nonprofit sector is viewed in this theory as a mechanism for satisfying demands for collective goods that are not satisfied by either the market or government.

One way to test this theory is to look at the behavior of nonprofit organizations in urban and rural settings. Because social welfare programs are typically less generous in rural or small-town settings than in more urbanized areas, this theory would predict that nonprofit attention to the poor would be more pronounced in rural than in urban areas.

As table 5.10 shows, however, our survey data provide little support for this hypothesis. Although the proportion of rural agencies that have some (that is, 21–50 percent) poor clients is slightly higher than the comparable proportion of urban agencies, and the proportion with few or no low-income clients slightly lower, these relationships are not statistically significant. This finding is all the more significant in view of the fact that income levels in the rural counties were well below those in the urban areas and the proportions of people in poverty and eligible for welfare were considerably higher.[10]

10. Median income levels in the four rural counties averaged some 16 percent below those in the urban areas, and the share of the population eligible for public assistance in the rural counties averaged 35 percent higher.

Funding Source

A second factor that might explain variations in nonprofit human-service agency attention to the poor is the funding structure of the agencies. As it turns out, a strong relationship exists between the funding structure of an agency and its client focus, though the relationship tends to support the "voluntary failure theory" more than the "market failure/government failure theory." Under the market failure theory, as we have seen, nonprofit attention to the poor should be most in evidence where government involvement in aid to the poor is least pronounced. This is the so-called "gap-filling" theory of nonprofit activity, the notion that nonprofits operate to "fill the gaps" left by government social welfare activity, permitting charitably inclined individuals to provide more relief for poverty and distress than the official government programs provide. The "voluntary failure" theory, by contrast, predicts that nonprofit attention to the poor will be greater where government involvement in assistance to the poor is greater, since government support allows nonprofits to overcome their own inherent limitations as providers of aid to the needy.

As table 5.11 shows, there is a strong and consistent relationship between government support and nonprofit attention to the needy, but in the direction predicted by the "voluntary failure theory" rather than the "market failure/government failure" theory. Thus, the agencies primarily serving the poor averaged 57 percent of their income from government in 1981 compared to only 29 percent for the agencies with no poor clients. Conversely, as the share of income from private charitable sources *increases,* the focus on the poor *goes down,* except for the agencies with no poor

TABLE 5.11 Funding Sources and Poverty Focus of Nonprofit Human Service Agencies, 1981

	Average Share of Income for Agencies Serving				
Source	Mostly Poor	Some Poor	Few Poor	No Poor	All Agencies
Government	57(%)	45(%)	33(%)	29(%)	38(%)
Private Giving	28	33	32	25	31
Dues	8	17	26	38	23
Other	7	5	9	8	8
Total	100%	100%	100%	100%	100%

NOTE: Shares are based on reported aggregate income for all agencies in each group.
SOURCE: Salamon/Urban Institute Nonprofit Sector Project Survey, rounds 1 and 2.

clients, which seem to operate in a more commercial vein, with close to 40 percent of their income from fees. These is thus little evidence here that private charity is filling in for inadequacies in the system of public support for the poor. To the contrary, the data seem to suggest that one of the major factors accounting for what limited focus the nonprofit human service sector gives to the poor is the availability of government financial support. By contrast, private charitable support seems to flow more heavily to agencies that are less focused on the poor.

This point can be seen even more clearly in table 5.12, which records the estimated share of income from each source going to support services for the poor and the share of total expenditures on services for the poor that came from each of the major revenue sources.[11] As this table shows, an estimated 47 percent of all government support to nonprofit human service organizations went to support services for the poor. By contrast, only 39 percent of all private giving and 25 percent of all fee income went to support such services. Among the sources of private charitable support, moreover, the only one that provided above average support for services to the poor was United Way.

Reflecting these patterns, table 5.12 also shows that government support is even more important to the financing of services to the poor than it is to financing nonprofit human service activities more generally. Compared to the 38 percent of all income it provides to human service agencies generally, government contributed 57 percent of the estimated costs of services to the poor. By contrast, while private giving accounted for 31 percent of all nonprofit human service agency income, it provided only 22 percent of the income going for services to the poor.

Determining the distributional implications of these findings is complicated by the fact that detailed information is not available on the contributions that different income groups make to these various revenue streams. Generally speaking, however, to the extent that the U.S. tax structure is mildly progressing (Pechman and Okner 1974), the extensive flow of government support to services for the poor through the nonprofit sec-

11. These data utilize an approach similar to that used in compiling the data in table 5.9. In particular, lacking any basis for allocating different sources of income differently among agency clientele, we assumed that agencies allocated all of their sources of income equally among the clients served by the agency. Because agencies differ in size, and have different revenue structures as well as different client focuses, however, important differences emerge in the extent to which different income sources support services for the poor once the results for all the agencies are aggregated. These aggregated results are reported in table 5.12.

TABLE 5.12 Sources of Revenues to Support Services to the Poor by Nonprofit Human Service Agencies

Revenue Source	Percentage of Total Revenue from Source Going to Services for Poor (1)	Percentage of Support for Poor from Source (2)	Percentage of Support for all Services from Source (3)
Government	47.0(%)	57.2(%)	38%
Private Giving	39.4	21.7	31
United Way	45.3	7.9	
Other federated	35.2	2.0	
Religious	37.3	1.4	
Individual	36.2	5.9	
Corporations	40.7	1.7	
Foundation	36.5	2.9	
Fees	25.2	13.4	23
Other (investment, etc.)	36.9	7.7	8
Total	39.5%	100.0%	100%

NOTE: Column 1 records the share of the revenue from each source going to the poor. Column 2 records the share of all expenditures on the poor that originate from the indicated revenue sources. Column 3 records the share of all expenditures for all clients that originate from the indicated revenue sources. All data were compiled by allocating the revenues from each source to poor clients in proportion to the share that the poor represent among the agency's clients. Thus if 30 percent of an agency's clients are poor, it is assumed that 30 percent of the agency's private charitable income, 30 percent of its government income, and 30 percent of its fee income goes to support the poor.
SOURCE: Salamon/Urban Institute Nonprofit Sector Survey, rounds 1 and 2.

tor is redistributive in character.[12] The same can probably also be said for fee income, which is most likely to be paid by middle- and upper-income clientele. Although it accounts for only an estimated 13 percent of the cost of nonprofit human service agency services to the poor, and although only an estimated 25 percent of all fee income finds its way into support for such services, there is probably still a meaningful redistributional dimension to this support.

The situation with respect to private giving is more complicated. In the first place, there is some evidence that giving is regressive, namely, that the poor contribute more as a percentage of their income than do the better-off (Hodgkinson and Weitzman 1990, 48–49). In the second place, the better-off receive tax deductions that significantly reduce the actual out-of-pocket cost of their gifts. If these deductions average 30 percent, and if only 40 percent of all private giving goes to support services to the poor and some of this comes from the poor or near-poor, then the redistributive effect of private philanthropy's contribution to human service agencies is open to serious question.

Religious Affiliation

According to the "supply-side" theory of the nonprofit sector, the existence of a need such as continued poverty is not a sufficient explanation for the existence of significant nonprofit activity. Equally important is the availability of a supply of "social entrepreneurs" willing to organize a charitable response. To a significant degree, moreover, such entrepreneurs have historically tended to emerge from one or another religious traditions. This suggests that the presence or absence of a religious connection should help to explain the extent to which a nonprofit organization focuses on the needs of the poor.

Two measures of religious affiliation were available in our survey to assess this dimension of nonprofit activity. One classified agencies according to whether they had "any formal religious affiliation." The other asked whether the agency "belong[s] to or receive[s] funds from any religious federation (e.g., Catholic Charities, Jewish Federation)." Altogether, about 15 percent of the agencies we sampled indicated one or both of these forms of religious ties.

---

12. This observation applies principally to the federal tax structure, rather than state or local taxes. Since about 70 percent of government human service spending comes from the federal government, this caveat probably alters the overall point only slightly.

When we related religious affiliation to the client focus of the agency, however, a curious result emerged. While religious affiliation does appear to be significantly related to the extent of poverty focus, the relationship is the reverse of what the "supply-side" theory would predict. In particular, as table 5.13 shows, agencies with a religious affiliation were *less* likely to have a primarily low-income clientele than agencies without such an affiliation. Thus only 25 percent of the agencies with a religious affiliation reported that most of their clients were poor, compared to 28 percent of the agencies without such an affiliation. By contrast, 58 percent of the religiously affiliated agencies reported few or no low-income clients compared to 51 percent of the remaining agencies. Although it will still have to be tested holding other factors constant, this finding seems to refute the conventional "altruism" view of the relationship between religion and nonprofit organizations and to lend credence to the alternative organization-theory view of how this relationship works.

Agency Age

One possible explanation of this unexpected result may be that agencies change their client focus over time. Put somewhat differently, the initial focus of the agency may not be so much on the problems of the poor as on the problems of a particular religious community that happens to start out poor. As the economic circumstances of this community improve, the client focus of the agency may appear to change away from the poor. In this sense, the agency might lose its poverty focus through "natural causes," namely the improvement of the economic status of the "community" on which it focuses its activities.

To the extent this occurs, however, it would run counter to one of the

TABLE 5.13 Religious Affiliation and Nonprofit
Human Service Agency Client Focus

| | % of Agencies by Religious Affiliation | | |
Client Focus	Yes	No	All
Mostly poor	25(%)	28(%)	27(%)
Some poor	17	21	20
Few or no poor	58	51	53
Total	100%	100%	100%

NOTE: Chi-square probability = .01.
SOURCE: Salamon/Urban Institute Nonprofit Sector Project Survey, rounds 1 and 2.

TABLE 5.14 Agency Age and Client Focus
(*n* = 1,469)

	Year Formed—% of Agencies				
Client Focus	Before 1930	1930– 1960	1961– 1970	1971– present	All
Mostly poor	23(%)	23(%)	29(%)	29(%)	27(%)
Some poor	28	23	18	18	21
Few or no poor	49	54	53	53	52
Total	100%	100%	100%	100%	100%

NOTE: Chi-square probability = .06.
SOURCE: Salamon/Urban Institute Nonprofit Sector Project Survey, rounds 1 and 2.

central tenets of organization theory, which holds that organizations tend to resist changes in their basic technologies or approach. Organization theory would thus predict that agencies that start out with a focus on problems of the poor would retain this focus over time.

To test these two possible hypotheses, we grouped agencies by their year of formation. Our expectation was that agencies formed during either of two periods would be most likely to start out being focused on the poor and therefore would be most likely, if the organization theory view holds, to retain that focus today. The first is the period prior to 1930, when the nonprofit sector was the only line of defense against poverty and distress. The second was the period of the 1960s, when poverty was "rediscovered," and voluntary organizations were formed to represent the poor and carry out antipoverty initiatives of various sorts.

When this notion is tested against the data, it finds little empirical support. As shown in table 5.14, agencies formed during the 1960s do seem to be more heavily focused on the poor, but only slightly so. By contrast, the pre-1930 agencies are among the least likely to focus on the poor. Overall, the relationship that exists between agency age and client focus is not statistically significant. If the two groups of agencies started out their lives heavily focused on the poor, something must have intervened to reduce that focus.

Agency Field of Service

One such possible intervening factor suggested by the literature is professionalization and changing agency operating technology. Cloward and Epstein (1965) and others have argued, as we have noted, that the field of social work underwent a significant metamorphosis in the period following the Great Depression. It became more professional, more preoccupied

161

with the techniques of individualized social "casework," and in the process lost some of its orientation toward the poor and toward advocacy. One reason that the 1930s agencies may be less oriented to the poor than we might have expected, therefore, is that they have taken on the coloration of this dominant profession.

This line of argument may explain the pattern of agency client focus reported in table 5.8. The professionalization argument would lead us to expect that social service agencies would focus less heavily on the poor than agencies providing employment, training, and income support, or legal services and advocacy since it is in the social service agencies that the practice of social casework is most clearly lodged.

As noted above, this is exactly what we found. The primarily social service agencies, which account for 34 percent of all the agencies in our sample, ranked among the lowest in terms of average proportion of clients who are poor. In particular, only 26 percent of the social service agencies focus primarily on the poor while 56 percent report having few or no poor clients. By contrast, over half of the employment, training, and income support agencies, and over 40 percent of the legal rights and advocacy agencies, focus primarily on the poor. What is more, these findings are statistically significant at the .01 level of probability (that is, they could have happened by chance less than one time in 100).

Despite these results, however, there is reason to question whether the dynamic that Cloward and Epstein identified in the mid-1960s is still at work as powerfully in the nonprofit sector as of the the early 1980s. In the first place, as we have seen, the rather weak showing of social service agencies in service to the disadvantaged seems to be due at least to some extent to the inclusion of numerous child day care centers among the social service agencies. More than other social service providers, agencies that provide day care seem to focus less heavily on the poor. Thus, only 24 percent of the day care providers focus principally on the poor compared to 28 percent of the other agencies. Similarly, 55 percent of the day care providers report few or no poor clients compared to 52 percent of the other agencies. While this relationship is not statistically significant, it suggests that the inclusion of day care providers may be one of the reasons for the relatively limited focus of social service agencies on the poor. What is more, this same point receives even stronger confirmation when we zero in on the agencies providing "individual and family counseling," which is the precise locus of the social casework mode of service. As it turns out, a statistically significant relationship exists between the provision of individual and family counseling and agency focus on the poor, but it is in a direction opposite to what Cloward and Epstein would predict. Agencies providing individual and family counseling are *more* likely rather than less likely to focus heavily on the poor. Thus, 33 percent of the agencies providing this service focus primarily on the poor compared to only 27 percent of all agencies. Conversely, only 43 percent of the individual and family counseling agencies serve few or no poor clients, compared to 52 percent of all agencies. Given the "ecological fallacy" problem mentioned earlier,[13] it may still be the case that the providers of individual and family counseling within these agencies may not serve the poor. But the weight of the evidence seems to temper the thrust of the Cloward and Epstein thesis. At the very least, some agencies seem able to combine their focus on professional casework services for a general population with attention to the problems of the poor.

Two routes for doing this may be to include within the activities of an agency some focus on social advocacy and the provision of material goods, even though these may not be the principal activities of the agency. Based on our survey data, numerous agencies do this. Thus, while only 4 percent of our sampled agencies were *primarily* involved in advocacy work, just over 20 percent reported some advocacy activity; and among these the proportion reporting that most of their clients are poor was 38 percent, compared to 27 percent of all agencies. Similarly, while only 6 percent of all the agencies were primarily involved in providing material assistance, 16 percent indicated that they provided some material assistance; and 48 percent of these indicated that most of their clients were poor.

In short, while there is some support for the Cloward and Epstein thesis that professionalization of the social work field has alienated it from the poor, it seems clear that many agencies delivering professional social casework services continue to serve the poor, at least in part, through advocacy and material assistance. Whether these activities represent a serious assault on the problems of the poor, or a thin veneer of activity intended chiefly to provide legitimacy to agencies that are supposed to be charitable but are largely not, is more difficult to say.

Professionalization

One way to shed further light on this issue is to examine the relationship between agency staffing patterns and client focus more directly. If professionalization is associated with loss of interest in the poor, we would ex-

13. See footnote 9.

pect that the agencies with the most reliance on professional staff would have the lowest levels of focus on the poor.

Unfortunately, our survey did not gather direct information on the professional degrees of agency staff. However, it did gather other information that makes it possible for us to explore this relationship, including information on the size of agency paid staffs and on the ratio of paid staff to volunteers. Generally speaking, this information provides little support to the professionalization thesis. In the first place, it appears that agencies with more paid staff focus more heavily on the poor than do agencies staffed entirely by volunteers or by only a handful of paid staff. This is evident in table 5.15, which relates the staff size of the agencies in our sample to their client focus. A clear, statistically significant relationship is apparent, but opposite to what the professionalization thesis would suggest. In particular, only 10 percent of the agencies staffed wholly by volunteers focused chiefly on the poor, whereas 77 percent reported few or no poor people among their clients. By contrast, among agencies with 100 and over paid staff, the comparable figures are 39 percent of the agencies serving mosly poor clients and only 36 percent serving few or no poor clients. This relationship may be due in part to the fact that "informal" organizations are excluded from our survey, reliance on volunteers instead of paid professional staff does not seem to be associated with attention to the needs of the poor, as is sometimes assumed.

As a second way to check on this relationship, we computed the ratio of paid staff to volunteers in our surveyed agencies. The basic notion here is that what is potentially important in determining agency responsiveness to lower-income clientele is not simply the *number* of paid staff, which may

TABLE 5.15 Agency Employment Levels and Client Focus

Paid Staff Size (FTE)[a]	% of Agencies with Indicated Clientele Focus			
	Mostly Poor	Some Poor	Few or No Poor	Total
None	10(%)	13(%)	77(%)	100(%)
1–2.5	17	20	65	100
3–13	28	20	52	100
14–99	34	23	43	100
100 and over	39	25	36	100
All Agencies	27%	21%	52%	100%

[a]Part-time staff converted to full-time equivalents (FTE).
NOTE: Chi-square probability = 0.000.
SOURCE: Salamon/Urban Institute Nonprofit Sector Project Survey, rounds 1 and 2.

TABLE 5.16 Staff-Volunteer Ratios and Client Focus

	% of Agencies with Indicated Client Focus			
Staff/Volunteer Ratio	Mostly Poor	Some Poor	Few or No Poor	Total
Low[a]	19(%)	17(%)	64(%)	100(%)
Medium[b]	30	22	48	100
High[c]	31	25	44	100
Very High[d]	27	17	56	100
All Agencies	27%	21%	52%	100%

[a]Less than 1 staff per volunteer.
[b]1–14 staff per volunteer.
[c]15–100 staff per volunteer.
[d]Over 100 staff per volunteer.
NOTE: Chi-square probability = 0.000.
SOURCE: Salamon/Urban Institute Nonprofit Sector Project Survey, rounds 1 and 2.

really be a proxy for the size of the agency, but the extent to which volunteer staff are also incorporated into agency operations. The results, however, reported in table 5.16, provide further support to the conclusion reached above. Thus, of the agencies with the lowest staff to volunteer ratios, only 19 percent primarily served the poor, whereas 64 percent reported few or no low-income clients. By contrast, among the agencies with medium or high ratios of paid staff to volunteers, about 30 percent focused principally on the poor and 44 to 48 percent reported few or no low-income clientele. In other words, extensive reliance on volunteers instead of professional staff is no guarantee of attention to the poor. Evidently, it is the volunteers who may be alienated from the poor, not the professionals. The one piece of contrary evidence is the finding that the agencies with "very high" ratios of staff to volunteers (that is, in excess of 100:1) tended to be less likely to focus on the poor, but the difference is not great.

As a final check on the relationship between professionalism and client focus, we asked agency directors whether they agreed or disagreed with the statement that "volunteers can be substituted extensively for paid professionals in nonprofit organizations without any significant decline in service quality." Not surprisingly, 80 percent of the respondents disagreed with the observation. Interestingly, however, the agency personnel taking the antivolunteer position were more likely to represent agencies primarily serving the poor than was the case with those who took the provolunteer position. Thus, 30 percent of those who disagreed with replacing professionals with volunteers worked in agencies primarily serving the poor compared to 20 percent of those who favored such replacement. Conversely, over 60 percent of those favoring volunteers over paid staff work in agencies with few or no poor clients compared to 47 percent of those who are more skeptical about the capabilities of volunteers.

Overall, there thus seems to be a strong relationship between professionalization within the nonprofit sector and attention to the needs of the poor. Whether fairly or not, efforts to cope with the serious problems of poverty and distress have come to be seen as requiring more than amateur approaches and volunteer activity. The good news in this is that professionalization may not alienate nonprofit organizations from the problems of the poor as much as some may fear. The bad news is that the costs of mounting a serious attack on the interrelated problems of poverty and despair may be higher than some are willing to pay, whether the approach uses the nonprofit sector or direct public intervention.

Bureaucratization

Quite apart from the level of professionalization of staff, the sheer size of an agency may have an impact on its client focus. According to organization theory, organizations "seek out environments that permit organizational growth and stability" (Dess and Beard 1984, 55). The larger an agency, the greater these pressures must be and therefore the greater the possibility of "goal displacement," of the substitution of the needs of the organization qua organization for those of the clients. To the extent that organizational survival requires moving away from the needs of the poor, agency size will therefore be associated with less attention to the poor.

As reflected in table 5.17, this line of reasoning finds little support in the data from our survey. Far from decreasing as agency size increases, attention to the poor increases. Thus, only 18 percent of the smallest agencies reported focusing most of their attention on the poor compared to 35 percent of the largest agencies. Conversely, among the small agencies, 65 percent reported few or no poor clients compared to only 41 percent among the large agencies. Large size thus does not appear to be an inhibiting factor in making nonprofit agencies responsive to the poor. To the contrary, it is small size that seems to inhibit attention to the poor.

Summary: Regression Results

What are we to make of these findings? To what extent do they refute the organization theory approach outlined earlier, as seems to be the case? Which of the theoretical perspectives on the nonprofit sector finds most support in the data reviewed here?

TABLE 5.17 Agency Size and Client Focus

	% of Agencies with Indicated Client Focus			
Agency Expenditures	Mostly Poor	Some Poor	Few or No Poor	Total
Small[a]	18(%)	17(%)	65(%)	100(%)
Medium[b]	30	23	47	100
Large[c]	35	24	41	100
All Agencies	27%	21%	52%	100%

[a]Expenditures under $100,000.
[b]Expenditures of $100,000–$999,999.
[c]Expenditures of $1 million or more.
NOTE: Chi-square probability = 0.000.
SOURCE: Salamon/Urban Institute Nonprofit Sector Project Survey, rounds 1 and 2.

To answer these questions properly, it is necessary to go beyond the cross-tabulation analysis that has been presented thus far to take account of the interrelationships among some of the variables we have been examining. A strong correlation exists, for example, between agency size and the share of agency income coming from government. This is so for the obvious reason that government support tends to come in rather large chunks. It is therefore important to try to sort out whether it is the source of the income or the size of the agency that is really the relevant factor. To the extent that the latter is at work, we will have found a basis for refuting the organization theory perspective, which holds that the larger and more bureaucratized the agency, the greater the maintenance and enhancement pressures and therefore the greater the incentive to extend the reach of the agency beyond the poor. To the extent it is the former, this theory will retain credence.

To sort out these interrelationships, we have developed a multiple regression model that seeks to assess the independent impact of the various factors that our theories suggest as possible explanations of the extent of nonprofit attention to the poor, while holding constant the impact of the other factors.

Table 5.18 summarizes the variables in the model, the theory or theories with which each is associated, and the direction of impact that the various theories suggest will exist between the factor and the extent of agency focus on the poor. Thus, the market failure/government failure theory would lead us to expect that the extent of agency focus on the poor will be positively related to the extent of private support an agency receives, and negatively related to the extent of government support, other things being

TABLE 5.18 Expected Relationships Between Agency Characteristics and
Extent of Poverty Focus

Theory	Variable	Expected Relation to Poverty Focus
Market Failure/	Government support (%)	−
Government Failure	Fee support	+
	United Way support	+
Voluntary failure	Government support (%)	+
	Fee support	−
Supply-side theory	Religious Affiliation	+
Organization Theory	Social service expenditures	−
	Employment/income support expenditures	+
	Legal services/advocacy expenditures	+
	Pre-1930s formation	+
	Expenditure size	−
	Staff size	−
	Professional/volunteers ratio	−

equal. The voluntary failure theory, by contrast, would lead us to expect a *positive* relation between government support and the extent of agency focus on the poor. For the supply-side theory, at least in its "religion-as-altruism" version, the key variable is the presence of a religious affiliation, and the expected relation between religious affiliation and attention to the poor is positive. Finally, organization theory posits negative relationships between agency poverty focus and adoption of the social casework method (percent of social services expenditure), agency size (expenditures and staff size), and professionalization (professional/volunteer ratio). This same theory would lead us to expect a positive relationship between the extent of poverty focus and agency involvement in employment and income support as well as legal services and advocacy, and agency age (on grounds that agencies formed prior to the creation of government social welfare programs in the 1930s would be more likely to focus on the poor and to retain this focus today).

Table 5.19 presents the results of this multiple regression analysis. As this table shows, five of the factors we have examined turn out to have a statistically significant independent effect on the propensity of agencies to focus on the poor. Three of these have to do with the *sources* of agency income—the share coming from government, which is positively related to

TABLE 5.19 Relationship between Agency Characteristics and the
Percentage of Poor in Agency Clientele

Factor	Predicted Relation to Client Focus (% Poor)	Actual Regression Factor
Government support (%)	+	0.1612**
United Way support (%)	+	0.2141**
Fee support (%)	−	−0.2498**
Religious affiliation	+	4.6374
Social service expenditures (%)	−	0.0039
Employment/income support expenditures (%)	+	0.2477**
Legal services/advocacy expenditures (%)	+	0.1720**
Pre-1930s formation	+	−4.3978
Expenditures	−	4.4980
Staff size	−	0.0276
Professional/volunteer ratio	−	−0.5466

$R^2 = 19.5\%$
Probability = 0.0001

** = Significant at the .01 level.
 * = Significant at the .05 level.

poverty focus; the share coming from United Way, which is also positively
related to poverty focus; and the share coming from fees and charges,
which is negatively related to poverty focus. The remaining two factors
have to do with the *service field* in which agencies concentrate. Thus the
propensity to focus on the poor is positively related to the share of agency
expenditures going into advocacy and the share going into employment
and income support (that is, direct material support) activities.

Interestingly, however, once these factors are taken into consideration,
there is no significant relationship between poverty focus and agency size,
year of formation, religious affiliation, extent of involvement in the provision of social services, or the ratio of paid staff to volunteers. Taken together, these factors lend support to the "voluntary failure" and "organization theory" models of the operation of the nonprofit sector. Far from
filling in for the inadequacies of government policies for coping with the
problems of the poor, as the "market failure/government failure theory"
would predict, nonprofit organizations seem to operate in the same fields
as does government and to rely extensively on government support to extend their reach to the poor. Aside from United Way, which provides relatively modest levels of support, private giving is not particularly available

to agencies focusing on the poor. Far from creating a conflict between agency survival and attention to the poor, the availability of government support has given agencies a way to avoid such a conflict.

The fact that agency size drops out as an independent explanatory factor once government support is included in the equation reinforces this interpretation. The expectation that large agencies would feel compelled to turn away from the poor in order to ensure their survival turns out not to be supported by the evidence, but this may not be because the basic organizational dynamic is not at work. Rather, the reason appears to be that government support became available to rescue at least some agencies from this dilemma. Thanks to government support, in other words, agencies were able to reconcile their organizational survival needs with at least limited service to the poor. The alternative would have been greater dependence on either fees or private support, neither of which seems congenial to service to the poor.

Finally, the data give little credence to the "supply-side" theories of the nonprofit sector, at least as they relate to the question of who the nonprofit sector serves. Religious affiliation and poverty focus are positively related to each other, as these theories predict, but the relationship is not strong enough to be statistically significant. Religious affiliation thus has no independent effect on the likelihood that agencies will serve the poor.

Conclusions and Implications

These findings have significant implications for the success of the social policies put into effect in the United States in the early 1980s and for the evolution of the nonprofit sector as a consequence. A central premise of these policies was that the private nonprofit sector could make a significant dent in filling the gaps left by cutbacks in government support for the poor. Underlying this premise was the assumption that the nonprofit sector remained oriented toward service to the poor and would redouble its efforts to attend to this obligation as government support declined.

The data presented here, however, suggest a rather different view of the dynamics at work within even the human service component of the nonprofit sector. What these data make clear is that nonprofit human service agencies, whatever else they may be, are first and foremost organizations. As such, they seek to maintain themselves as viable systems. But as nonprofits, they find themselves in a particularly vulnerable position, in what Hasenfeld and English (1974, 100) term a "state of dependency," "dependent on external units for the procurement of resources without having sufficient countervailing powers vis-à-vis these units." To cope with this situation, nonprofit human service agencies have had to develop internal routines, mission concepts, staffing approaches, and definitions of their clientele that allows them to come to terms with the realities of their environment. This has involved a broadening of the concept of social services that has extended the domain of nonprofit human service agencies well beyond the needs of the poor, the development of a mode of task accomplishment congenial to the professionalization of agency staff, and the legitimization of a source of funding—fees for service—that provides some relief to dependence on the vagaries of private largesse.

The upshot of these pressures, however, has been to shift the focus of nonprofit human service agencies to a significant extent away from the poor. As we have seen, fewer than 30 percent of the agencies surveyed reported that the poor constitute half or more of the agency's clientele. By contrast, over half of the agencies reported serving few or no poor clients and over 60 percent of the resources went to the nonpoor. What is more, this pattern held across most of the service fields in which human service agencies operate—social services, mental health, health, institutional and residential care, and even housing and community development. Only employment, training and income support agencies, and legal rights and advocacy organizations differed markedly from this pattern, and these agencies make up a very small proportion of the sector.

The one truly effective countervailing force in the system has been the availability of government funding targeted to the poor. Based on our statistical analysis, it has been the availability of such funding that has allowed or encouraged the nonprofit sector to focus on the poor to the limited extent that it has. Other factors thought to be associated with attention to the poor—such as agency traditions, religious affiliation, private giving, and high levels of voluntarism—turn out to have little or no effect.

In view of these findings, the recent decline in government spending, at least to the extent that it translates into a decline in government support for nonprofit organizations serving the poor, seems more likely to produce a *decline* in nonprofit service to the poor than an increase. At the very least, it seems reasonable to expect that during a time of government retrenchment agencies focusing most heavily on the poor will not fare as well as agencies focusing on the nonpoor. Over time, such a situation can lead to a further shift of attention of the nonprofit human service sector away from the poor.

TABLE 5.20   Change in Nonprofit Revenue, 1981–83, by
Poverty Focus of Agencies

	Inflation-adjusted Change in			
Client Focus	Government Support	Private Giving	Fee Income	Total Expenditures
Mostly Poor	−15(%)	+4(%)	+29(%)	−6(%)
Some Poor	−17	−8	+10	−8
Few Poor	+3	+8	+7	+5
No Poor	+4	+4	+16	+8

SOURCE: Salamon/Urban Institute Nonprofit Sector Project Survey, rounds 1 and 2.

Although the data available make it difficult to assess definitively whether this dynamic has indeed come into play, there is some reason to believe that it has. Table 5.20 thus reports the changes in revenues and in total expenditures experienced by the agencies we surveyed between 1981 and 1983, the first years of the Reagan budget cuts. As this table makes clear, despite the pressures to focus private resources on the poor as government cutbacks occurred, the agencies serving few or no poor people performed much better during this period than did those with a much higher poverty focus. Thus the agencies with no or few poor clients actually increased their total expenditures during this period by 8 and 5 percent, respectively. By contrast, agencies with some or mostly poor clients experienced expenditure *declines* of 8 and 6 percent, respectively. Even more strikingly, the agencies with few or no poor clients actually enjoyed greater growth in private giving than did the agencies with larger proportions of poor clients. While private giving grew, in other words, much of it went to agencies serving mostly the nonpoor. Finally, and perhaps most distressingly, the agencies principally serving the poor had to turn increasingly to fee income during this period to avoid an even more severe drop in activity. Thus the agencies primarily serving the poor lost, on average, $90,000 in government support per agency between 1981 and 1983 but gained only $6,055 in private support. To make up part of the loss, these agencies boosted fee income by 29 percent, yielding $21,485 per agency in additional income. Since the poor are least able to pay for the services they receive, it is reasonable to conclude that these agencies had to skew more of their energies into service for the nonpoor. What is more, this situation also affected the agencies serving at least moderate proportions (20–50 percent) of poor people. For these agencies, however, private giving as well as government support declined in real terms.

The obvious implications of these findings is that the still somewhat limited progress made during the 1960s and 1970s in reorienting the private, nonprofit human service sector toward its charitable roots may have become significantly unraveled during the 1980s. To be sure, countervailing forces are also at work—a rise in consciousness about the problems of the poor, the emergence of new agencies and new personnel committed to the traditional charitable mission of the nonprofit sector, and a steady if not dramatic growth of private giving. But whether these new forces will prove capable of overcoming the more enduring dynamics revealed by this analysis in the context of shrinking government budgets is open to serious doubt.

6

Arts and Culture

Dick Netzer

The creation of nonprofit organizations to produce cultural services in the nineteenth century was, in part, done to elevate and improve the working classes, like many other initiatives of the movers and shakers of the business world in that era. However, the redistributional goal from the outset often was very secondary to the primary goal of establishing clubs to make possible cultural experiences that would be enjoyed, if not solely by the very rich who were the initial organizers and backers, then by the relatively educated and affluent upper-middle-class. The nonprofit cultural subsector remains, as we will see, one that does not generate much redistribution in an equalizing direction, unlike much of the rest of the nonprofit sector. It is also unlike most other nonprofit activity in that its rivals, or substitutes, are not to be found in the for-profit sector of the economy.

I. The Arts and Culture Subsector

Direct governmental production of cultural services is relatively modest.[1] Of the roughly 3,800 museums other than those run by educational institutions (and therefore included in data for the education subsector), nearly 2,500 are under private nonprofit auspices. There are a few large art museums run by state and local governments and there are some very large federal museums, but most of the 1,350 or so governmentally run museums are very small historical museums. If the federal museums are excluded, the nonprofit museums probably account for between 70 and 80

1. The definition of the subsector used in this chapter excludes libraries, a field in which government production is substantial, in the form of "public libraries" that are in fact operated by governmental rather than nonprofit entities, libraries in the public sector of higher education, and libraries within governmental agencies. The "public libraries" operated by nonprofit organizations with most of their operating budgets provided by local governments comprise a substantial component of the universe of libraries, but the available data make it very difficult to distinguish the finances and clienteles of the nonprofit and government-operated components.

percent of the total budgets of all museums.[2] There are governmentally owned performing arts centers, but many are operated by nonprofit organizations. Some public broadcasting stations are owned and operated by state and local governments or public educational agencies, but most are under nonprofit auspices, including the big-budget television stations in the major cities.[3]

On the other hand, for-profit production is very large. The total income of all the public broadcasting stations was $1.1 billion in 1985; advertising expenditures for commercial television and radio and subscription revenue of cable systems amounted to $36.2 billion.[4] In the 1982 Census of Service Industries, total receipts of tax-exampt organizations in the live performing arts amounted to $1.1 billion; total receipts of taxable firms were $3.3 billion (*1989 Sourcebook,* table 4–68). Motion picture box office receipts in 1985 were $3.7 billion; it is doubtful that all nonprofit film organizations combined (excluding those in educational institutions) had revenues of as much as $100 million.[5] Similar disparities between substantial for-profit volumes and tiny nonprofit activity exists in literature and the creative visual arts, both fields in which the nonprofit sphere (again, outside educational institutions) consists of a relatively small number of organizations, all modest in budget, that provide supporting services for individual artists and writers and, in literature, small presses and literary magazines (many mom-and-pop operations in scale).

By and large, nonprofit cultural organizations produce high culture, while for-profit firms produce mass culture. But the lines are often blurred. The production and distribution of paintings and sculpture is overwhelmingly the province of for-profit firms and the self-employed, as is the case for literature; opera stars and celebrated classical musicians tour under commercial auspices; a large proportion of Broadway plays are high cul-

2. The number of museums is based on tables in *1989 Sourcebook,* chapter 7. The most recent reported count is for 1979; the figures cited in the text exclude visitor's centers in parks. In a 1971–72 survey of 1,821 museums, private nonprofit museums accounted for 77 percent of the total income of museums exclusive of federal museums (U.S. National Endowment for the Arts 1975).

3. Over time, there has been some shifting to operation by newly created nonprofit entities, even if the license continues to be held by the state or local government, as occurred in the 1980s for the New York City municipal broadcasting stations.

4. U.S. Bureau of the Census, *Statistical Abstract of the United States, 1989,* tables 908, 910, and 920.

5. The American Film Institute, which may account for as much as half of the revenue of the entire nonprofit film field, had revenues of $12.6 million that year (*1989 Sourcebook,* tables 8–1 and 8–21).

ture by any definition (which does not mean that they are good); Texaco has sponsored broadcasts of the Metropolitan Opera on commercial radio stations since 1940.

Nonprofit cultural organizations are not uniformly high-brow, for their part. Much of the repertoire of nonprofit theater companies is very middle-brow indeed, as is some of the cultural fare on public television (like popular Hollywood films of the 1930s and 1940s). The nonprofit subsector includes organizations self-consciously devoted to activities that their sponsors intend to be mass culture, rather than high culture—crafts, folk arts, much of the ethnic arts and most of what the arts bureaucrats call "expansion arts." [6] Nonetheless, for the nonprofits, the stereotype is valid: most of the money and resources consumed by the nonprofits is devoted to activities that are seen as, and meant to be, high culture.

Size of the Subsector

Statistical information on nonprofit arts and culture organizations is incomplete and contradictory, even by the standards of other parts of the nonprofit sector. The National Endowment for the Arts explicitly decided in the late 1970s not to take a direct role in improving data on the subsector, but instead to subsidize the discipline-based service organizations to develop and maintain statistical series based on membership annual reports.[7] Those series provide very good data for core groups of organizations that have responded regularly for some years, but otherwise the coverage is incomplete: in some cases, not all members respond regularly and the membership does not comprehend the universe of those fields. A second principal source of data is the quinquennial Census of Service Industries, which has tabulated data for the live performing arts and for museums separately for taxable and tax-exempt organizations since 1977.

6. Officials of the National Endowment for the Arts, state arts agencies, and the lobbying and advocacy organizations that surround the public agencies have a penchant for using catchy, nondescriptive labels for programs and activities. That penchant is surpassed, at the Endowment, only by the attitude toward disseminating information about its activities that has prevailed since the founding in 1965: puffery is good, silence is acceptable, full disclosure can kill you.

7. In the late 1970s, while still under the leadership of Nancy Hanks, the Endowment hired a number of consultants to make recommendations on the organization and content of new statistical series, which the Endowment would finance. The consultants designed a statistical system based on data that were then required from grant applicants and recipients (although often not supplied, with no adverse consequences to the noncomplying organization), paralleled by substantial improvements in the arts coverage of the Census of Service Industries. The National Council on the Arts and a new chairman rejected those recommendations.

Although the Census coverage of the tax-exempt organizations appears to have improved substantially since 1977, the coverage in 1982 remained incomplete; in some cases, service organization surveys had more respondents than the Census.

The estimates of the universe in the first five columns of table 6.1 combine data from the 1982 Census with data from service organizations, with detail on the source of contributed funds estimated from data on the funding sources. Column seven, "other," includes organizations in visual, media, folk and design arts, literature, crafts, humanities (excluding those covered elsewhere in the table and excluding educational institutions), and many small organizations on the fringes of the live performing arts disciplines covered in the first four columns, but unlikely to have been counted in the sources for those columns.

Public broadcasting is a significant element of the nonprofit cultural sector. The total expenditure of the entire system—the central organizations and the local stations—was about $1.1 billion in 1985, all but a trivial portion of which came from public funds and private contributions.[8] The Corporation for Public Broadcasting data for public television show that approximately 20 percent of broadcast hours was classified as cultural in the 1984–86 period and that cultural programming accounted for 23 percent of "audience hours" and one-third of prime-time "audience hours" (*1989 Sourcebook*, tables 8–59 and 8–60). The cultural programming is substantially more expensive to produce, per hour, than is other programming. Public radio is a small share of the public broadcasting system, but within public radio, cultural programming probably accounts for 80 percent of the total hours and costs. It seems reasonable to ascribe at least 40 percent of public broadcasting income and expenditure to the arts and culture. This is done in table 6.1.

The results show that the subsector is a small one, with total income (and operating expenditures) of less than $5 billion in 1985.[9] Although the mainstream live performing arts organizations covered more than 60 per-

8. There was some earned income from the sale of cassettes and books and it can be argued that much of the corporate support really amounts to payment for commercial messages lightly disguised as contributions.

9. In the 1960s, a good many cultural organizations of all sizes had substantial operating deficits in most years. The exhaustion of endowments, the insistence on the part of some major donors (notably the Ford Foundation) that recipients have proper budgeting regimes, the occasional sacking of managements that were casual about deficits, and the salutary example of actual disbanding of some insolvent cultural organizations in the 1970s and early 1980s made most organizations very cautious about operating deficits. The data in table 6.1

TABLE 6.1 Estimated Income of the Nonprofit Arts and Culture Subsector, 1985[a] (In millions of dollars)

	Live Performing Arts[b]					Museums[c]	Other[d]	Public Broadcasting[e]	Total
	Theater	Opera	Dance	Classical Music	Subtotal				
Total income	470	305	168	480	1,423	1,650	1,197	440	4,710
Earned	350	182	99	261	892	460	600	39	1,991
Contributed	120	123	69	219	531	1,190	597	401	2,719
Government	35	18	25	57	135	220	161	215	731
Federal	16	8	13	20	57	45	75	72	249
State	17	6	11	26	60	70	68	40	238
Local	2	4	1	11	18	105	18	103	244
Private	85	105	44	162	396	970	436	186	1,988
Corporations	17	13	8	25	63	98	160	68	389
Foundations	17	12	11	33	73	115	26	17	231
Individuals	51	80	25	104	260	757	250	101	1,368

[a]This table has been pieced together from data generated by the Census Bureau (on service industries), organizations serving the various arts disciplines and federal and state arts agencies, which appear in tables in the 1989 Sourcebook and the Statistical Abstract of the United States. In general, the procedure was: (1) establish a total income for the activities of a given type in 1985 from 1982 Census of Service Industries data and/ or special surveys that had comprehensive coverage; (2) fill in missing pieces of the breakdown of total income in the columns on the basis of other survey data and using data on grants made by the various types of funders; and (3) use data on funders as control totals for the relevant rows. The results differ somewhat from those shown in Hodgkinson and Weitzman (Independent Sector 1989), mainly—but not entirely—because of the difference in the numbers for museums. That publication appears to be internally inconsistent with regard to the arts and culture subsector (nearly half the receipts are uncounted for on the expenditure side) and at odds with some of the data in published sources, including Census data.

[b]Total income, except for dance, based largely on using trend data from service organization surveys for parts of the universe to extrapolate 1982 Census of Service Industry totals to 1985. For dance, the total income estimate is based on the methods used in Netzer (1987).

[c]Data on the universe of museums are not only sporadic and inconsistent, but are also plagued by a seemingly deliberate effort to prevent separating the data by type of governing authority: for most financial categories, the data in from surveys done by museum organizations cover, inextricably, both governmental and nonprofit museums. Totals in this column are based on extrapolating 1982 Census of Service Industries data, and detailed data for 1985 on art museums. Hodgkinson and Weitzman show total operating expenditures of museums in 1982 to be $1.0 billion, compared to total revenue in the 1982 Census of $2.6 billion, which presumably includes receipts for capital purposes.

[d]Built upon the basis of data, for funding agencies, on their grants for activities not covered in the first five columns of the table, including an estimate of National Endowment for the Humanities grants for cultural programs other than those made to organizations covered in other columns of this table and excluding grants made to educational institutions.

[e]The arts and culture share of the public broadcasting system is estimated to be 40 percent of all the financial magnitudes; see text.

cent of their operating budgets from earned income—mainly box office receipts—the other components of the subsector depend mainly on grants from government and private philanthropy. For the subsector as a whole, contributed income accounted for 58 percent of total income in 1985, with direct grants from government amounting to only about one-fourth of contributed income and gifts from individuals accounting for about two-thirds of private-sector contributions.

Government support of the arts and culture is more extensive than table 6.1 indicates: the table excludes the funding of government-owned museums (important both for the federal government and for local governments), grants to individual artists (a significant share of National Endowment for the Arts expenditure), and grants that flow through educational institutions (especially important for the National Endowment for the Humanities). For the activities that *are* covered in the table, the two National Endowments, the Corporation for Public Boradcasting, and the Institute of Museum Services are the main actors at the federal level; the state arts councils dominate the state role, although there is a good deal of direct legislative appropriation to favored enterprises; and local government support consists mainly of subventions to the leading local institutions, notably museums, and support of public broadcasting, especially from school funds.

II. Nature of the Benefits

Like all other components of the economy, the arts and culture sector generates benefits that accrue to the immediate consumers of the goods and services the sector produces, benefits to the factors of production employed in the sector, notably in this case—since there is not supposed to be any pecuniary return to investors—to the specialized labor employed in the sector, and indirect benefits to third parties. The issues that concern us are how the various types of benefits are distributed by income class, how much redistribution is involved, and how distribution will change in response to marginal changes in policy or the external environment.

Direct Benefits Internalized by Consumers

The most obvious of the benefits of the operations of nonprofit arts and cultural organizations is the pleasure derived by those who attend the

---

are supposed to apply only to current operating income, not receipts for capital purposes, but the table probably does include some capital receipts. However, capital expenditures are very small in the aggregate, except for museums.

events presented, visit museums, watch and listen to broadcast perform-ances, read literary magazines, and so on. With the exception of school children conscripted for museum visits, the choice of whether to consume the cultural service at the subsidized price (which may be zero) is almost entirely voluntary and truly discretionary: there are close substitutes for many of the products of nonprofit cultural enterprises, usually low-cost substitutes, in the unsubsidized commercial arts and entertainment world. Despite the presence of the close substitutes, the price elasticity of demand for one major component of the arts and culture subsector, the live per-forming arts, appears to be quite low.[10] This suggests that, despite theoret-ical objections to so doing, it is reasonable to measure the distribution of consumer benefits by income class on the basis of use by income class.[11]

There are extensive data, albeit shaky (see below), on the income char-acteristics of audiences for the main live performing arts and of museum visitors, but not much for other nonprofit cultural activities: music other than classical music and musical theater; visual arts aside from art mu-seums; literature; film-making; architecture as art; the arts in public broadcasting; art education via nonprofit organizations; local arts and cul-tural centers and councils; and others. According to the estimates in table 6.1, these activities account for one-half of total direct public subsidy to the arts and culture and one-third of private giving.[12]

The surveys of "public participation in the arts" discussed below asked numerous questions about cultural activities and preferences that might be suggestive about the income distribution characteristics of the direct bene-ficiaries of subsidies to activities other than the main types of live perform-

10. Aggregate data in studies done over a good many years show low price elasticities rela-tive to all other goods and services and relative to commercial entertainment and leisure-time activities (Baumol and Bowen 1966, 274–78; Withers 1980). Studies for specific organiza-tions and markets that deal with cross-elasticities among live performing arts organizations tend to confirm this, with some exceptions, especially smaller and lower-ranking companies, like small dance companies in London (Gapinski 1986).

11. Strictly speaking, as Estelle James pointed out in comments on drafts of these papers, net benefits equal willingness to pay less actual payments. Usage will not be a proxy for net benefits when costs exceed willingness to pay, or when income elasticity of demand varies with income, both of which probably are true for components of this subsector. The data are so sketchy, however, that it is not feasible to go beyond the simplifying assumption used here.

12. These activities accounted for about one-third of National Endowment for the Arts grants in fiscal 1985, according to the NEA annual report for that year, most of the arts-related expenditure of the National Endowment for the Humanities, and, of course, all of the arts-related expenditure of the Corporation for Public Broadcasting. The data for foundations reported in DiMaggio (1986) suggests that nearly one-third of all foundation giving to the arts an culture in the mid-1980s was for such activities.

ing arts and museums. For example, there are questions about reading and television-watching habits, about music preferences and about amateur music playing. One might assert that the benefits of subsidies to literature are distributed by income class in proportion to reported reading of books. There are two difficulties with this assertion. First, there is little reason for believing in the validity of the association: subsidies to literary activities are directed at younger writers, small presses, and small literary magazines, whose audiences are probably quite unlike the universe of buyers of best-sellers; the subsidies are not distributed in proportion to revenue from sales of books. Second, the volume of artistic activities, active and passive, reported in the surveys is suspiciously high, given that most respondents must devote most of their waking hours to earning a living, attending school, and fulfilling the other nonartistic obligations of everyday life.

So, we must rely mainly on audience surveys for a few types of mainstream, high-culture arts activities. There have been audience surveys done for a long time—for at least thirty years in Broadway theaters. A 1978 study (DiMaggio, Useem, and Brown) was able to find 270 earlier studies of audiences in specific cities and for specific institutions or attractions that were sufficiently well documented to permit analysis of the results. However, it is not possible to aggregate the results of the organization-specific studies: the questions, definitions, and categories differ wildly, as do the sampling procedures (typically, the sample consists of any members of the audience at a given performance who bother to fill out and return the questionnaire left on the seat or handed out with the printed program). Moreover, there are large and erratic gaps in the extent to which arts organizations conduct surveys at all.

There are, however, surveys with more systematic coverage of parts of the universe of arts and culture. The nature and weaknesses of these surveys are discussed in the appendix to this chapter. In brief, the surveys of the entire population appear to report more people attending and, especially, attending more frequently, than is consistent with the data on admissions collected from arts-producing organizations.

Although it is likely that the disparities between the survey results and recorded attendance are explained to some extent simply by good-natured exaggeration on the part of the respondents, two other explanations are the ones most frequently advanced. The first is a common problem in market research: respondents recall events that occurred some time earlier as recent occurrences, so that attendance at a ballet performance two or three years ago is recalled as having taken place "within the last twelve months" and, even more, two visits to a museum within the space of a year are recalled as having taken place within four or five months.

The second explanation is that the activities covered by the survey questions and in the respondents' understanding of those questions are considerably broader than the activities covered in the attendance reported by art museums and professional performing arts organizations. For example, the NEA survey asks about visits to art museums and art galleries (using that wording to avoid excluding museums with the word "gallery" rather than "museum" in their names). But "art galleries" also include commercial art galleries, including establishments in tourist areas that are little more than souvenir shops. Similarly, the survey questions do not exclude attendance at children's performances in proprietary music and dance schools, at solo recitals organized by for-profit concert managers, and at amateur theatrical and musical performances. The ideal data for the purposes of this chapter would exclude the activities of the for-profit sector, which presumably do not involve redistribution. Nor is there redistribution entailed in the clublike activities of most nonprofessional arts groups.

Nonetheless, there is no alternative to use of the survey data. It is unclear whether there is any systematic variation in the extent of overstatement of attendance by income class. There are reasons for both an inverse and a direct relation between the extent of overstatement and income, for attendance at events for which redistribution is relevant—that is, excluding for-profit and clublike activities—but there is no way to resolve the issue.[13]

Income and attendance

The starting point for study of the distribution of attendance in the data derived from the National Endowment for the Arts 1985 survey is the findings on the percentage of the adult population, by income, that reported attending at least once in the previous twelve months, shown in table 6.2. For each of the six types of activities, the percentages rise steeply with income, with the highest income class a large multiple of the second from the bottom class. The only exception to this pattern is the below-$5,000 in-

---

13. For example, the single most powerful determinant of participation in cultural activities—in *all* survey findings—is educational level. The positive association between income and educational level and the presumably greater familiarity with what the question means that goes with more education would tend to support the argument that overstatement is an inverse function of income. Nonetheless, there is a good deal of evidence that participation in amateur and professional arts activities is complementary, so relatively high-income people who report frequent attendance may well be reporting a considerable volume of attendance at nonprofessional events.

TABLE 6.2 Adult U.S. Population Attending Selected Arts Events at Least Once in the Previous 12 Months, as Reported in the 1985 NEA Survey

I. Percent of adults in each income group attending at least once[a]

	Classical Music	Opera	Musicals	Plays	Ballet	Art Museums
All income groups	13%	3%	17%	12%	4%	22%
Income						
Under $5,000	9(%)	2(%)	10(%)	8(%)	3(%)	16(%)
$5,000–$9,999	7	1	8	4	2	12
$10,000–$14,999	8	1	11	8	3	15
$15,000–$24,999	11	2	12	9	4	19
$25,000–$49,999	15	3	22	14	5	28
$50,000 and over	30	8	37	28	11	45
Not ascertained	12	2	17	11	3	19

II. Percent distribution of ever-attenders, by income group[b]

	All Adults[c]	Classical Music	Opera	Musicals	Plays	Ballet	Art Museums
All income groups	100%	100%	100%	100%	100%	100%	100%
Income							
Under $5,000	7.0(%)	4(%)	5(%)	4(%)	4(%)	4(%)	5(%)
$5,000–$9,999	11.8	6	4	5	4	5	6
$10,000–$14,999	11.2	6	4	7	7	7	7
$15,000–$24,999	20.8	16	14	13	15	17	16
$25,000–$49,999	33.7	35	33	40	37	34	38
$50,000 and over	15.5	32	41	31	34	34	28

[a]Source: John P. Robinson, Carol A. Keegan, Marcia Karth, and Timothy A. Triplett (1987, table 3.3, p.98).
[b]Calculated from data in section I of this table and data on the distribution of all adults by income. The "income not ascertained" category is ignored, thus implicitly assuming that the characteristics of this group are identical with those for whom there are income data.
[c]Based on the Current Population Survey tables appearing in the 1987 *Statistical Abstract of the United States*.

come class, which has percentages that are higher than in the next class; removing students from the distribution does not eliminate this (see Schuster 1988). The phenomenon is no doubt explained by the usual difficulty with the composition of the bottom class in most distributions of current money income—the large number of temporary members of that class in addition to students and the deliberate understatement of income by some respondents. In any event, as section II of the table shows, adults in the upper half of the income distribution include between two-thirds and three-fourths of all those who reported attending at least once; those in the top sixth of the distribution include between 28 and 41 percent of the ever-attenders.

The next stage in the analysis is to develop data on the income distribution of total attendance and museum visits, using the survey responses on the frequency of visits by those who attended at least once. The museum data in table 6.3 are from Schuster's monograph (1988), but the performing arts estimates in that table have a more convoluted derivation. Robinson et al. (1987) does not present data on frequency of attendance by income class.[14] However, all the data they do present on frequency show a strong positive relation between frequency of attendance and the likelihood of attending at least once. I used a regression equation based on those data to estimate frequency by income class;[15] reduced reported frequencies by 20 percent (as Robinson et al. suggests); used the lower bounds of frequency class intervals as multipliers; and eliminated attendance at performances in schools and churches—on the grounds that such performances either involve no redistribution (as club goods) or are subsumed in the redistributive effects of the education and religion sectors.[16]

The results in table 6.3 show that, as one would expect, total attendance is even more concentrated in the upper part of the income distribution than is participation in the sense of attending at least once a year. For example,

14. It would have been possible to extract those data from the survey tapes, as Schuster did for museums, at considerable cost in time and money.

15. I used both the 1982 and 1985 survey summary volumes, including every observation for which both the percentage attending at least once a year and frequency of attendance was reported. A simple bivariate regression equation explained about 60 percent of the variation in reported frequency. The equation was: frequency of attendance (in a year) = 2.63 + (13.0 × the probability of attending at least once a year, in percent). The coefficient is significant at the 1 percent level.

16. To the extent that schools and churches provide venues for outside groups, the latter point will not be valid. However, it seems probable that many of the reported performances in these locations are school plays, liturgical music at the Christmas season, and similar events.

TABLE 6.3 Estimated Attendance at Performances and Museum Visits by U.S. Adults in the Previous 12 Months, Based on the 1985 NEA Survey[a]

Income	Classical Music	Opera	Musicals	Plays	Ballet	Art Museums	All Types in Survey	All Adults
				Number				
Under $5,000	2,384	617	3,571	2,722	874	10,118	20,285	
$5,000–$9,999	2,955	503	4,560	2,023	951	12,858	23,852	
$10,000–$14,999	3,310	478	6,504	4,381	1,406	15,268	31,348	
$15,000–$24,999	9,256	1,850	13,586	9,460	3,619	36,019	73,789	
$25,000–$49,999	22,683	4,651	51,234	27,313	7,565	85,766	199,212	
$50,000 and over	28,837	6,754	52,514	34,318	9,228	63,558	195,210	
All incomes	69,425	14,853	131,971	80,217	23,644	223,587	543,697	
				Distribution by Percent				
Under $5,000	3.4	4.2	2.7	3.4	3.7	4.5	3.7	7.0
$5,000–$9,999	4.3	3.4	3.5	2.5	4.0	5.8	4.4	11.8
$10,000–$14,999	4.8	3.2	4.9	5.5	5.9	6.8	5.8	11.2
$15,000–$24,999	13.3	12.5	10.3	11.8	15.3	16.1	13.6	20.8
$25,000–$49,999	32.7	31.3	38.8	34.0	32.0	38.4	36.6	33.7
$50,000 and over	41.5	45.5	39.8	42.8	39.0	28.4	35.9	15.5
All incomes	100.0%	100.0%	100.0%	100.0%	100.0%	100.0%	100.0%	100.0%

[a]The estimates for the performing arts begin with data in Robinson et al. (1987). The data in the report on frequency of attendance by those who attended at least once in the previous year are adjusted for the overstatement noted in the report, and the lower bounds of the intervals are used as multipliers. Also, attendance at performances in schools and churches is excluded. Where the published data for these adjustments are not presented by income class, allocations by income were made by the author. The "income not ascertained" category (see table 6.2) is ignored, thus implicitly assuming that the characteristics of this group are identical with those for whom there are income data. The estimates for the frequency of attendance per visitor for art museums are based on Schuster (1988). The income distribution used is not the distribution that is derived from the survey volumes, but rather the distribution from the Current Population Survey, appearing in tables in the 1987 *Statistical Abstract of the United States.*

those with incomes of $50,000 or more were 32 percent of all those who attended classical music performances even once, but they accounted for 41.5 percent of total attendance. Predictably, opera attendance is more concentrated at the top of the income scale than is the case for any other of the activities, but classical music and theater are not much less concentrated. Ballet attendance and visits to art museums both are noticeably less concentrated, especially the latter.[17]

It was noted early in this chapter that public broadcasting is a significant element of the nonprofit cultural sector, especially as a user of governmental and private contributed funds. The NEA 1982 and 1985 surveys contain data on participation in the arts via media. Some of that reported participation no doubt is viewing of or listening to arts programs on commercial broadcasting stations (and cable), especially in the case of classical music on radio, but the bulk of this participation surely involves noncommercial broadcasting. Using some simplifying assumptions (see the notes to table 6.4), I have calculated a composite distribution of cultural consumption by income class, shown in table 6.4.[18] The tilt in consumption toward the higher-income classes is relatively mild and may not exist at all if lower-income adults who watch cultural programs on television devote more hours a week to that kind of viewing than do more affluent adults who watch cultural programs—which is the case for television watching in general.

External Benefits

The survey data presented above confirm, unsurprisingly, that the output of the arts and culture subsector of the nonprofit sector is consumed mainly by individuals and households whose income, wealth, and social

17. The income distribution that is implicit in the NEA 1985 survey is considerably more even than the one I derived from Current Population Survey data for 1985, in which I distributed adults living in households by household money income. The NEA survey distribution implies a household income for the median adult that is well below the median income of households as $23,618 in 1985; my distribution implies a household income for the median adult *above* the distribution for households—$24,625—which seems logical. The data shown in this paper on attendance use the CPS income distribution.

18. The reported participation rates for some of the media cultural attractions are suspiciously high, like those reported for live events. For example, more than 20 percent of adults say they watch classical music and/or plays on television. The broadcast of *The Civil War*, in September 1990, attracted an all-time high in public television viewing, according to newspaper reports, with about 10 percent of the viewing population at prime time in major markets and perhaps 6 to 7 percent of households in those markets (and a slightly smaller percentage for the entire country).

TABLE 6.4 Participation in the Arts via Broadcast Media, by
Income, 1985[a]
(Percent distribution)

Income class	Number of Adults	Percent of Adults in Income Class Participating[b]	Weighted Distribution of Participation[c]
Under $5,000	7.0(%)	11(%)	4(%)
$5,000–$9,999	11.8	12	8
$10,000–$14,999	11.2	13	9
$15,000–$24,999	20.8	15	18
$25,000–$49,999	33.7	19	37
$50,000 and over	15.5	26	24
All incomes	100.0 %	16 %	100 %

[a]The data on participation from which this table is derived are from table 9-17, *1989 Sourcebook,* and in turn come from one of the NEA 1985 survey monographs.

[b]The source table shows participation (meaning any listening or viewing of the type of art described) for twelve types of art via the broadcast media. Jazz was excluded, on the grounds that respondents might view much music carried on commercial radio as jazz. For the other ten types (classical music, opera, musicals and plays on both television and radio, and ballet and art museums on television only), a pooled regression equation was estimated, using the estimated midpoint of each income class and the reported participation rate for that cell. The composite percentages shown in this column are derived from the equation: composite participation rate (in percent) = 9.96 + 0.25 (income, in thousands). The *t* statistic for the sixty observations is 4.78.

[c]The weighted (by population) distribution assumes that there are no systematic differences by income in the frequency or duration of viewing or listening, either among or within types. Moreover, it is assumed that there are no systematic differences by income in the extent to which the viewing or listening involves commercial, rather than nonprofit, stations.

attributes are well above the national averages. In this, the subsector is like its close relative in the nonprofit world, higher education. Like higher education, the distributional effects of the subsidies to the subsector would be considered objectionable by many people, were it not for the positive external benefits the subsector is believed to generate. Like higher education, the reality and relevance of some of these indirect benefits look shaky on close examination: either an ample plenty of the indirect benefits would be generated as byproducts of transactions between unsubsidized sellers and the direct beneficiaries, or the alleged indirect benefits amount to double-counting of the direct benefits, or the indirect benefits accrue to the direct beneficiaries and others with similar economic and social status.

A considerable fraction of the literature of cultural economics is devoted to the case for (and against) subsidy to the arts and culture, particularly subsidy involving the use of tax-generated funds. Much of the case involves cataloging the benefits to third parties—or to society at large—that allegedly would not be generated without subsidy. However, if the external benefits are real, whether or not their generation requires subsidy, those benefits should be considered for our purposes, provided that their distribution by income class differs from the distribution of direct benefits and provided that there are data to support the analysis of the distribution of indirect benefits.[19]

By and large, the indirect benefits claimed for the arts and culture do appear to be distributed in ways that are very similar to the direct benefits, that is, most of the alleged indirect benefits are enjoyed by potential consumers and producers, people whose socioeconomic characteristics should be very much like those of actual consumers and producers. For example, the indirect benefits include succeeding generations' enjoyment of what is usually called "preservation of the cultural heritage," that is, the transmission of that heritage from one generation to the next.[20] Some current consumers of cultural goods and services may be more than willing to pay higher prices in order to assure that their children and grandchildren also will be able to enjoy those goods and services, and thus the benefits to their posterity can be counted as direct benefits to today's consumers. But others in the following generations have no agent among today's consumers and are thus indirect beneficiaries.

Similarly, within a single generation, some consumers derive utility from the very existence of cultural goods that they themselves never consume, but whose replacement would be immensely costly—like historic buildings (there is an obvious parallel with many of the supporters of wilderness preservation who themselves do not visit—or ever expect to do so—threatened wilderness areas). Consumers who value the existence of a splendid old symphony hall or opera house, but never attend performances there (perhaps because they don't care for opera or symphonic music, but do care for architectural beauty) are external to the market exchanges that determine whether the building will continue to stand.

Then there are the benefits that some consumers enjoy from the existence of cultural facilities and services that they seldom, if ever, use, but which they believe they might use, someday. Again, there are analogies in national parks and similar outdoor attractions, where option demand does

19. If the indirect benefits are very widely diffused, there is no basis for distributing them by income class that is not entirely arbitrary. See McGuire and Aaron (1969) for a theoretical treatment of this.

20. A good exposition of the points in this paragraph is in Frey and Pommerehne (1989, 19).

seem to explain much of voters' willingness to devote tax funds to facilities few of them ever do visit.[21]

Another indirect benefit of specific cultural activities is, by definition, confined to the arts and culture sector, the cost-reducing and quality-enhancing interactions among different types of cultural activities, such as the use of local symphony orchestra musicians for the local opera company, which gives only a few performances each season (see Netzer 1978, chapter 2, for more examples). Clearly, it is most unlikely that the income characteristics of the direct beneficiaries of these related activities differ greatly. This may not be the case for an analogous type of indirect benefit, the extent to which commercial mass media, entertainment, publishing, and even some less conspicuously artistic enterprises benefit from artistic talents and products developed under nonprofit auspices. Presumably, the income characteristics of the consumers and producers in these industries are not the same as is true for the nonprofit sector's direct beneficiaries. The net differences, however, are not self-evident.[22]

There is one class of indirect benefits whose distribution *must* be different from the distribution of direct benefits, the alleged strongly positive effects of local production of arts and culture on local economic development. The literature on this subject is characterized by extravagant claims.[23] The case has a number of components. First, in some places, art and culture is an export industry of consequence. New York and southern California do export cultural goods and services to the rest of the world in some volume, and there are a fair number of places in which the arts are an important ingredient of the local tourist industry, like the Spoleto Festival in Charleston, the Santa Fe Opera, and the collection of summer festivals in western Massachusetts. Like other export industries, this one has a local multiplier effect, albeit with major leakages for small communities.

21. Survey evidence suggests that there is indeed widespread public support for the use of government funds to realize these types of benefits. The most careful evidence is in Throsby and Withers (1983) for Australia and in Frey and Pommerehne (1989), using evidence from referenda in Basle, Switzerland.

22. The commercial sector does generate some indirect benefits for the nonprofit sector (like celebrity actors performing for union scale in nonprofit theater productions); also, while pop culture audiences generally are less affluent than high-culture audiences, the main indirect beneficiaries of this type may be extremely well-paid producers in the commercial sector. In addition, the most obvious such indirect commercial beneficiary of the nonprofit sector, the Broadway theater, has audiences that are at least marginally more affluent than the audiences at the regional nonprofit theater.

23. See the essays by Seaman and Gapinski in Radich (1987) for careful (and skeptical) treatment of the claims.

Second, on a very small geographic scale, all cultural activities are exported services: from the perspective of an area of only a few blocks, all the people in the audience for the local theater are "foreigners" who bring export earnings to that area. Thus, advocates argue for subsidies to cultural activities to revive central business districts, to benefit declining central cities, and to develop weak regions within states. Third, it is argued that cultural activities are an important element of the "quality of life" in a place and that quality-of-life considerations are important in the location decisions of firms and households. Therefore, cultural activities confer indirect benefits in the form of higher income and wealth to local households.

Whatever the merits of this case—and it seems a very weak one, except for the few places where the arts and culture are consequential local export industries, clearly the geographic extent of the positive externalities must be very narrow. The extent is not national, and therefore these indirect benefits should not be considered here.

There are other indirect benefits that may be real, but which are so general in nature that their distribution by income class must be arbitrary. One is the utility provided by the arts and culture in the form of national prestige (something that obviously is of importance to nonconsumers in some countries, notably France). The politicians who make decisions on public subsidies for the arts seem to believe that voters attach significant prestige value to the existene and flourishing of many kinds of cultural institutions and activities and are willing to pay taxes to elicit that element of value by subsidizing the arts. "Another general benefit is the uncompensated educational value of the arts: Artistic activities . . . may help a society to foster creativity, to improve the capacity for cultural evaluation and to develop aesthetic standards, aspects that benefit all persons in a society. The corresponding utilities are difficult, and sometimes impossible, to internalize within the market" (Frey and Pommerehne 1989, p. 19).

Even if the advocates' claims with regard to external benefits were less shaky, those claims afford little basis for allocating the external benefits by income class, either because the positive externalities clearly should have distributional effects that parallel the direct benefits to cultural consumers and producers, or because the indirect benefit in question is highly diffuse, or because there is no way of making quantitative estimates. Therefore, the summary data on the distribution of benefits presented below deal only with the distribution of the direct benefits to consumers and producers.

Benefits in the Form of Increased Compensation

Marginal changes in the fortunes of the subsector, notably marginal increases or decreases in the contributed income of the subsector, will result in changes in the quality and/or quantity of output and prices (usually, ticket prices) charged, with obvious effects on the benefits received by consumers. It is plausible that the earnings of those at work in the subsector also will be affected. This presumably will be true, to some extent, for all except those for whom the nonprofit arts and culture subsector is a minor element in the demand for labor, like maintenance and custodial workers. Conceivably, a considerable share of the direct benefits from arts subsidies might accrue to the people who work at producing cultural services, rather than the audiences. Certainly, some share does: the handful of world-class opera companies, all heavily subsidized (and most far more so than American opera companies) bid aggressively for the star singers, whose fees would surely be lower if all these companies had less subsidy money. And some portion of the subsidy must be captured by much more ordinary participants in the production process.

The question is, *what* share? In *The Subsidized Muse* (1978), I attempted to estimate the effects of subsidy on the economic behavior between 1966 and 1974 of nonprofit theater and opera companies and symphony orchestras that constituted about 90 percent of the universe of professional artistic activity in those fields.[24] The period chosen was one in which there had been very large increases in both government and foundation support for the performing arts (the National Endowment for the Arts was created in 1965, and no state arts council made significant grants before then), and for which there were good data, but not good enough to implement anything beyond a highly oversimplified model. I found that subsidy had increased the number of performances, lowered ticket prices, increased attendance, and increased compensation, relative to what would have occurred in the absence of the change in contributed income. The increase in earnings of those engaged in production attributable to subsidy was substantial, as was the increase in attendance; the reduction in ticket prices

24. See Netzer (1978, 97–110). The data were collected by the Ford Foundation for the seasons 1965–66 through 1973–74 in two separate surveys, the first with 166 respondents and the second with 153. Unlike all previous surveys of arts-producing organizations and many subsequent ones, the responses were carefully edited to correct anomalies and fill gaps (by followup calls).

was modest. In the case of the theater companies, the total dollar value of the "excess" wage rate increases was equal to almost the entire increase in contributed income.

Increasing the compensation of artists was an explicit goal of arts funders in the 1960s. The largest of all foundation programs in the arts and culture field, the Ford Foundation's massive program of aid to symphony orchestras announced in 1966, had as one of the principal goals increasing the earnings of orchestral musicians substantially, to improve the quality of orchestras over time. However, by the 1980s, increasing the earnings of artistic and support personnel in the major fields was no longer an explicit (or even implicit) goal of funders. Moreover, the single most important way of increasing earnings in the performing arts in the 1960s and 1970s, the lengthening of seasons, was no longer at work: in general, seasons did not lengthen in the 1980s. For other fields of the arts and culture, increasing earnings may remain a goal of subsidy policy. Surely, in some fields, like folk arts and much of "expansion arts," the object of funders has been to professionalize and regularize what had been casual and intermittent artistic activity.

However, the data do not permit the implementation of aggregative models that would tell us the overall extent, for all fields combined or by field, of the division between consumers and producers. In a later section, it is simply assumed, in one variant, that one-half of the benefits accrue to producers and one-half to consumers. To implement that assumption, it is necessary to consider the income distribution of the people who work in the arts and culture subsector. The stereotype is of artists who, on average, earn very little indeed as artists, the "starving artist" stereotype immortalized in *La Bohème*. The only really careful analysis of the question, a study by Filer (1986) using a large sample from the 1980 Census, concluded that "artists do not appear to earn less than other workers of similar training and personal characteristics" (p. 56) and that there is no lifetime earnings penalty attached to the decision to enter the field and stay in it.

The raw data tend to support the stereotype, which attributes the low earnings of artists to the fact that they are not employed as artists for much of any given year. This is especially true of artists who are largely self-employed, but it is also true of the large majorities of actors, singers, and dancers—who work for commercial and nonprofit enterprises—and report periods of unemployment of four weeks or more in a year (*1989 Sourcebook*, table 2–26). However, very high rates of unemployment are not the case for musicians, curators, film editors, and the large number of people in supporting trades and occupations. Overall, the result is relatively low annual earnings for two of the three main types of tax-exempt organizations in the subsector and not especially high annual earnings for the third type. The following expresses annual payrolls divided by employment relative to the average for all industries in 1985:[25]

All industries	100
Public broadcasting	111
Live performing arts	81
Museums	71

However, the relevant statistics for measuring the distributional effects are those on the incomes of the households that people who work in the arts form or live in. That income includes the nonartistic earnings of artists, the earnings of other household members, and nonlabor income. When so measured, the distribution of household income for the main types of performing artists is very much like that of the entire U.S. population (*1989 Sourcebook*, table 2–29). For others, like writers and people in "broadcast occupations," the distribution is skewed far to the right of that for the whole population. No doubt there are occupations for which the reverse is true. On balance, it seems appropriate to assume that the income distribution of those who work in the arts subsector is similar to that of the whole population.[26]

III. Distribution and Redistribution
The Distribution of Direct Benefits

In table 6.5, direct benefits are distributed by income on three bases. In the first two columns, all benefits are ascribed to consumers and allocated on the basis of the audience distributions shown in table 6.3 and 6.4. Consumer benefits from the "other" category in table 6.1, for which there are no comparable audience data, are allocated on the basis of the distribution of public broadcasting audiences, the most equal of the distributions. Conceivably, the "true" distribution of these audiences could be very much more skewed in either direction.

Tables 6.3 and 6.4 show estimated attendance by income class for vari-

25. Based on 1982 Census data updated to 1985 on the basis of *County Business Patterns* data for 1982 and 1985.
26. It is probably the case that marginal changes in the income of the subsector have especially pronounced effects on the earnings of those at the top of the income scale within the subsector, like star performers and celebrity museum directors. There are no data to support empirical expressions of this hypothesis.

TABLE 6.5 Distribution of Direct Benefits From the Arts and Culture Subsector by Income Class, 1985[a]

(In percent)

Income class	All Benefits Assigned to Audiences, Weighted by Income of Different Types of Activity[a]		Half of Benefits Assigned to Audiences, Half to Producers[b]	Income Distribution of All Adults[c]
	Total Income	Contributed Income		
Under $5,000	4.2	4.3	6.3	7.0
$5,000–$9,999	6.0	6.3	9.8	11.8
$10,000–$14,999	6.8	7.1	9.6	11.2
$15,000–$24,999	15.7	16.2	18.9	20.8
$25,000–$49,999	36.4	36.8	34.4	33.7
$50,000 and over	30.9	29.4	20.9	15.5
All incomes	100.0%	100.0%	100.0%	100.0%

[a]The distribution for the four main types of live performing arts and museums is based on the distribution of attendance shown in table 6.3. The distribution for public broadcasting is based on the distribution of audiences shown in table 6.4. The distribution for the "other" category shown in table 6.1 uses that for public broadcasting (see text for the reasoning). The six separate distributions are combined by using the size of the income of each of the types of cultural activities as weights. In the first column, total income is used as the weight. In the second column, contributed income is the weight.

[b]The share of benefits assigned to "producers," meaning artistic and supporting staff, is distributed on the basis of the distribution of all U.S. households; see text for the reasoning.

[c]Based on the Current Population Survey tables appearing in the 1987 Statistical Abstract of the United States.

ous types of cultural activities separately. The next question is how to combine the benefit allocations for each of the types of cultural activities. In the first column of table 6.5, it is assumed that the total consumer benefits for each type of activity is proportional to total current expenditure (or income) for the activity, so that, for example, total benefits for theater and classical music are roughly equal, while total benefits for opera and ballet are much smaller (see table 6.1). In the second column, total benefits for each type are assumed to be proportional to its contributed income (also from table 6.1); in this case, total benefits for classical music are nearly twice as important as those for theater. The reason for the distinction is the argument that the voluntary exchange represented by consumers' purchases of services is not relevant to a study of distribution.[27] The distinction turns out not to be important empirically: in both cases, just about two-thirds of the audience benefits are allocated to adults in the upper half of the income distribution and about 30 percent to the top group, which contains about one-sixth of the adult population.

In the third column, half the benefits are assigned to consumers and half to producers. That makes the distribution of benefits close to that of the adult population for all income classes except the top one: its disproportionately large share of benefits is offset by shares for the below-$25,000 income groups that are disproportionately small, but narrowly so.

There are two major reasons why the estimates in table 6.5 may understate the pro-rich pattern of the distribution of benefits. First, the audience benefits probably are not a simple function of attendance or usage. If, as is probably the case, the demand of low-income consumers for cultural activities is more sensitive to price than is true for high-income consumers, subsidies that reduce admissions prices do not generate much more attendance by upper-income people, but make them better off (and able to use the funds for other purposes). Meanwhile, all or most of the benefits enjoyed by low-income consumers are in the form of additional attendance and are reflected in the usage data. Second, if—as the findings of Filer (1986) can be construed to imply—the earnings of most people working in the arts are unaffected by subsidy and the only real gainers are the most specialized

27. No doubt there is some cross-subsidization among ticket purchasers: if ticket prices are higher for the first three rows of the mezzanine than for the rest of that section, surely the difference in benefits, in the sense of sight and sound, between a seat in row C and one in row D is less than the difference in the ticket price. On the other hand, the price difference may do no more than reflect the willingness of the purchaser of a seat in row C to pay a premium to avoid the risk of sitting in row P, in the typical advance purchase situation (where the purchaser has no way of knowing just what seats she will be assigned).

and most celebrated talents, then the producer benefits should be assigned largely to the top income groups.

How Much Redistribution Is There?

Obviously, a set of activities that generates direct benefits two-thirds of which accrues to people in the upper half of the income distribution, 30 percent to people in the top 15 percent of the distribution (as in the first two columns of table 6.5) and, possibly, an even more skewed distribution of indirect benefits, will not entail much net redistribution. Nonetheless, there is some, if the table 6.5 estimates are generally valid.

Tables 6.6 and 6.7 present estimates of the distribution by income class of the sources of the contributed income—about $2.7 billion in 1985—of the arts and culture subsector. It is not obvious that private giving, net of the tax advantages, should be regarded as any different from voluntary exchange, especially for this subsector.[28] Considerations of prestige play a conspicuous role in much of the giving, which buys glamorous and well-publicized connections that tend to be less transitory than, say, the brush with celebrities at benefit dinners for other charities. Power is also a commodity that giving buys; there may be a lot less power to be had in dealing with so puny a component of the economy than is true in other parts of the nonprofit sector but, just the same, large donors may have more power to actually affect decisions on the content of the arts than is the case in other subsectors that are better equipped to fend off interventions by donors.[29]

In addition, both large and more modest individual donors are likely to see their contributions as buying more of the private consumption goods they prefer, if they believe—as they are constantly told—that their contributions are essential if the show is to go on. That is, they might be content with art enterprises that practice perfect price discrimination, charging several thousand dollars for a few seats and next to nothing for others, and that live entirely from earned income.[30] However, such regimes are simply

28. See chapter 1, in which this issue is discussed.

29. See Feld, O'Hare, and Schuster (1983, chapter 5), for a systematic discussion of giving and decision making.

30. "Perfect price discrimination" means charging each buyer the price that she or he is willing to pay for that service rather than do without. It means not only a very wide range of ticket prices for many events, but also many gradations within that wide range, in some cases a different price for every buyer. In the real world, in each ticket price range, there are some buyers who would have been willing to pay a higher price, and by not having to do so, enjoy what economists call "consumer surplus."

TABLE 6.6 Estimated Sources of the Contributed Income of
the Arts and Culture Subsector, 1985[a]
(Dollar amounts in millions)

PRIVATE PHILANTHROPY		
Individuals	1,368	
Less: income tax deduction offset[b]	385	
Equals: net cost to individuals		983
Corporations	389	
Less: income tax deduction offset[c]	163	
Equals: net cost to shareholders		226
Foundations	231	
Less: equivalent of income-tax deduction[d]	109	
Equals: net cost to donors		122
Net costs, all classes of givers		1,331
GOVERNMENT FINANCED		
Direct support from tax revenue		729
Income tax deductions, revenue to be made up—		
Individuals	385	
Corporations	163	
Foundations	109	
Equals: net cost to taxpayers		1,385

[a]The totals by type of income are from table 6.1.

[b]This estimate begins with a distribution of individual giving by income class. The only data on this are from 1970 (*Giving in America* 1975, 61); it was assumed that the *relative* distribution by income class, with class intervals expressed in 1985 dollars—and adjusted crudely from an adjusted gross income to money income basis—was the same in 1985 as in 1970. Next, *Statistics of Income* data on marginal tax rates, the proportion of itemized deduction returns and deductions by nonitemizers for 1985 were used (with the income basis adjusted) to estimate the value of federal income tax deductions by income class. State and local income taxes were taken into account by increasing the deductible amount uniformly by the ratio of state-local individual income tax revenue to federal individual income tax revenue, net of the deductibility of those taxes against the federal taxes, calculated as for the federal deduction for contribution.

[c]The offset is the ratio of federal corporate income taxes paid to corporate income subject to tax, as shown in *Statistics of Income* data.

[d]The offset is the combined federal and state-local marginal individual income tax rate for the $50,000 and over money income class, as used in the calculations described in note b.

not feasible in most cases. Arts enterprises do not have the information needed for perfect price discrimination even where admission is, or can be, charged, and even when the enterprise is a near-monopoly. So, the contribution is then a supplement to the price, meant to subsidize tickets for others only to the extent that the subsidy assures that the show does go on for the donor.

TABLE 6.7 Estimated Distribution of the Origins of the Contributed Income of the Arts and Culture Subsector, by Income Class, 1985[a]

Income class	Net Private Giving[b]	Taxation[c] Pechman variant—		Combined Private and Governmental Support Pechman variant—	
		1c	3b	1c	3b
Under $5,000	0.3(%)	0.7(%)	1.0(%)	0.5(%)	0.7(%)
$ 5,000–$ 9,999	1.6	2.3	2.9	1.9	2.2
$10,000–$14,999	2.6	8.0	8.5	5.4	5.6
$15,000–$24,999	6.8	12.7	13.2	9.8	10.1
$25,000–$49,999	38.1	35.8	36.1	36.9	37.1
$50,000 and over	50.6	40.4	38.3	45.4	44.3
All incomes	100.0%	100.0%	100.0%	100.0%	100.0%

[a]Total amounts to be distributed from table 6.6.
[b]Estimating methods described in note b, table 6.6.
[c]Assumes that the cost of deductibility is offset by uniform increases in all the existing tax revenue sources. The distribution given in the revised tables (1987) to Pechman (1985) was converted to the income basis and income classes used here. Variant 1c is the most progressive distribution, variant 3b the most regressive.

There is no such conceptual ambiguity about the redistribution attached to support from tax revenues, including the additional tax revenues that must be generated to make up for the deductibility of contributions. Table 6.6 shows that half of total contributed income for the subsector is derived from taxation, and table 6.7 shows that the distribution of the tax burden is somewhat more progressive than the distribution of direct benefits shown in table 6.5 (the taxes distributed are all taxes collected by federal, state, and local governments in 1985).[31] The people who make up the top half of the income distribution bear about 75 percent of the tax burden and are two-thirds of the audience and a somewhat smaller share of the total when direct benefits are assigned to producers. The costs of the net redistribution are borne entirely in the above-$50,000 class; there is no redistribution at all for the $25,000–$50,000 class. In the benefit variant in which all benefits are allocated on the basis of audiences, the gains for the classes between $10,000 and $25,000 are small. At the bottom, the gains are relatively larger, not because the poor loom large in audiences (or among producers) but because their tax burdens are a small share of the total (even in the most regressive of the Pechman allocations).[32]

If private giving, net of the tax advantages, is considered redistribution, the extent of redistribution rises, even for the income class just below the median. Of course, the conclusions on redistribution depend heavily on the rather weak data on attendance, as well as on the assumption that consumers benefits are proportional to attendance. If those data and the assumption are seriously in error, the error results in overstating benefits in the lower part of the income distribution. Correction for such overstatement almost certainly would lead to the finding that there is little or no redistribution from the upper to the lower half of the income distribution, but

31. Payroll taxes for social insurance are included in the taxes distributed in table 6.7. It can be argued that these taxes (nearly 40 percent) of federal tax revenues in 1985 and 29 percent of the tax revenues of all governments, according to *Survey of Current Business,* July 1989, tables 3.1–3.3) should be excluded, since they are not available for other purposes. A case also can be made for confining the analysis of the distribution of revenues to finance income tax deductibility for contributions to income taxes.

32. In Pechman (1985), there are a number of different sets of findings on the distribution of the overall tax burden, differing in the assumptions used regarding the incidence of specific types of taxes. The major differences concern the property tax and the corporate income tax. In the most progressive variant (1c), the burden of these taxes is held to be borne entirely by owners of capital (which is the consensus view among economists studying the distribution of the burden of the nation's taxes). In the most regressive variant (3b), part of the burden of these two taxes is held to be borne by consumers.

significant redistribution from the highest income-receivers to the one-third just above the median.[33]

The Potential Distributive Effects of Marginal Changes

Fiscal stringency and the effects of tax rate reductions and reform on contributions have been having marginal—and in some cases, not so marginal—effects on the level of support for the nonprofit arts and culture subsector since the late 1970s. Federal appropriations have remained roughly constant in current dollars since 1978, which means a large decline in real terms. State and local government funding has increased substantially in the aggregate, but not in all places. For example, there have been substantial declines in real terms in New York. Moreover, state government support has been highly volatile, with huge increases in at least one year in thirty of the fifty states, but year-to-year declines, often as much as 25 percent in current dollars, at least once during the 1980s in forty-five states (Netzer 1990).[34]

The time-series data for the larger organizations in the main fields show growth in output over the 1980s, financed by increases in earned income—notably higher admissions prices in real terms—and by continued increases in contributions by individuals, and for some types of organizations, by corporations until late in the decade. In the light of the highly progressive distribution of contributions to the arts and culture by individuals, the reduction in federal marginal income tax rates between the 1980 and 1988 tax years should have had a substantial negative effect on the subsector. It certainly did have such an effect on charitable giving in total (see Clotfelter 1990). For arts and cultural organizations, there was not much sign of this expected effect before the 1986 Tax Reform Act. The

33. One complication is not considered here, because the refinements involved seem inappropriate, given the imprecision of the data. Nearly half of the tax support, direct and via deductibility, comes from state and local taxation. That is a larger fraction than is the case for the entire tax system of the country in 1985, and, therefore, use of the aggregate Pechman findings overstates (slightly in variant 1c, more in variant 3b) the progressivity of the taxes levied to finance the benefits of this subsector. Also, it is conceivable that the revenue structure of the states that heavily subsidize the arts differs systematically from that of the states that do not, which would affect the tax burden distribution. I have tested this hypothesis with data for state appropriations to state arts councils, one component of total state-local subsidies from taxation, and found no statistical associations at all between a state's tax structure and the relative level of state funding of its arts council.

34. In the aggregate, state legislative appropriations for the arts agencies declined in fiscal 1991, by 2.5 percent, for the first time in thirteen years (National Assembly of State Arts Agencies 1990).

limited evidence for the years since 1986—mostly in the form of complaints from directors of institutions—suggests that there has indeed been a significant decline for museums, partly from the decline in marginal tax rates and partly because of the less favorable tax treatment of gifts of appreciated property.[35]

To a considerable extent, the effects of fiscal restraint on government support have been borne by the more established organizations and fields. The Arts Endowment and those state arts councils that have not done well have tended to concentrate their real-terms reductions in grants on the established, while protecting the fringe fields and organizations; by the same token, when state arts councils have had sudden large increases in funding, much of the increase was passed through to establishment organizations, sometimes ones that were on the edge of financial collapse. If the income distribution profile of the audiences for the establishment organizations is more skewed to the right than is the case for the fringe organizations and fields, which is by no means clear, then a continuation of this strategy for allocating declining government support will elicit more instances of shrinkage of output and even collapse among the establishment organizations—assuming no offsetting increase in private giving or in earned income—and a change of the distributional pattern that is somewhat pro-poor. Nevertheless, the prospects of bankruptcies could lead to changes in emphasis, with the real-term cuts borne to a greater extent by the nonestablishment components of the subsector.

The likely effects of marginal reductions in private giving are obvious, if the reasons for the reduction are the ones that now seem important: tax law changes for individuals and mergers and other reorganizations for corporations. The reductions in corporate support should affect, in particular: public television with a negative impact mainly on quality—which may be of concern mainly for the more affluent among the audience; the local symphony orchestra, ballet company, and the like in medium-sized cities, with a negative impact on the quantity of performances, probably of most concern in the upper-middle reaches of the income distribution; and a good many small, local nonestablishment enterprises supported out of civic duty.

As for reductions in individual contributions, museums are more at risk than the live performing arts, simply because individual giving is so much more important for museums. To the extent that the reduction in the re-

---

35. In the October 1990 budget settlement, the pre-1987 treatment of appreciated-property gifts was restored, for the 1991 tax year.

ceipts of museums mainly affects acquisitions and scholarship, with a limited impact on exhibition and opening hours, the immediate distributional effects will not be regressive. However, the audiences at museums are clearly less affluent than those at the main types of live performing arts, so that, if reductions in individual giving do reduce opening hours, the distributional impact will indeed be regressive.

The employment effects of reductions in support are worth attention. Reductions in the scale of output, like numbers of performances, will increase unemployment among professionals and crafts people with specialized talents and limited alternatives, except in the long run. The short-term distributional impact may be quite regressive; over time, the most protracted periods of unemployment may be suffered by people in occupations that are not now poorly paid, like symphony orchestra musicians and theater crafts people.

IV. CONCLUSION

The bulk of the benefits of the activities of nonprofit arts and cultural organizations are realized by people in the upper half of the income distribution, but the frequent allegation that support of the subsector from tax funds and tax-deductible gifts is a transfer from those in the middle of the income distribution to those at the top of the distribution is a caricature. It is impossible to say just how badly distorted the caricature is because of the many weaknesses in the data on the subsector. Better data would help support answers to such policy questions as the distributive effects of reductions in direct public support of the arts and culture or of substitution of public funds for declines in charitable contributions, as well as the distributive effects of changes in the allocation of funds among types of cultural activities and institutions. However, the subsector is a small one, so changes in its distributive effects at the margin may be of no real concern for anyone except the activists and participants in the field. Even so, the usual policy analyst's call for better data seems appropriate.

APPENDIX
SURVEY DATA ON PUBLIC PARTICIPATION IN THE ARTS

The first effort to study the cultural activities of the population as a whole, rather than the characteristics of audiences at specified performances or in particular settings (like museums) was the survey of the audience for the performing arts done for the Twentieth Century Fund in 1964–65, in connection was the Baumol and Bowen study (1966) that is rightly considered *the* pioneering work in the economics of the arts. Beginning in the late 1960s, Louis Harris Associates and a newly formed subsidary, National Research Center of the Arts, began making surveys of the entire adult population and asking questions about participation in cultural activities, including attendance, with extensive background questions on individual and household characteristics. The sample selection procedures were those used by the Harris organization in its regular public opinion survey work. The initial Harris participation surveys were done in individual states, sponsored by the state arts agency (although usually financed from National Endowment of the Arts grants money).[36] In the 1970s, Harris did three nationwide surveys, under the aegis of the Associated Councils for the Arts (an advocacy organization), but with Endowment funding. A fourth was done in 1984 and a fifth in 1988.

At first, the results of the Harris surveys made their sponsors—the Endowment, state arts agencies, organizations of art institutions and other advocacy groups—happy. The surveys showed that there was an unexpectedly large audience for the arts (far larger than was implied by the scattered data on actual ticketed attendance for the main professional performing arts organizations), vast amateur participation in cultural activities, and much good will toward the arts and public subsidy of the arts. By the late 1970s, however, there was considerable dissatisfaction, with doubts about the credibility of the findings and concern with the high cost of the Harris surveys.[37] In the 1980s, the Endowment contracted with the Census Bureau to conduct arts participation surveys in conjunction with its regular inter-censal population survey work. Such surveys were conducted in 1982 and 1985. The basic results were presented and analyzed in one monograph for each year, by a University of Maryland team, and a series of monographs explored further particular dimensions of the survey results.[38] The results used in this chapter are from the NEA 1985 survey (Robinson et al. 1987).

It is not at all surprising that respondents would tend to exaggerate the extent that they participate in highly regarded activities, especially if they think that this is the answer the sponsor would like to hear. Thus, in the first Harris nationwide survey, just under half of all American adults reported that they had visited an art museum in the preceding twelve months (which is probably far above the ratio that one would expect to find in a survey confined to the faculty of a typical

36. The Harris organization also began to conduct surveys of arts institutions (all those in a state, or all museums, for example), with questions on organization, operations, finances and audiences, based on a similar funding pattern.

37. Another factor was the Harris organization's assertion that its data tapes were "proprietary," and available neither to the public agency paying for the survey nor to other researchers (except at a fee, or when the researcher proposed to do something that the Harris people were interested in doing themselves). Otherwise, only the published results—with few cross-tabulations, limited detail, and frequent use of percentages rather than absolute numbers—were available. The Harris position was almost certainly in contravention of federal law (as one can see by reading the "boilerplate" attached to federal research contracts and grant awards), but the Endowment chose not to challenge Harris on this.

38. As with most of the research sponsored by the Endowment in the 1980s, little of this material was published through the Government Printing Office. Most remains fugitive material, available (on microfiche) via NTIS or ERIC.

American university). Gratifyingly, participation rates reported in the NEA surveys were dramatically smaller than in the Harris surveys.

Table 6.A1 compares the results of the earliest of the Harris surveys with the results of the most recent NEA survey. Translated into numbers of adults, the two surveys in combination suggest that the number of adults visiting art museums at least once in the preceding year declined from 69.8 million in 1973 to 37.4 million in 1985; the number attending live theatrical performances at least once declined from 46.6 million in 1973 to 36.3 million. Whether the same thing can be said about concerts and opera depends on the extent to which the 1973 survey respondents included popular music concerts, and the 1985 respondents did not. According to the former survey, 39.3 million attended live concerts and opera at least once in the previous twelve months; according to the latter, the number was 22.8 million. In contrast, estimates of the number attending dance performances increased, from 11.6 million in 1973 to somewhat over 13 million in 1985.[39] These comparisons are a bit facetious, for the later Harris surveys continue to report very high, and not credible, participation rates. For example, the 1984 Harris survey reported rates well above the 1973 results for theater—60 percent versus 21.3 percent in the NEA 1985 survey—and for art museums—58 percent versus 21.9 percent in the NEA 1985 survey.[40]

But are even the more modest NEA survey results believable? Attendance—that is, the number of visits, rather than visitors—calculated from the NEA surveys seems to be far in excess of the attendance figures reported by the major types of performing arts producing organizations to the service organizations that collect data on the different art disciplines. Consider the following comparisons, for 1985:[41]

—The American Symphony Orchestra League has collected data from a rather complete universe of orchestral groups, in 1985 from 1,572 orchestras, including youth and chamber groups with budgets below $70,000. They reported a total 1985 attendance of 23.7 million, including free performances in parks and

39. My estimates of total dance attendance at performances of professional companies in 1984 (see Netzer 1986, 1987) suggest that ballet companies accounted for about 55 percent of total attendance, exclusive of "Nutcracker" performances (where most of the audience usually consists of children). If the frequency of attendance among those who attend at least once is the same for ballet and modern dance (there is some fragmentary evidence that frequency is higher for the latter), then the member of adults attending modern dance at least once in 1985 would have been about 6.0 million, with the ballet attendees in the 1985 NEA survey 7.3 million.

40. The disparities for art museums and their causes are discussed in some detail in Schuster (1988, 40–45). The causes include the placement and wording of the questions, the under-weighting of the bottom socioeconomic group with lower participation rates in calculating aggregates, and sample selection biases in the Harris surveys. Schuster notes that "the arts research community has generally been critical of Harris for producing advocacy documents pretending to be 'objective research.' This applies not only to the questions asked, but also to which calculations are made, which results are chosen to be presented, and how they are presented" (p. 42).

41. Attendance data from table 397, *Statistical Abstract of the United States, 1989,* and from *1989 Sourcebook.*

TABLE 6.A1 Two Surveys of Public Participation in the Arts: Percentage of Respondents Attending at Least Once in the Preceding Twelve Months, by Art Form[a]

	Harris 1973	NEA 1985
Ballet and Modern Dance	8	
Ballet		4.3
Concerts and Opera	27	
Classical Music		12.7
Classical Music and Opera Combined[b]		13.4
Theater	32	
Musicals		16.6
Other Plays		11.6
Musicals and Other Plays Combined[b]		21.3
Art Museums	48	21.9

[a]Harris survey results from National Research Center of the Arts (1975, tables 46 and 47). NEA survey results from Robinson et al. (1987, table 3.2a, 3.3, and 3.5). The Harris survey was conducted in January 1973 and involved 3,005 interviews; the universe was the 145 million Americans sixteen years of age and older. The NEA survey was conducted in waves during 1985 and involved 13,675 respondents; the universe was 170.6 million Americans eighteen years of age and older. As the stub shows, the two surveys used somewhat different categories.

[b]Combined on the basis of data on overlapping audiences in table 3.5 (Robinson et al. 1987, 209).

similar places. Anecdotal evidence suggests that the free attendance estimates tend to be generous, as would be expected, since the donors who sponsor such concerts are pleased with high attendance. The NEA 1985 survey suggests that total attendance at classical music performances (adjusted as the Robinson et al. report proposes and excluding attendance at performances given in schools and churches) was nearly 70 million.

—The service organization for opera reported data for 1,123 companies, which include some very small community groups with negligible budgets in 1985. Total reported attendance was 14.1 million, but close to one-third of performances were musical plays, rather than operas per se; musicals constitute a separate category in the NEA surveys. Some of the larger, more heavily subsidized companies (notably the Metropolitan Opera) give free performances in parks; the estimated attendance at such performances is included in those totals and may be even more exaggerated than is the case for symphony orchestras. Probably, attendance at the opera performances of these companies was no more than 9 million. The NEA 1985 survey results (adjusted as in the previous case) indicate total attendance of nearly 15 million at operas.

—During the 1984–85 season, about 22 million tickets were sold for the Broad-

way and road-show for-profit theater. For-profit dinner and summer performances and other types of for-profit theater may account for a similar number in
total; they did in the last NEA study, done for the 1976–77 season (*1989
Sourcebook,* table 4-13). The Theatre Communications Group's surveys of
nearly two hundred nonprofit theaters cover a very large fraction of the nonprofit universe and report attendance in recent years of about 14 million (*1989
Sourcebook,* table 4-11b). Attendance at college and community theater performances not included in any of above categories could conceivably be as high
as 20 million. So, the data we have on attendance suggest a total of not more
than 80 million. The adjusted NEA 1985 survey indicates total attendance at
musicals and plays of more than 210 million.

In an earlier paper (Netzer 1987), I made a more systematic comparison of
attendance data for dance with the NEA survey results for "ballet" (the word is in
quotations marks because some respondents may well have interpreted it to cover
other types of dance performances). In the 1983–84 season, there were roughly
5,000 professional dance performances in the United States, with an estimated
total attendance of perhaps 5.2 million, excluding children attending "Nutcracker" performances in the Christmas season. Of this total, about 2.9 million
appears to have been at ballet performances and 2.3 at modern dance company
performances. But the NEA 1985 survey (as adjusted) suggests a total attendance
at ballet performances of more than 23 million. If the mean number of performances attended by individual members of the audience was as low as 1.5, then my
data suggest that only 1.9 million adults attended ballet performances and another
1.6 million attended modern dance performances, compared to the figure of 7.3
million attendees at ballet performances in the NEA 1985 survey.[42] (In this earlier
volume the tables were inadvertently omitted, but are available from the author.)

42. Data for the New York area suggest that the mean number of dance performances
attended in a year by those who attend any at all is more than three.

7

Foundations

Robert A. Margo

Some charitable contributions are made directly to individuals or to non-profit organizations. Other charitable contributions are provided through an intermediary. The philanthropic foundation is a principal example of a charitable intermediary: foundations do not "initiate charitable transfers ... [they] complete them" (Clotfelter 1985, 253). Ranging in size from miniscule, obscure organizations to huge, multinational agencies, foundations in the aggregate spend billions of dollars annually. Since the early twentieth century, donors have been permitted tax exemptions for setting up private foundations; income from foundation assets is not taxed at corporate tax rates. In return for this tax exemption, and subject to certain restrictions, foundations influence the pattern of resource allocation in the economy, for example, by allocating dollars for medical research or supporting art museums. It is important therefore, to analyze the distributional impact of foundations—what foundations spend their income on, what variations in expenditure patterns are a function of, and what long-term trends have been.

Certainly there is no shortage of opinion on the distributional impact of foundations. Since the early twentieth century, foundations have been denounced as dangerous concentrations of wealth and political power or as tax dodges (Nielsen 1972, 3–20, 373; Freemont-Smith 1965, 21; Karl and Katz 1981, 249). Others have charged that the development of a "culture of philanthropy" among wealthy Americans, of which the establishment of foundations is a key element, has led to a disproportionate share of philanthropic dollars being allocated to established and frequently wealthy institutions that largely perpetuate a social and economic elite (Odendahl

I am grateful to Elizabeth Boris, Clive Bell, Edward Buffie, Charles Clotfelter, Estelle James, Al Rees, conference participants, and several anonymous referees for helpful comments, and to Amy Phillips for research assistance. Research support from the Center for the Study of Philanthropy and Voluntarism, Duke University, is gratefully acknowledged.

1990, 3–4; Fisher 1983).[1] In turn, foundations have justified their existence by claiming that the goods and services financed by their grants are worthy of public support (via the tax exemption) and might not have been produced otherwise in a timely manner.[2]

As will become apparent, answering the question, "Who benefits from the tax exemption for private, philanthropic foundations?" is not possible with available published data. The data are simply too aggregated for a detailed study of all the various issues involved in measuring distributional impact. Even if the data were disaggregated, no useful analytical models of foundation behavior have been developed as interpretive guides.[3] Nevertheless, the evidence is sufficient to set forth a number of working hypotheses for further study.

Section I defines terminology and presents a brief, nontechnical theoretical discussion of the distributional impact of foundations. Section II presents data on long-term trends in the size of the foundation sector and foundation finances, while section III considers expenditure patterns. Section IV is concerned with the unequal distribution of foundation assets and expenditures across regions. Conclusions are presented in section V.

I. THE DISTRIBUTIONAL IMPACT OF FOUNDATIONS: AN INTRODUCTION TO THE ISSUES
Definitions

Legally, private foundations are tax-exempt organizations as classified by the Internal Revenue Service under its Code, Section 501(c).[4] For analytical purposes, it is useful to distinguish four different types of foundations. *Independent foundations,* also referred to as *private, nonoperating foundations,* are the principal type; the largest examples of these, such as Ford Foundation, are what is popularly meant by a foundation.[5] Typically, independent foundations are established by an initial grant from one or more

1. See Karl and Katz (1987) for a critique of the argument that foundations are (and were) established to perpetuate a ruling class elite.

2. A superb example is Weaver (1967), who provides testimony from eminent natural and social scientists extolling the timely benefits produced by foundation grants to their disciplines.

3. An exception to the nonanalytical nature of the literature on foundations is Clotfelter (1985).

4. See Foundation Center (1989, v–li) for an excellent background discussion of the different types of foundations and the various legal requirements governing foundation behavior.

5. The foundations are "nonoperating" because they do not provide goods or services to clients directly.

donors, made either while the donor is alive or as a bequest. Subsequently, the foundation may receive contributions from the donor or the donor's descendants.[6] Depending on the size of the foundation's *payout rate* (grants as a fraction of assets), the assets of the foundation may accumulate over time.[7] If assets grow sufficiently, or for other reasons (death of the donor), control of a foundation's affairs may pass from the donor to professional managers.

The legal purpose of an independent foundation is the making of grants. In principle, the scope of foundation grants can be very wide; in practice, most foundations confine their grants to a relatively narrow range of activities. Approximately 70 percent of independent foundations restrict grants to the state (or metropolitan area) in which the foundation is located (Foundation Center 1990b, vii).

Community foundations are a second type of foundation. The primary purpose of a community foundation is to centralize administration for diverse charitable funds that may exist in a metropolitan area. By centralizing administrative functions, certain economies of scale are obtained and more dollars are available for charitable purposes. The directors of community foundations are generally drawn from the metropolitan area, and the grants made are to local organizations.

Company-sponsored foundations are established by firms to facilitate the receiving and distribution of corporate contributions to charity. As such, they are conceptually closer to independent foundations than are community foundations. Decisions on grants are typically made by company officials; grants are restricted to activities of corporate interest, or which benefit the community in which the corporation is located. An economic advantage of company foundations is their ability to "smooth"

---

6. A foundation may be *self liquidating;* that is, the donor requires that assets be fully distributed by a particular date. A famous example is the Rosenwald Foundation. Established by Julius Rosenwald, a Chicago merchant, the foundation distributed matching grants for the construction of *de jure* segregated schools for black children in the South in the early twentieth century. On the role of foundations in fostering black education in the early twentieth century South, see Anderson (1987).

7. The following accounting identity is useful in this regard:
$$A_t = A_{t-1}(1 + r - p) + C_{t-1} - X_{t-1}$$
where A represents the real value of foundation assets, r is the real rate of return on assets, C are contributions, X are expenses (for example, salaries and overhead), p is the payout rate, and t indicates the year. For a given level of contributions and expenses, the greater is the difference between the rate of return and the payout rate, the greater will be wealth accumulation (assuming that r is positive).

charitable contributions over cyclical fluctuations in profits; that is, contributions can remain relatively stable even if the company experiences hard times (Siegfried and McElroy 1981).

Finally, *operating foundations* are nonprofit organizations or endowments that produce research or provide services directly to clients. Unlike the other types of foundations, operating foundations rarely make grants. Conceptually, they are closer in function to the typical nonprofit firm than are the other types of foundations.

As a consequence of their tax-exempt status, foundations are subject to a variety of complex regulations involving the administering of grants, minimum payout rates, maximum allowable expenditures for administrative purposes, ownership of businesses, and self-dealing.[8] The majority of these rules were established as part of the Tax Reform Act of 1969, with occasional amendments since then. Currently, foundations are required to pay out grants equal to at least 5 percent of the current value of their asset holdings; in addition, they are subject to a 2 percent excise tax on net investment income. Up to 30 percent of cash contributions to independent foundations (20 percent for appreciated property) can be deducted from the donor's income tax liability. Somewhat more generous tax deductions are allowed for contributions to community or operating foundations; contributions to community foundations are generally fully deductible. For federal estate tax purposes, however, charitable gifts to all types of foundations are fully deductible. Foundations are also required to file IRS Form 990-PF on an annual basis, which is a publicly available document containing information on finances and grantmaking activity (Clotfelter 1985, 264; Foundation Center 1989, vii–viii).

Table 7.1 shows the distribution of assets, contributions received, and grants by foundation type for 7,581 foundations in 1989. The foundations included in the table comprise 25 percent of all private grantmaking foundations as defined by the IRS, accounting for 96 percent of all assets held by foundations and 93 percent of grants awarded.[9] About 86 percent of assets and 75 percent of grants are attributable to independent foundations. Company foundations are more numerous than community foundations, but the latter are significantly wealthier. Grants by company foun-

8. Self-dealing refers to a set of illegal practices involving foundations and donors; for example, a foundation is not permitted to make interest-free loans out of endowment to the donor.
9. The criteria for inclusion in the table are assets in excess of 1 million dollars or $100,000 or more in annual grants. See Foundation Center (1990a, v–vi).

TABLE 7.1 Distribution of Assets, Gifts Received, and Grants: By Foundation Type, 1989

Type	Number	Assets	Gifts Received	Grants
Independent	82.6(%)	85.9(%)	62.3(%)	74.1(%)
Company-sponsored	12.5	4.3	23.3	18.9
Community	2.5	4.7	11.0	5.7
Operating	2.4	5.1	3.4	1.3

SOURCE: Foundation Center (1990a, vi).

dations, however, are a higher proportion of assets than grants by community foundations. Operating foundations constitute a minor part of the foundation sector.

Distributional Impact

It is useful to begin by considering a simple model of the distributional impact of foundations. The idea is to trace through the distributional consequences of a small expansion of the foundation sector, ignoring any induced changes in factor prices or dynamic effects.[10]

Imagine a change in federal tax policy that leads to a marginal increase in the value of foundation assets. Although the precise distributional effects depend on the type of change, for the sake of argument suppose the increase in assets is financed by a more generous tax deduction for current contribution. By lowering the "price" of charitable contribution, this change in the tax code can be expected to increase contributions to foundations, which would increase the amount of assets held by existing foundations, and could possibly result in new foundations being established.[11] In turn, the increase in assets would generate a higher level of foundation

10. For a general discussion of such effects in evaluating the distributional impact of nonprofits, see chapter 1, this volume, by Clotfelter.

11. See Clotfelter (1985) for an extensive discussion of the impact of tax deductibility on charitable giving. If the change in the tax code were a permanent one, there would be an additional incentive for the rich to accumulate wealth for charitable purposes, as opposed to say, squandering assets in conspicuous consumption or sheltering wealth in various ways to avoid taxation. By permitting foundations to exist—generically, an institutional form by which the donor, descendants of the donor, or professional managers retain control over the disposition of assets—overall wealth accumulation in the economy might be greater. The cost to society, however, may be that the overall pattern of resource allocation is changed; fewer resources might have been devoted to art museums and more to drug treatment centers, if the tax deduction for foundations did not exist. The idea that foundations are a compromise solution between society's desire to appropriate a fraction of private wealth for charitable purposes against the donor's wishes to control how the money is spent is discussed by Karl and Katz (1987, 8–9).

grants, the size of the increase depending on payout rates and administrative expenses. Throughout the economy, there are various organizations, each of which receives a share (possibly zero) of the increase in foundation grants. The firms use the additional funds to increase their output. For example, a hospital might expand a research program with its share; a theater company might offer discount tickets for senior citizens; a private university might offer additional scholarships to needy students.

Eventually, the increased output will be consumed; a simple way of measuring distributional impact is to compare the change in consumption across deciles of the income distribution. For example, suppose that foundations allocated all of the increase in grants to shelters for the homeless. Because usage of homeless shelters is presumably concentrated among persons in the lowest centile of the income distribution, it would be reasonable to conclude that, in this instance, foundations were pro-poor.

Before using this approach, however, several problems must be addressed. First, the distributional consequences of the method of financing the increase in foundation grants would also need to be considered. The change in the tax code proposed above would reduce tax revenues; as a concrete example, suppose the revenue is made up by reducing tax deductions for middle-income households.[12] In this case, the conclusion that foundations were pro-poor would arguably be unchanged. But it is easy to imagine tax scenarios in which the overall distributional impact would be neutral, or possibly reversed from the pattern of consumption across income groups.

Second, the allocation of benefits across income groups may not be readily determined in some cases as in the homeless example, particularly for public goods like medical or scientific research. Although one might, as a practical matter, allocate benefits equally in the case of research, the amount of grant dollars may be a very poor proxy for the actual benefits received. Gunnar Myrdal's book *An American Dilemma* (1944), financed by the Carnegie Corporation in the late 1930s, provided intellectual grist for important civil rights legislation in the late 1940s as well as fundamental evidence cited in the Supreme Court's landmark desegregation case, *Brown vs. Board of Education* (Southern 1987, 120, 127).[13] Exactly how

12. Alternatively, the government might reduce its expenditures in certain areas; that is, crowding-out may occur. For example, if foundations increased their grants to the arts, the federal government might cut back its own spending.

13. For an excellent history of the Carnegie Corporation, including its financing of Myrdal's study, see Lagermann (1989).

one would gauge the book's distributional impact is unclear, but it would clearly be inadequate to do so by allocating the dollar amount of the Carnegie grant equally across income groups.

Third, and most important, economic theory suggests that the change in *consumer surplus*—willingness to pay less actual expenditure on a good— is the appropriate measure of distributional impact, not usage patterns. A rich person might value attendance at an opera performance much more highly at the margin than a poor person. Even if a foundation grant allowed an opera company to lower its ticket prices so that the share of lower-income persons attending performances increased, the additional consumer surplus enjoyed by the wealthy might change the overall distributional impact from progressive to regressive. As a practical matter, however, the measurement of consumer surplus is fraught with difficulties; even if the surplus approach were used, it would still be necessary to determine the distribution of foundation grants across nonprofit firms.

II. Foundation Growth and Payout Rates

The simple model of distributional impact suggests a number of empirical issues to explore; in particular, the size of the foundation sector, payout rates and administrative expenses, and the distribution of foundation grants. This section examines evidence on the growth of foundations and various aspects of foundation finances, from the 1930s to the present, while section III studies the allocation of foundation grant dollars. At the outset, it is important to acknowledge that the data analyzed in this section, and in section III, are drawn primarily from aggregate statistics compiled and published on a irregular basis by the Foundation Center and its predecessors. These data have numerous flaws; while I have attempted some corrections, it is impossible to fix all the inconsistencies. Data collection has become more systematic in the 1980s, but there is no question that a much richer study of distributional impact could be attempted by collecting data on a random sample of individual foundations.[14] As an illustra-

14. Several recent studies of foundation behavior using microeconomic data are Boris (1987), Rudney (1987), Ylvisaker (1987), Nelson (1987), and Salamon and Voytek (1989). Boris collected survey information on a stratified random sample of 1,009 independent foundations, which she used to study asset values, dates of birth, and characteristics of donors. Rudney's study, which is based on a sample of 367 foundations, is similar to Boris'. Ylvisaker allocated grants made by forty-seven large foundations over the period from 1955 to 1979 into categories similar to those in my table 7.5. Nelson collected balance sheet information on eighty-eight large foundations to study asset values, payout rates, and expenditures in 1962 and 1981. Salamon and Voytek conducted and analyzed a survey of investment and payout policies of 478 foundations.

tion of the potential value of disaggregated evidence, a brief analysis of such data is presented in section III.

Growth of the Foundation Sector

As a type of charitable institution, foundations date back to at least the Roman Empire; civilizations throughout history appear to have had foundations in one form or another. Although available data are extremely sparse, there does not appear to have been an upward trend in the formation of new foundations in the United States until the twentieth century.[15] Americans did found private foundations in the nineteenth century, but the number was very small.

Rapid economic growth after the Civil War, coupled with the emergence of large corporations and well-developed financial markets, led to a sharp increase in the number of personal fortunes in the United States.[16] The establishment of the federal income and estate taxes during World War I and the estate tax exemption for charitable donations (in 1919) appears to have led to an initial surge in the formation of private foundations.[17] Figure 7.1 charts the dates of establishment of 717 foundations based on a survey from the mid-1950s. There is little evidence of an upward trend in the annual number of foundations founded prior to World War I. After the recession of the early 1920s, however, the foundation growth rate nearly doubled.

The early years of the Great Depression witnessed a sharp fall in the rate at which new foundations were established. Once economic recovery ensued in the mid-1930s, the growth rate rose once again. Foundation growth rates slowed during World War II but increased in the late 1940s and into the early 1950s.

My analysis of figure 7.1 might be criticized, however, because the distribution of dates of birth is derived from cross-sectional data, as opposed to annual records of foundation births.[18] As long as the population of

15. Useful studies of the foundation sector providing historical background are Andrews (1956), Weaver (1967), and Nielsen (1972, 1985).

16. For evidence on the evolution of the distribution of wealth in the late nineteenth century United States, see Williamson and Lindert (1980).

17. I do not wish to suggest that the imposition of an income tax was the sole force behind the initial growth of foundations. Other factors, such as donors' personal motives and rising concern for social welfare during the Progressive era, clearly played an important role; see Karl and Katz (1987, 5–20). Boris (1987, 78–82) provides an illuminating discussion and some survey results on the motives of donors for establishing foundations.

18. Boris (1987) and Rudney (1987) also use cross-sectional evidence on foundation dates of birth to infer long-term trends and cyclical fluctuations.

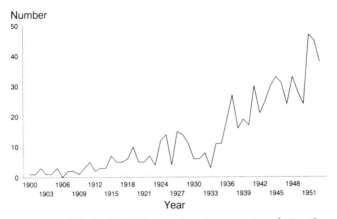

Number

FIGURE 7.1 Dates of Birth of 717 Foundations (Source: Foundation Center 1960, xi)

foundations was growing (which it was), we should expect more foundation births in the late 1940s than in, say, the late 1920s, because the survey represented in figure 7.1 was taken in the mid-1950s. For the pre–World War II period, however, the same annual patterns appear in a survey of 359 foundations taken in 1944 (Harrison and Andrews 1946, 20), suggesting that any cross-sectional bias is small.

Table 7.2 shows distributions of foundation dates of birth by decade, taken from surveys at different points after 1960. From the survey taken in

TABLE 7.2 Distribution of Foundations by
Date of Establishment

| | Date of Survey | | |
Year of Birth	1963	1972	1987
<1900	0.4(%)	0.8(%)	0.7(%)
1900–09	0.4	0.7	0.3
1910–19	1.5	2.3	1.1
1920–29	3.4	4.9	2.3
1930–39	5.7	7.4	2.7
1940–49	32.4	23.9	10.2
1950–59	56.2	40.3	24.4
1960–69		19.6	19.0
1970–79			10.8
1980–87			15.0

SOURCES: 1963: Foundation Center (1963, 13); 1972: Foundation Center (1975, xiv); 1987: Foundation Center (1989, iv).

1963, it might have appeared reasonable to conclude at that time that the growth rate of the foundation sector was accelerating: fully half of the foundations then in existence had been founded in the 1950s. In retrospect, that expectation was clearly premature: the surveys taken in the 1970s and 1980s show *fewer* foundations established in the 1960s and 1970s than in the 1950s. The evidence from the 1980s is not yet in, but there were more foundation births between 1980 and 1987 than in the 1970s.

The post–World War II data demonstrate there was a bulge in foundation births from the early postwar period through the 1950s, and a dearth of new institutions were founded in the 1970s. At the time the bulge was occurring, commentators on the foundation scene attributed it to pent-up demand—a delay in establishment of new foundations resulting from, in part, depression and war—and to high marginal income tax rates in the late 1940s (Foundation Center 1960, xii, xxv; Foundation Center 1964, 15).[19] Many of the independent foundations established in the aftermath of World War II were family-run organizations that began with limited assets and which never grew very large. Numerous firms established company foundations in the early 1950s, allegedly in response to higher corporate tax rates (Foundation Center 1967, 17).

What factors, then, account for the decline in foundation growth during the 1960s and 1970s? One possibility is the Tax Reform Act of 1969. In addition to imposing an excise tax on foundation investment income, the legislation established a minimum payout rate, as well as numerous regulations involving grantmaking and other aspects of foundation behavior. The act, in other words, reduced the incentives for establishing and maintaining a foundation. Compared with the 1950s and 1960s, foundation births in the 1970s were indeed lower; in the next section I will argue that the tax on investment income permanently raised administrative expenses, which may have lowered the growth of foundation assets. However, the fact that the bulge occurred in the late 1940s and early 1950s suggests that the number of foundation births in the 1960s might have been relatively low anyway, whether or not tax reform had been instituted (Clotfelter 1985, 269). Sluggish economic growth in the 1970s may have contributed independently to a slowdown in foundation births. This much is suggested by analogy to the Great Depression and by the fact that foundation growth rates increased once again in the 1980s, when economic growth was ro-

19. Similar conclusions on the effects of business cycles, war, and tax rates are reached by Boris (1987, 82, 91) and Rudney (1987, 190, 196).

TABLE 7.3 Per Capita Foundation Grants:
Decadal Averages

	In 1967 dollars	Percent of Per Capita Income
1930–39	$1.44	0.00088
1940–49	1.23	0.00055
1950–59	2.52	0.00098
1960–69	5.30	0.00170
1970–79	5.73	0.00120
1980–89	6.94	0.00140

SOURCE: 1930–69: calculated from data in U.S. Department of Commerce (1975, 10, 210, 225); 1970–89: calculated from figures for 1972, 1975, 1977, 1979, 1981, 1983, 1985, 1987 in Foundation Center (1989, xxii) and U.S. Department of Commerce (1989, 7, 424).

bust. The recent surge in income inequality (Levy 1987) may have contributed to the establishment of new foundations in the 1980s by increasing the pool of available donors.

Thus far I have examined the growth of foundations in terms of numbers of foundations. Table 7.3 provides additional evidence on the absolute and relative size of the sector. Measured in constant 1967 dollars, annual grants per capita were 4.9 times higher, on average, in the 1980s than in the 1930s. Growth in per capita grants was especially rapid in the 1950s and 1960s and has slowed since then. Foundations grants, however, are (and always have been) a trivial fraction of per capita income and foundation assets a trivial fraction of national wealth.[20] In 1987, for example, I estimate that foundations owned about 0.005 percent of aggregate assets (U.S. Department of Commerce 1989, 458; Foundation Center 1989, v). At the other extreme, were foundation assets confiscated, sold at market value, and the proceeds redistributed to persons below the poverty line, the amount per person would have been $3,427 in 1987.[21] Measured in financial terms, foundations are a very small part of the American economy, but the potential for redistribution is there.

Payout Rates and Administrative Expenses

As defined earlier, the payout rate is the ratio of grants to assets. A very low payout rate may be a signal of excessive administrative costs; or of

20. See Nelson (1987, 130) for a similar conclusion.
21. Calculated from U.S. Department of Commerce (1989, 452–53, 458) and Foundation Center (1989, v). In making this point, I am not suggesting that confiscation was ever a threat, even when the tax exemption for foundations was first established; see Karl and Katz (1987, 9).

low current income, which may be a consequence of poor management; or, of the desire to accumulate assets.[22] A high payout rate indicates that foundations are using the income generated by their assets for charitable ends. A very high payout rate, however, may result in the spending of assets ("invading corpus").

Table 7.4 gives estimates of the average payout rate from the early 1930s to the late 1970s. In the late 1930s and early 1940s, payout rates averaged slightly less than 4 percent of assets. By the late 1950s, the payout rate had risen to over 5.4 percent, and to nearly 6 percent in the mid-1960s. After a brief fall in the early 1970s, payout rates rose until the early 1980s and have declined since that time. The table also shows that, historically, payout rates have been higher for company foundations than for community or independent foundations.[23]

Table 7.4 also contains estimates of foundation administrative expenditures, expressed in cents per dollar of grants.[24] The method by which these administrative cost ratios were derived assumes that administrative expenses equal the difference between total expenditures (which include grants) and grants. Although there is some evidence that this is a reasonable procedure, at least on average, it would be preferable to base estimates on actual accounting data (Foundation Center 1975, xvi). For what they are worth, the estimates show that the ratio of administrative expenses to grants ranged between 7 and 9 percent in the 1960s. The figures for the 1970s and 1980s, however, are about double the 1960s average, displaying no trend after 1972.

Previous studies suggest that the minimum payout rate established by the Tax Reform Act of 1969 may have ratified an upward trend in place before the legislation was passed (Clotfelter 1985, 266). Table 7.4 supports this conclusion, but it also suggests that the excise tax on investment income permanently increased administrative expenses by an amount approximately equal to the tax.[25] Because payout rates were higher in the

22. See Steuerle (1977) for a detailed discussion of these points.

23. The relatively high payout rates for company-sponsored foundations are a consequence of the fact that such foundations receive a disproportionate share of current contributions to foundations (see table 7.1). These contributions derive from employee gifts and firm profits. As is apparent from column 2 of Table 7.4, some of the increase in overall payout rates in the 1970s was due to an increase among company-sponsored foundations.

24. The definition of "administrative" here includes all costs associated with the making of grants, including taxes, compensation of officers, legal fees, and so on. For a detailed accounting of the different types of foundation administrative expenses, see Riley (1989, 33).

25. Similar effects on payout rates and administrative cost ratios were found by Nelson (1987, 161) in his analysis of financial data of eighty-eight large foundations, which he attrib-

TABLE 7.4 Payout Rates and Administrative Cost Ratios: U.S. Foundations, 1937–89

Year	National Average	Grants/Assets (% × 100) By Type of Foundation			Administrative Expense per $ of Grants, National Average (in cents)
		Company	Community	Independent	
1937	4.1(%)				
1940	3.8				
1957	5.4	13.4(%)			9.9
1963	5.4	12.1	4.2(%)		8.7
1966	6.1	13.5	4.0		6.4
1969	6.0				8.7
1972	4.9	13.0	4.2		14.9
1975	6.3	20.1	6.0	5.7(%)	16.3
1977	6.4	19.5	6.8	5.7	14.9
1979	6.4				
1981	7.3	26.9	8.4	6.2	16.3
1983	6.5	26.8	8.7	5.5	16.3
1985	6.0				
1987	5.9	25.0	7.9	5.2	14.9
1989	5.6	15.6	8.0	4.7	17.6

NOTE: Administrative expense = expenditures − grants; see Foundation Center (1975, xvi) for a justification of this calculation; national average refers to all foundations in the sample in the specific year.

SOURCES: 1937: Seybold (1939, 21); 1940: Seybold (1942, 25); 1957: Foundation Center (1960, xiv, xxii); 1963: Foundation Center (1964, 16–17, 22); 1966: Foundation Center (1967, 14–15, 27); 1969: Foundation Center (1971, x–xi); 1972: Foundation Center (1975, xvi–xvii, xix); 1975: Foundation Center (1977, xi, xviii); 1977: Foundation Center (1979, xiv); 1979–81: Foundation Center (1983, xiii); 1983: Foundation Center (1985, vi, x); 1985–87: calculated from Foundation Center (1989, v, xi, xxii); 1989: Foundation Center (1990, vi–vii, xi).

1970s than in the 1960s, one potential consequence was a reduction in the real value of foundation assets. In fact, a reduction did occur; between 1972 and 1979, the real value of foundation assets declined by 30 percent (Foundation Center 1989, xxii). The reduction, however, was not a permanent one. Fueled by economic recovery in the 1980s, the value of foun-

---

uted to the effects of the excise tax and various regulatory burdens imposed on foundations by the Tax Reform Act. The original tax rate was 4 percent of investment income. Recalculating administrative expenses as a fraction of *expenditures*, the average ratio in the 1960s is about 9 percent, while the average in the 1970s is about 13 percent, precisely equal to the tax rate. I say "permanently" in the text because, while the tax rate was reduced to 2 percent in 1978 (Clotfelter 1985, 264), the administrative cost ratios after 1978 are about the same as in the 1972–78 period.

dation assets rose 80 percent between 1981 and 1987 (Foundation Center 1989, xxii).

As a matter of simple arithmetic, it would appear from the evidence in table 7.4 that payout rates *could* be higher, particularly for independent foundations. Nothing prevents a foundation from paying out, say, 50 percent of its assets. Nevertheless, were the typical foundation to do so, it would go out of business very quickly. How high the average payout rate could be, and still avoid widespread self-liquidation, requires some notion of what the long-run, real rate of return to foundation assets is. Recent studies suggest that a plausible estimate of the long-run, real rate of return is about 4 percent (Williamson 1977, 1650–51; Salamon and Voytek 1989). This rate is below the average payout rate because foundations, on average, receive annual contributions equal to roughly 2 percent of assets (Foundation Center 1989, v). Unless independent foundations could dramatically raise the return on assets or cut administrative costs, it is doubtful if payout rates in, say, the 10 percent range could be sustained for the long run. Even so, the minimum payout requirement, currently set at 5 percent, does appear to be consistent with the long-run rate of return and the level of current contributions, without doing serious damage to the growth or size of the foundation sector, measured in terms of numbers or asset values.

III. Expenditure Patterns

As the model of section I suggests, the distribution of foundation grants across the nonprofit sector is crucial for evaluating distributional impact. Aggregate evidence on the distribution of foundation grants by expenditure category from the early 1930s to the late 1980s is shown in table 7.5. As noted in the section II, the data, which are drawn from published compilations by the Foundation Center and its predecessors, should be treated cautiously. In particular, the rules by which grants were allocated to different categories changed over time; specifically, a change in the allocation procedure occurred in 1980 (see below). Despite these caveats, I believe that the relative ranking of categories, as well as broad trends, are useful indicators of foundation spending patterns, in the long and in the short run.

Before World War II, the health category claimed the largest share of foundation expenditures, followed by education and then scientific research. Pre–World War II foundations allocated relatively few dollars to

TABLE 7.5 Distribution of Foundation Grants Across Broad Expenditure Categories

Year	Education	Health	Social Welfare	Scientific Research	Culture	Religion	International Activities	Other
1931	24.9(%)	31.4(%)	12.9(%)	23.4(%)	3.2(%)	0.7(%)	3.4(%)	0.1(%)
1934	27.0	26.8	16.9	21.6	4.3	0.1	3.1	0.2
1937	23.8	35.1	15.0	18.4	4.3	0.7	2.3	0.4
1940	29.0	30.4	13.3	18.8	3.5	3.0	1.7	0.3
1957	46.9	14.2	8.8	15.0	4.2	3.4	7.5	—
1966	23.8	9.4	12.1	10.4	17.7	5.1	21.3	—
	[37.7]							
1970	35.4	15.3	17.2	11.8	10.3	6.4	7.4	—
	[41.3]							
1976	27.0	21.0	23.1	12.1	15.2	1.6	—	—
	(28.9)	(18.8)	(13.8)	(16.6)	(10.8)	(1.6)	(9.5)	
1978	27.0	23.1	24.3	9.9	13.5	2.0	—	—
	(28.3)	(20.0)	(16.1)	(17.2)	(10.6)	(1.9)	(6.0)	
1980	22.4	25.1	24.5	12.1	13.5	2.4	—	—
1982	23.9	20.8	25.9	13.4	14.1	1.9	—	—
1984	17.4	23.7	27.5	15.1	14.0	2.3	—	—
1986	21.9	20.5	26.4	15.2	14.7	1.3	—	—
1988	17.1	20.2	27.0	19.1	14.5	2.0	—	—

NOTE: Figures in [ ]: allocates a portion of international grants to education; figures in ( ): uses pre-1980 allocation rules. Other: miscellaneous plus grants to governments.

SOURCES: 1931–57: Foundation Center (1960, xxviii); 1966: Foundation Center (1967, 36, 39); 1970: Foundation Center (1971, xvi); 1976–78, figures outside parentheses: Foundation Center (1979, xi); 1976–78, figures in parentheses: Foundation Center (1981, ix); 1980–86: Foundation Center (1987, xii); 1988: Foundation Center (1989, xi–xii).

religious organizations, a pattern that has continued to the present. Despite the prominent example set by such institutions as the Russell Sage Foundation, among others, social welfare activities received less than one-fifth of foundation giving. Cultural institutions attracted only 3 to 5 percent of foundation dollars, considerably less than the proportion allocated in the 1970s and 1980s.

By the mid-1960s the allocation of foundation grants toward international activities had increased substantially. A significant portion of such grants, however, were for the purpose of establishing various programs at American universities. Following a suggestion made at the time by the Foundation Center (1967, 39), I have reallocated the educational portion of international grants to the education category. A similar adjustment was made for 1970, assuming that education accounted for the same fraction of international grants as it did in 1966 (74 percent).

The adjusted figures demonstrate that foundations were actually allocating a larger share of grants to education from the late 1950s to 1970 than in the 1930s. Compared with the pre–World War II period, allocations to health and scientific research had fallen, while the share received by social welfare was approximately the same. Grants for cultural activities increased, and there is evidence of a modest rise in grants to religious organizations.[26]

As noted above, the Foundation Center's procedures for allocating grants to expenditure categories changed in 1980. In particular, the international activities category was discontinued, and grants formerly allocated to this category were reallocated to other categories. Other reallocations occurred as well, but I have been unable to determine from published sources precisely what the definitional changes were. Fortunately, estimates of expenditure shares for 1975 to 1979 were prepared using the pre- and post-1980 definitions; thus the consequences of the change in allocation procedures can be observed, albeit for a brief period of time. The figures for 1976 to 1988 without parentheses use the post-1980 allocation procedures. The figures in parentheses for 1976 and 1978 use the pre-1980 definitions.

It is clear that the burst of foundation spending for education in the 1960s had declined by the late 1970s and continued to decline in the

---

26. The very high percentage spent on cultural activities in 1966 reflects the Ford Foundation's record gift ($85 million) to symphony orchestras in that year.

1980s. The share of grants for social welfare and scientific research increased steadily from the mid-1970s to the late 1980s, while the shares allocated to health and culture remained roughly stable.

More detailed distributional evidence for a single year (1988) is shown in table 7.6. The first section of table 7.6 demonstrates that, within the education category, approximately 64 percent (= 10.9/17.1) of grants in 1988 went to higher education. By comparison, adult education, vocational training, and elementary and secondary education received relatively few foundation dollars. In several of the other categories, grants for "general purposes" were most important, reflecting the difficulty (and arbitrariness) of allocating grants for specific purposes. For example, approximately 40 percent of the social welfare category was for general purposes; among grants that can be specifically allocated, the largest relative shares went to community affairs, environmental programs, and urban development.

The second section of table 7.6 offers a different perspective on distribution, in terms of recipient organization. Approximately sixteen cents of every foundation grant dollar in 1988 was given to private universities and colleges, 44 percent of total grants to education. Direct service agencies and medical care facilities received about 29 percent of the dollar value of grants, while approximately 10 percent was allocated to museums and performing arts groups.

Since 1980, data on the distribution of foundation grants to specific population groups has been reported. The final section of table 7.6 shows these data for 1988. As with the first section, it should be kept in mind that a grant is allocated to a specific group only if the group is identified in the grant, or if the organization clearly provides services to members of the specific group.

Approximately 30 cents of every foundation grant dollar in 1988 was allocated to minorities, the elderly, children, and various disadvantaged population groups. To the best of my knowledge, similar aggregate compilations were not made in the 1960s and 1970s. Some fragmentary evidence suggests that the share allocated to these population groups is higher today than in the recent past. Data from 1966 suggest that 0.4 percent of foundation grants was then allocated to the elderly, compared with 2.5 percent in 1984. A study conducted in the mid-1970s discovered that foundation grants to organizations serving Hispanics equaled 0.0037 of total grants between 1962 and 1971 (National Council of La Raza 1977,

TABLE 7.6 Foundation Grants: Detailed Distributions, 1988

By Expenditure Categories	
Cultural Activities	
General	4.5(%)
Art and Architecture	2.9
History	1.0
Language and Literature	1.0
Media and Communications	1.7
Music	1.6
Theater and Dance	1.8
Education	
General	1.2
Adult and Continuing	1.1
Elementary and Secondary	3.6
Higher	10.9
Vocational	0.3
Health	
General	1.1
Medical and Health Education	2.8
Medical Care and Treatment	5.4
Medical Research	4.5
Mental Health	1.9
Public Health	4.5
Religion	
General	1.1
Religious Education	0.9
Natural Science	
General	4.2
Life Sciences	1.8
Physical	1.7
Technology	1.6
Social Science	
General	1.3
Anthropology	0.5
Economics	1.1
Law and Legal Education	0.8
Political Science	6.1
Social Welfare	
General	6.5
Business and Employment Programs	2.6
Community Affairs	3.8
Crime and Law Enforcement	0.8
Environment and Energy	3.6
Equal Rights and Legal Services	2.1
Recreation	2.5
Rural Development	1.6
Urban Development	3.6
TOTAL	100.0%

TABLE 7.6 continued

By Recipient Organization	
Educational Institutions	
Private Universities and Colleges	15.6(%)
Public Universities and Colleges	10.4
Graduate Schools	7.0
Junior/Community Colleges	0.3
Elementary and Secondary Schools	2.5
Direct Service Agencies	23.8
Hospitals and Medical Care Facilities	5.2
Research Institutes	11.7
Associations and Professional Societies	12.3
Museums and Historical Societies	6.3
Performing Arts Groups	3.9
Government Agencies	3.2
Community Funds	2.7
Libraries	2.5
Churches and Temples	0.9
TOTAL	100.0%

By Specific Population Groups	
Elderly	2.5(%)
Alcohol and Drug Absuers	0.5
Children	13.3
Criminal and Ex-Offenders	0.4
Handicapped	2.5
Minorities	
Blacks	1.6
Hispanics	1.6
General and Other	3.4
Women	4.0
TOTAL	29.8%

NOTE: Figures are percentages of total foundation grant dollars.

SOURCE: Foundation Center (1989, xli, xliii, xlv).

1925).[27] Since then, the share of grants to Hispanics has increased, although it is still quite small (1.6 percent in 1988).

Thus far I have examined data on *average* shares. Such data do not necessarily reveal how a marginal change in the level of foundation grants would be distributed across the different categories. To explore the issue of marginal change, I estimated time-series regressions, using annual data

27. Ylvisaker's (1987, 368) sample of forty-seven large foundations, gives similar results for Hispanics, but also suggests that foundation support for organizations serving blacks was somewhat higher in the late 1960s than in the late 1980s. As Ylvisaker points out (p. 369), his sample and the data underlying my table 7.6 are not strictly comparable.

(1976–88) on percentages of foundation grant dollars allocated to particular categories (for example, social welfare).[28]

The results suggest that an increase in the level of foundation grants (measured in per capita terms) would, other things being equal, reduce the shares allocated to health and social welfare.[29] An increase in the level of grants has a positive effect on the share of grant dollars going toward education, the humanities, and scientific research. On this evidence, grants for scientific research, education, and culture are luxury goods; health and social welfare are necessities. Overall, however, the marginal effects are small and generally insignificant statistically, suggesting that the average shares do approximate how an increase in the level of foundation grants would be allocated in practice.[30]

Crude as they are, the data on foundation grant patterns suggest some tentative conclusions. First, the distribution of foundation grants has changed over time and, by inference, may do so again in the future. The increase in college enrollments after World War II, coupled with growing federal involvement in funding medical and scientific research, may account for the relative movements in the education, health, and research categories through the 1970s.[31] Conversely, federal cutbacks in research and social welfare might explain the rising share of foundation spending on both categories since the early 1980s.[32]

Second, the fact that cultural activities and higher education, particularly private colleges and universities, have accounted for a greater share

28. The dependent variables are the percentages of grant dollars allocated to particular categories (from 1976–88), and the independent variables were the real value of foundation grants per capita (1988 dollars) and a time trend. The coefficients of the grants per capita and the R^2's are shown in table 7.A1, in the appendix to this chapter. Because the sample sizes are small and because no account has been taken of possible feedback between the dependent variable and grants per capita (in econometric terms, grants per capita may be endogenous, if foundations respond differently to "permanent" as opposed to "temporary" increases in income), the regression results should be interpreted as provisional evidence, nothing more.

29. Regressions for the religion category are not reported because the share of foundation grants for religious purposes is very small.

30. The average value of grants per capita over the sample period was $8.53. A 25 percent increase in this average value would imply (using the regression coefficients) a 1.9 percentage point increase in the share of grants going to education, a 2.0 percentage point decrease in the share going to social welfare, and 2.1 percentage point increase in the share going to scientific research, a 0.4 percentage point increase in the share going to culture, and a 1.8 percentage point decrease in the share going to health. The implied elasticities are small; less than 0.4, except for scientific research (0.6).

31. The interaction between foundation and public sector expenditures, particularly at the federal level, is stressed by Karl and Katz (1987, 37).

32. Recall that the health category does not include medical research.

of foundation grants than has social welfare, might suggest that foundation grants were regressive in the aggregate. In my opinion, such a conclusion would be very premature, for three reasons. First, while attendance at private universities and colleges is a positive function of income, the distribution of subsidies *within* private institutions (scholarships) is strongly pro-poor (see Chapter 3, this volume). Second, while attendance at cultural activities rises with income, Netzer (chapter 6) found no evidence that the distribution of *net* benefits (that is, benefits adjusted for payments made for services rendered) disproportionately favored the wealthy. Furthermore, the combined shares of education and culture have decreased since the mid-1970s.

Third, the data also show that foundations currently allocate a numerically significant fraction of grants to medical care and human service agencies, many of which provide subsidized services to the poor. For example, according to Lester Salamon's study (chapter 5), the typical client served by a significant fraction of service organizations (27 percent) falls below the poverty line. Scientific research funded by foundations may be a public good, the benefits of which accrue to society at large and, in some cases, disproportionately to low-income groups.

Finally, it is important to stress again that the data on grants are aggregated, which may obscure important distributional effects. In particular, some foundations may be more pro-poor than others; some grants may be pro-poor even if other grants in the category are not. As an illustration of the potential insights that disaggregation can deliver, I randomly sampled twenty-five foundations from the 1990 edition of the *Foundation Grants Index* (Foundation Center 1990b). From this sample, I selected four foundations for detailed study—Fireman's Fund (a company foundation, located in California); the Community Foundation of Washington, D.C.; the McKnight Foundation, located in Minneapolis; and the Andrew Mellon Foundation, located in New York City.[33] The latter two are independent foundations.

I then classified the dollar value of each foundation's grants, as reported in the *Index,* into ten broad categories, as shown in table 7.7.[34] The sum of the figures in these categories equals 100 (the categories are inclusive). I

33. The four foundations were selected randomly, after stratifying the sample into community, company, and independent foundations.
34. The categories differ slightly from those in tables 7.5 and 7.6; the Foundation Center has introduced new categories in its latest *Grants Index,* and I have chosen to use the new categories in constructing table 7.7. Nothing substantive would change if the old categories

TABLE 7.7   Expenditure Patterns: Four Foundations, 1989

Category	Fireman's Fund	Comm. Fund of D.C.	McKnight	Mellon	National Average
Arts/Culture	30.8(%)	13.9(%)	6.8(%)	38.8(%)	14.0(%)
Education	1.8	5.7	4.0	29.0	22.0
Environment	4.1	1.6	0.0	5.9	4.9
Health	6.1	43.4	4.3	3.6	17.3
Human Services	40.5	16.6	45.0	0.6	15.2
Public Benefit/Advocacy	14.3	15.3	30.8	1.0	10.0
Scientific Research	2.4	3.1	0.0	16.6	11.0
International	0.0	0.5	6.3	4.5	3.9
Religion	0.0	0.0	0.0	0.0	1.4
Other	0.0	0.0	2.9	0.0	0.1
Low-Income/Minority	5.4	20.3	46.1	12.9	
	[26.1]	[20.3]	[50.1]	[12.9]	
High-Income	5.7	3.8	0.0	15.6	

SOURCE: Calculated from Foundation Center (1990b, 29–31, 133–34, 308–11, 483–88).

also created a second classification scheme: low-income/minority and high income. A grant was allocated to the low-income/minority category if, on the basis of the information in the *Index*, it was given to an organization specifically providing services to low-income or minority households, or was clearly intended for that purpose. For example, grants for the homeless, for orphans, and for emergency food banks were included in the low-income category, as were scholarships for minority students.[35] The figures in brackets count donations to United Way campaigns in the low-income/minority category; the figures without brackets exclude such donations. The high-income category includes certain grants to arts organizations; in particular, grants to symphony orchestras, ballet, dance, and legitimate theater. I assume that the benefits of such grants accrued largely to higher-income households even though, as previously noted, Netzer (chapter 6)

---

were used (the public-benefit/advocacy and human services categories are equivalent to the social welfare category; "environment" would be classified under social welfare, "other," or, in some cases, under research or international affairs). The classifications into categories are my own, but spot checks of individual grants against the index provided by the Foundation Center (1990b), which also classifies grants, revealed no major inconsistencies. For the most part, the data refer to 1989, although some grants were allocated in 1988.

35. Examples of other types of grants included in this category were grants for child/spouse abuse, for the physically and mentally handicapped, and for low-interest housing loans for the poor. A complete list is available from the author on request.

found that the rich do not benefit disproportionately from the arts net of their own expenditures. Obviously, neither the low-income/minority or high-income categories, as I have defined them, are fully inclusive, but my goal here is simply to explore the uses of disaggregated data on foundation grants, not to defend a particular classification scheme.

The first point to emerge, as noted above, is variation across foundations. For example, Fireman's Fund and the Mellon Foundation allocated a much larger fraction of their grant dollars in 1989 to arts and culture than did the Community Foundation of Washington, D.C., or the McKnight Foundation. Slightly less than one-third of Mellon's grant dollars went for education, the majority to institutions of higher learning; this was a percentage vastly larger than what the other foundations spent. The disaggregated data suggest, as a provisional hypothesis, that the average foundation may be a statistical illusion. Most foundations specialize to some extent, and aggregate expenditure patterns reflect the composition of foundations at any point in time.

Second, all of the foundations, except for Mellon, allocated a larger fraction of grant dollars to the low-income/minority category than to the high-income category.[36] Among the four foundations studied, the most pro-poor was McKnight; close to half of its grant dollars went to organizations serving low-income/minority households. Although most of the low-income grants were given to social welfare organizations, the human services and public benefit/advocacy categories were not synonymous with the low-income/minority category. For example, Fireman's Fund made a $7,500 grant for the purpose of training minority youth to serve as museum guides; the grant was given to a museum (and thus classified under arts and culture), but the immediate beneficiaries were the youths, who received salaries and training. The Mellon Foundation allocated a miniscule fraction of its grant dollars to human services organizations. Yet the foundation also made multimillion dollar contributions to historically black colleges in the South, the United Negro College Fund, and to encourage minority graduate education.[37] It is also noteworthy that, for each of the foundations, less than half of arts and culture grant dollars were included

36. Many of Mellon's humanities grants were given for projects that ultimately should improve the quality of services provided by elite arts organizations. Thus, in Mellon's case, the gap between the high- and low-income figures is probably understated.

37. Grants for minority education comprise the entirety of Mellon's low-income/minority figure, unlike the other foundations.

in the high-income category. Clearly, further work is needed, but this brief analysis suggests the potential value of using disaggregated data in future studies of the distributional impact of foundations.

IV. REGIONAL VARIATION IN FOUNDATION ACTIVITY

The discussion thus far has largely focused on aggregate foundation statistics. There is, however, a regional dimension to foundations. Table 7.8 gives information on the regional distribution of foundation assets in 1954, 1969, and 1988. In the early 1950s, approximately two-thirds of foundation assets were concentrated in the Mid-Atlantic states, primarily New York. Between 1954 and 1969, the Mid-Atlantic share had declined by 15 percentage points; and the share fell by another 15 percentage points between 1969 and 1988. Nevertheless, it is clear that regional differences are still pronounced; measured on a per capita basis, for example, residents of the East North Central states have access to more than twice as much foundation wealth as residents of the South Atlantic states.[38]

A plausible explanation of the initial regional disparity in foundation assets is historical; many of the individuals who established foundations before 1950 either lived or made their fortunes in the Northeast (Foundation Center 1989, x). As the geographic distribution of very wealthy individuals became more uniform spatially and as the institutional form itself became widely known, foundations were established in other regions of the United States. My purpose in this section, however, is not to unravel the historical reasons for the unequal spatial distribution of foundation assets. Rather, I seek to evaluate the following hypothesis. As previously noted, a majority of foundations restrict grants to local organizations. Because large (wealthy) foundations are more likely to have a national focus in making grants, however, grants by such foundations may counteract the unequal regional distribution of foundation assets (Foundation Center 1989, x).[39]

To investigate the hypothesis, I collected state-level data on foundation grants received, foundation assets, and other variables over the period

38. Ylvisaker (1987, 360) also emphasizes regional differences in his analysis of assets and spending patterns of forty-seven large foundations.

39. Even so, locally oriented foundations may give a larger share of grants to social welfare organizations than nationally oriented foundations; this much is suggested by the microdata studied in section III. Having a national focus, in other words, does not necessarily imply that a foundation's grants are pro-poor *within* states, even if the flow of grant dollars is from high-income to low-income states, on average.

TABLE 7.8 Regional Distribution of Foundation Assets

	1954	1969	1988	1988 Per person relative to U.S. average (= 1.00)
New England	3.4(%)	4.0(%)	4.4(%)	0.83
Mid-Atlantic	64.7	50.1	34.9	2.28
East North Central	14.1	18.6	21.2	1.24
West North Central	3.2	4.7	5.0	0.69
South Atlantic	7.2	8.3	9.4	0.54
East South Central	0.8	0.7	1.1	0.17
West South Central	2.9	6.7	8.2	0.75
Mountain	1.1	1.3	2.0	0.37
Pacific	2.6	5.5	15.1	0.91

SOURCES: 1954: Rich (1955, xx); 1969: Foundation Center (1971, x, xi); 1988: Foundation Center (1989, xi); population estimates from U.S. Department of Commerce (1989, xv).

from 1984 to 1986.[40] The grants data pertain to all awards in excess of $5,000 made by foundations included by the Foundation Center in its *Directories*.

Using these data, I estimated three regressions.[41] The first regression documents a key implication of spatial differences in foundation assets: a positive association between assets and per capita income. Because much foundation giving is local, organizations in higher-income states would appear to have access to a disproportionate share of foundation assets.[42]

The second regression reveals that a positive and highly significant association exists between per capita income and grants received. Organiza-

40. Observations for Alaska, New York, and the District of Columbia were deleted for the regressions. Based on preliminary runs, Alaska appears to be an outlier. New York and the District of Columbia were excluded because many nonprofits maintain national headquarters in New York City or in D.C., and because per capita incomes are higher in New York and in D.C.

41. The regression coefficients are reported in table 7.A2. The dependent variable in the first regression is foundation assets per capita. The independent variables are state per capita income and dummy variables for region and year. In the second and third regressions, the dependent variable is per capita grants *received*. The unemployment rate was also included as an independent variable, to test whether foundation grants responded in any measurable way to short-run economic fluctuations over the period. Per capita assets, grants received, and income are expressed in logarithms.

42. It does not follow, of course, that all organizations receiving foundation grants serve a local clientele. For example, a private university in the Northeast receiving foundation grants may educate students from other parts of the United States; its faculty may engage in research benefiting society at large. Still, many organizations receiving foundation grants do serve a local or regional clientele—performing arts groups, or social service agencies, would be examples—thereby justifying an analysis of regional differences.

tions in higher-income states, in other words, receive more foundation dollars than do organizations in lower-income states. The positive correlation between grants received and income, however, may reflect the fact that foundation wealth is concentrated in higher-income states. This possibility was demonstrated by the third regression. Controlling for per capita foundation assets, grants received and per capita income were *negatively* related, confirming the principal hypothesis of redistribution of grants by large foundations toward lower-income states.[43]

Although the distribution of foundation grants is biased toward high-income states, the bias is a consequence of the historical concentration of foundation assets in certain regions, coupled with the local orientation of much foundation grant activity. The behavior of large, nationally oriented foundations, however, appears to offset unequal regional variation in foundation assets, at least in part. To the extent that future growth in foundations will continue to be more broadly diffused geographically, or that more foundations decide to increase the geographic scope of their activities, regional differences in grants received will be further diminished.

V. Conclusion

This chapter examines historical and contemporary data on foundations, with the aim of putting forth a set of working hypotheses about their distributional impact. The size of the foundation sector appears to have been fueled by long-run economic growth and tempered by short-run business cycle fluctuations and variations in federal tax policy. Since the early 1970s, foundations in the aggregate pay out an average of 6 percent of their assets annually, a figure that assures that most foundations will not self-liquidate but which does not appear to lead to excessive accumulation of assets. There have been significant shifts over time in the allocation of foundation grants across different types of expenditure categories. Although only a minority of foundation grant dollars can be readily classified as pro-poor, it would be premature to conclude that foundations were regressive in their impact; low-income households may ultimately benefit

---

43. The income coefficient, however, was small in absolute value and statistically insignificant. The coefficients of the unemployment rate were positive—other things being equal, higher unemployment rates increased the flow of foundation grants to a state, but the effects were small and statistically insignificant. Regional variation in grants received, as indicated by the coefficients of the regional dummies, generally remained large and statistically significant even after controlling for per capita income and foundation assets, suggesting that other factors not included in the regressions influenced the spatial distribution of foundation grants.

from foundation grants for medical and scientific research, and some foundations are more pro-poor than others. Foundation wealth is concentrated in higher-income states, but the behavior of large foundations tends to offset, in part, the unequal regional distribution of assets. The validity of all of these hypotheses, however, rests primarily on aggregate data of uncertain quality. Further detailed study of microeconomic data are necessary to advance our understanding of the economic behavior of foundations and their distributional impact.

APPENDIX

TABLE 7.A1 The Marginal Effect of an Increase in the Level of Grants on the Allocation of Foundation Grant Dollars across Categories

	Mean	Coefficients of Per Capita Grants (in 1988 dollars)	R^2
Education	0.218	0.0087	0.62
Health	0.224	− 0.0082***	0.08
Social Welfare	0.256	− 0.0096**	0.59
Research	0.140	0.0095	0.54
Humanities	0.143	0.0017	0.19

Mean value of per capita grants = $8.53
Number of observations per regression = 13
NOTES: The results of five time-series regressions are reported. The dependent variables are the percentages of total foundation grant dollars allocated to the particular category (e.g., education). The independent variables are the real value of grants per capita (1988 dollars) and a time trend. Observations are weighted by population counts (i.e., the denominator of grants per capita). Regressions were not estimated for the religious category since the share of foundations grants for religion is very small in all years.
* Significant at the 10 percent level.
** Significant at the 15 percent level.
SOURCES: Calculated from data reported in U.S. Department of Commerce (1978–89), sections on "Population" and "Social Insurance and Human Services."

TABLE 7.A2 State-Level Regressions: Assets and Grants

	Dependent Variable		
	Assets per capita	Grants per capita	Grants per capita
Constant	−30.38	−7.98	8.77
	(5.86)	(1.36)	(1.95)
Per capita income	2.97	1.10	−0.54
	(5.50)	(1.84)	(1.17)
Assets per capita			0.65
			(10.94)
Unemployment rate		−5.31	−1.33
		(1.24)	(0.42)
Region:			
Mid-Atlantic	0.98	0.12	−0.60
	(3.57)	(0.46)	(2.88)
East North Central	0.83	−0.03	−0.70
	(3.27)	(0.11)	(3.35)
West North Central	0.26	−0.25	−0.43
	(0.88)	(0.90)	(2.17)
South Atlantic	0.05	−0.74	−0.79
	(0.20)	(2.98)	(4.38)
East South Central	−0.21	−0.90	−0.85
	(0.59)	(2.60)	(3.38)
West South Central	0.70	−0.26	−0.80
	(2.45)	(0.93)	(3.80)
Mountain	−0.19	−0.88	−0.78
	(0.58)	(2.87)	(3.54)
Pacific	0.48	−0.11	−0.54
	(1.94)	(0.42)	(2.76)
Year:			
1985	0.31	0.02	−0.19
	(2.42)	(0.13)	(2.10)
1986	0.40	0.10	−0.16
	(3.00)	(0.85)	(1.69)
N	144	144	144
R^2	0.55	0.38	0.67

NOTES: Absolute value of t-statistics in parentheses. Left-out region dummy is New England; left-out year dummy is 1984. Dependent variables and per capita income are measured in logs. Observations from Alaska, New York, and Washington, D.C., were deleted from the sample; see footnote 40.

SOURCES: Foundation Assets and Grants Awarded: Foundation Center (1985–87), tables on "State Distribution of Grants and Grant Money Reported" and "Fiscal Data of Foundations by Region and State"; Per Capita Income and Unemployment Rate: calculated from data reported in U.S. Department of Commerce (1986–88), sections on "Income, Expenditures and Wealth" and "Labor Force, Employment, and Earnings"

8
Commentaries

Henry J. Aaron
Estelle James
Frank Levy

Commentary

Henry J. Aaron

As our volume editor has requested, my comments are focused on two of the chapters presented here, those by Salkever and Frank and by Netzer. Each is interesting in its own right. Each faithfully addresses the topic of the conference: the distributional consequences of the nonprofit sector. In thinking about distributional effects of various policies, the authors use the incidence framework to which we are all accustomed. I shall suggest that this framework may not be the right one for the problems at hand. I shall also succumb to some musings about the role and function of the nonprofit sector and, more specifically, about the policies that caused the nonprofit sector to be born and to thrive.

In reading the chapters, I found myself thinking repeatedly, "What do these results mean for policy? Should the federal or state governments change their policies? And what should those changes be?"

I. Salkever and Frank on Health

With this set of questions in mind, I found myself sympathizing with the challenge David Salkever and Richard Frank faced in estimating the distributional effects of nonprofit enterprises in the health services sector. Their procedure is straightforward. They divided the health services sector into categories: community hospitals, nursing homes, mental health services, and alcohol and drug treatment facilities. Based on a variety of surveys, they report the differences among nonprofit, profit, and government-owned facilities. They note the differences associated with form of ownership in the income, methods of payment, and other characteristics of patients served. In particular, they focus on the distributional characteristics of "beneficiaries," defined as those who receive subsidized health care services. The conclusion, in general, is that public facilities serve the neediest, for-profit facilities serve the least needy, and nonprofits fall somewhere in between.

The first question is whether such data give any real idea about the distributional effect of the nonprofit health care sector and whether that question even makes sense in the case of health care services. My tentative answer to both questions is: no.

This answer, I want to stress, is no criticism of what Salkever and Frank have written. They took the data at hand, assembled it informatively, and described the patterns they observed.

I have two related reasons for this negative conclusion. The first is that the nonprofit sector is a source of supply, not of demand. What would be the distributional effects of the disappearance or expansion of, say, General Motors? That there would be distributional effects is beyond question. But they would not be indicated, even to a first-order approximation, by differences between the characteristics of purchasers of General Motors cars and those of buyers of other types of automobiles. For similar reasons, one cannot infer the distributional effects of the nonprofit health care services sector from differences between the characteristics of users of that sector and characteristics of users of other health care providers.

In contrast, one could infer something about distribution from differences between the characteristics of users of public facilities and those of users of other facilities. But that inference would have some legitimacy because the public sector facilities are usually heavily subsidized and are often free. In short the "public-other" provider comparison makes sense because it would focus on the effects of demand-side subsidies, not of supply-side quirks.

A second way of looking at the same point is to note that the nonprofit health services sector is part of a system apart from which the nonprofit sector has no particular meaning. The health services sector is a complex of interacting institutions designed to serve a variety of objectives. The importance of the nonprofit sector in the provision of different services ranges from very important to dominant. Were the nonprofit sector to disappear or to expand, distributional effects would surely ensue, just as they would from the disappearance of General Motors. But one cannot reasonably infer from such disappearance or expansion that those whom the nonprofit sector serves would be neglected. Similarly, one cannot infer that if the nonprofit sector were somehow transmuted into for-profit enterprises or into publicly owned facilities, the characteristics of the groups they served would suddenly resemble those now served by for-profit or publicly owned facilities.

But, if one cannot make some such assumption, what do the tables showing differences among the characteristics of those served by different types of facilities really mean? Well, they mean that we have in one way or another allowed facilities with different types of management to assume differing functions. That is interesting to know. It may even tell us something about the sign of the effects on distribution of plausible changes in public policy concerning reimbursement for health care or tax policy; but it gives almost no guidance about the magnitude of the effects.

To illustrate my point, suppose that tax laws were changed so that charitable contributions—to hospitals or any other entity—were allowed only to the extent that total contributions exceeded, say, 5 percent of adjusted gross income. Gifts to nonprofit hospitals might well decline. Suppose further that one could estimate the reduction in the size of the nonprofit community hospital sector and the induced expansion of the for-profit and public sectors. I am willing to bet that no one—and certainly not observers as knowledgeable as David Salkever and Richard Frank—would use the tables presented here to calculate the shift in services by income group or method of payment.

What all of this means is that while it is meaningful to talk of the distributional consequences of the particular method of health care financing and delivery that we have chosen relative to some other system, it is not meaningful to speak of the distributional consequences of a single component. One could as readily speak of the effect on an automobile's horsepower of its water pump. The car has horsepower. To produce it, the car needs something that does what a water pump does. If the water pump isn't there, something else would have to be fashioned to do the job. The alternative might work better or worse. And the horsepower of the car might change. But one wouldn't have a very good idea from observing that the water pump pumps water and that the carburetor vaporizes fuel about what those effects might be. If this analogy is strained, then it may suffice to assert that in some cases partial equilibrium analysis just isn't justified, and that I think this case is one of them.

Salkever and Frank respond to my comment by misconstruing its nature. They assert that I hold that the supply of subsidies provided through nonprofit entities is insensitive to their existence. My criticism of their paper is rather different. I am simply observing that it is unreasonable to assume that if the large majority of hospitals (which happen to be nonprofit) were to disappear, the subsidies those hospitals now convey would disappear.

The current method of paying for health care is remarkably complex. It involves a host of explicit and indirect subsidies. The fee structures and

admitting policies of nonprofit hospitals and other entities depend sensi-
tively on the existence of Medicaid and Medicare and on the widespread
use, at least until recently, of charges well in excess of cost. To think that
one learns much about the distributional significance of the prevalence of
nonprofit hospitals from observing that one type of institution admits
more Medicaid patients than another type of institution strikes me as un-
justified.

If Salkever and Frank had provided data on the differences between payments by or on behalf of various patient groups and the cost of serving
those groups, they would have provided something of enormous interest.
Were data available to do such analysis, I believe they would have done it.
But such data are not available. They did not do that analysis. It is not
legitimate to justify one type of analysis by claiming to be applying another
type of analysis from which one excuses oneself because, as the authors
state, it would require econometric analysis, which they dismiss as beyond
the scope of their study.

II. Netzer on Arts and Culture

The issues Dick Netzer raises in his examination of the distributional effects of the nonprofit sector in arts and culture are unlike those raised by
Salkever and Frank, primarily because he approaches the question of distribution in a way quite different from theirs. He examines the distributional effects of some of the subsidies that companies and individuals engaged in producing art and culture receive. I think that this approach is
informative, and for the life of me I couldn't defend any given alternative
as superior to his. But for reasons to be listed presently, I find the exact
estimates conceptually unsatisfactory.

Some of the subsidies to the arts are conveyed through tax subsidies
linked to nonprofit status, but many are not. Netzer's general approach is
to assume that public subsidies, whether explicit (National Endowment for
the Arts) or indirect (deductibility of contributions to exempt organizations) are financed from a proportional claim on all federal taxes paid. And
federal taxes are assumed to be distributed according to the estimates prepared by Joseph Pechman. Similarly, Netzer assumes that the benefits from
these subsidies are distributed in proportion to attendance at artistic and
cultural events.

I have two comments about this approach. The first concerns the distribution of tax burdens. Netzer cites Pechman's estimates from the mid-
1980s on the distribution of personal and corporation income taxes in

table 6.6. The proportion of taxes paid by Netzer's top bracket is about 45 percent, regardless of incidence assumptions. After looking at similar estimates prepared by the Congressional Budget Office based on Pechman's methods, I surmise that these estimates refer to all taxes or just to personal and corporation income taxes. If so, then Netzer's conclusions about progressivity are strengthened. If one focuses on the loss of revenues from deductibility and assumes that the loss would be made up from higher income tax rates, one should exclude social insurance taxes on the grounds that these taxes are earmarked for a self-financed social insurance system. The share of the top decile of taxpayers in 1988 of individual and corporate income taxes was even higher than Netzer reports, about 50 percent. This number slightly strengthens his conclusion that subsidies to the arts are slightly progressive, a conclusion that arises because the financing is more progressive than the distribution of benefits is regressive.

The second comment concerns the distribution of benefits. Is it really plausible that the benefits of subsidies to the arts are proportional to attendance, as assumed in column (b) of table 6.5?[1] I don't think it is. To accept that conclusion, one would have to believe either of two hypotheses, some weighted average of the two hypotheses, or some alternative (that I shall argue is equally implausible) about what would happen in the absence of subsidy.

According to one hypothesis, attendance and costs of production would be unaffected, but prices would rise by exactly the increase in net costs of production (that is, costs less subsidy). If current subsidies are the same proportion of gross costs of production for events attended by all income brackets, the benefits of current subsidies would be distributed in proportion to attendance.

According to another hypothesis—one that takes consumer surplus into account—attendance would be curtailed by the higher prices but the product of the percentage change in attendance and lost consumer surplus of those who ceased to be attendees would be proportional to attendance under subsidy.

While either of these hypotheses is logically possible, neither is conceptually plausible. Furthermore, as Netzer stresses, many of the benefits claimed for subsidies to the arts are alleged to be external to the actual attendees. If the marginal social costs of subsidies to the arts and culture are roughly equal to the marginal social benefits, a necessary condition for

---

1. Similar comments would apply to the estimates in column (c).

the assumption that total benefits, ignoring consumer surplus, approximately equal total costs, the whole approach of focusing on attendees is flawed.

I would have preferred to see some attempt to estimate what would happen to attendance in the absence of subsidy to the arts. We can be fairly sure that it would have been smaller because higher ticket prices would reduce the quantity demanded. We can also be fairly sure that the fall in attendance would not be proportionately distributed across income brackets. Plausible estimates of attendance losses, I suspect, would have strengthened Netzer's conclusions about overall progressivity of subsidies.

I am less sure about the other distributional effect of reduced subsidies, the change in incomes of producers of art and culture. I suspect, however, that the losses would be larger for the stars, who now receive fees that are mostly economic rents than for the journeymen and journeywomen, who might be driven to higher-paying, if less satisfying, work. However the results might come out, I think that this approach would come closer to giving an accurate picture of how subsidies to the arts and culture change the distribution of income.

III. General Comments

In my opinion, the important questions about the nonprofit sector do not concern issues of distribution but ones of function and control. Religious congregations provide the best example. Our constitution requires the legal separation of church and state. Yet our political system, our views of rights and obligations, and so many aspects of our culture that we cannot even keep track of them are suffused with religion. The United States is the most religiously developed country in the world, measured by attendance at religious services, and there is no close second.

One can, to be sure, estimate the gainers and losers with the traditional instruments of differential tax incidence, as Netzer does, or by assigning to institutions the subsidies users of those institutions receive from public programs and other sources, as Salkever and Frank do. But the real function of the tax advantages to religious institutions is to provide encouragement free of direct administrative or political control to an institution that an overwhelming social consensus has long regarded and still regards, rightly or wrongly, as essential to the formation of the bedrock values of our society and political system. Furthermore, by connecting such subsidies to a legal form that excludes the explicit pursuit of profit by the owners, legislators have tried to enable those controlling such organizations to pursue objectives other than those enforced by the profit motive. Much the same is true of foundations, social service organizations, and educational institutions, as well as cultural and artistic organizations.

In each case, if in varying degrees, the objectives are largely political rather than economic. If one could accurately estimate the distributional effects as economists use the concept, it might be interesting and informative. Even if the objectives of providing tax subsidies linked to nonprofit status are largely political, as I think they are, we might be encouraged to modify policies if there was clear evidence that the effects were powerfully regressive or progressive.

To reach such a conclusion, one would have to be able to point to a clearly defensible "counterfactual," as Clotfelter points out in chapter 1. I am skeptical that one can do so. For this reason, I am skeptical that clear conclusions about the distributional effects of the subsidies linked to nonprofit status are possible.

One is left with the fact that the U.S. government seeks to encourage activities by private nonprofit entities that other countries provide, if at all, through direct government actions. This unique American approach may be a good idea or a bad idea, but the matter rests on judgments about whether services adequately or inadequately meet perceived needs and about whether or not it is desirable to leave control over these activities in the hands of managers who are not subject to political control much more than it rests on inevitably dubious estimates of distributional effects of the actions taken.

Commentary

Estelle James

In my comments, I start by making some general remarks about the definition of net benefits used in these studies and about what our a priori expectations should be concerning the distributional consequences of the nonprofit sector. I follow by making some more detailed comments about the chapters on foundations and human services, in particular, whether their findings are consistent with our predictions.

I. Distribution of Nonprofit Services versus Redistribution through Nonprofit Services

According to Charlie Clotfelter, the conference was interested in the distribution across income classes of the net benefits of nonprofit organizations, that is, the redistributional effects of nonprofits. Net benefits are to be defined in the usual way, as the amount households are willing to pay minus any charges they actually pay.

However, when I read the chapters I found that none of them had used this definition. The reason is not hard to find. We simply do not know how much different households are willing to pay for most nonprofit services.

If we were dealing with private goods that are allocated by price rationing, we would have an observable measure of willingness to pay for the marginal unit: it is the price people actually do pay. Since people pay exactly what they are willing to pay for the last unit purchased, there would be no net benefits at the margin and Charlie's question about the distribution of net benefits would be irrelevant, at least as applied to small changes. (Of course, there could be inframarginal net benefits, and this consumer surplus may differ from one household to another).[1]

In contrast, for public goods, or for private goods that are rationed by nonprice mechanisms (such as first-come, first-served, or SAT scores, or

1. For a discussion of consumer surplus, see chapter 1.

third-party payers and decision makers), there may be net benefits at the margin, since willingness to pay may exceed actual payments for some people but they are unable to purchase more. In this case, Charlie's question about the distribution of net benefits becomes relevant but, ironically, it also becomes difficult to measure because we cannot observe willingness to pay. This is the case with respect to many services provided by nonprofits. Thus, it is not surprising that none of the studies actually use the definition that Charlie proposes.

What then do they do? The most common approach in this situation is to assume that net benefits are proportional to usage and that the distribution of net benefits across income classes is the same as the distribution of usage. This approach is adopted by most of the authors, albeit with a few wrinkles. For example, in the chapters on education, arts and culture, and religion, we find usage patterns by income class, and in the chapters on health and human services, we find data on usage by the poorest groups. For arts and culture, these data are supplemented by information about the distribution of wage benefits that producers (that is, artists) may be receiving; for education, they are supplemented by information about the distribution of public and institutional subsidies; and for religion, a distinction is made between activities that help members and activities that help nonmembers, who presumably have low incomes, but the basic approach taken by all of the authors is to assume that net benefits are proportional to consumption. Most of these studies find that consumption rises sharply with income, casting doubt on the redistributive function of nonprofits.

A basic problem with this approach is that some users receive much smaller net benefits than others, and these differences may be systematically related to income. A simple example makes this point: Based on the income class of users, postsecondary proprietary schools look more redistributive than nonprofit colleges and universities, but in actual fact their net benefits are zero at the margin, since these schools use price rationing. Similarly, movies look more redistributive than operas or concerts, based on usage patterns, although their marginal net benefit also is zero. I summarize below the key problems with the usage-based approach to estimating net benefits. Most (but not all) of these problems have the effect of overstating the net benefits received by the poor; I believe the picture would be more income-biased if appropriate adjustments were made.

First of all, this method is too crude to capture quality differences. If richer people are more adept at getting access to higher-quality services (because they have better information or can afford to pay an incremental fee), aggregate consumption shares understate the quality-adjusted share of total benefits. (For example, it is possible that Medicaid patients, having less choice or information, get lower-quality medical services than privately insured patients).

Second, where nonprice rationing is used, the marginal willingness to pay will exceed actual charges by different amounts for different households. In general, if the goods are normal, for any given quantity the marginal willingness to pay of high income households will exceed that of low income households. Thus, for example, we can assume that upper-class families have a greater willingness to pay for an education at selective colleges than lower-class families, that for any given tuition fee they receive a higher net benefit, and that relative enrollment shares consequently understate the income bias in net benefits. The public and institutional subsidies that are received disproportionately by low-income students imply that they are paying a below-average charge which may compensate for their below-average willingness to pay, but in that case the subsidy is simply helping to equalize net benefits across income classes; it is not necessarily giving an above-average benefit to poorer students.

Third, in most public consumption studies, including the present ones, people are assigned to income classes according to current income rather than permanent income. But many people who "look" poor on the basis of their current income may really be middle class from a longer run point of view; key examples are students and retirees. Indeed, these groups are disproportionate users of nonprofit services, such as health, education, and high culture. In these cases, the use of current rather than permanent income as the measure of economic status overstates the usage of and net benefits received by the poor.

Of course, the opposite may also happen to some extent, but I believe less frequently. The most important counterexample probably concerns higher education, since the parents of college students are likely to be at the peak of their life cycle of earnings (while the students themselves are at the trough). As I have shown elsewhere (James and Benjamin 1987), when we look at the distribution of college enrollments according to parental income, the pattern is very income-biased both at public and private institutions, but this bias drops precipitously when we shift to a permanent income or income-within-cohort measure.

Fourth, along similar lines to this life cycle effect is the social insurance function of services for the poor, such as unemployment compensation or employment retraining. Suppose we think of these services as a kind of social insurance to which we will all have access if our income suddenly drops. From this vantage point, middle and upper classes benefit from the "option demand" for a safety net, even when their income is high and they are not using these services; looking only at current income of actual users understates the share of benefits received by these upper-income groups.

Fifth, it is possible (indeed likely) that producers as well as consumers capture some of the benefits of nonprofit expenditures, for example, by receiving higher wages than they would have otherwise. Only Dick Netzer's chapter takes account of this possibility and in the arts it turns out that producers have a lower income distribution than consumers. In other sectors, such as health and human services, we would probably get the opposite result.

Finally, some of the goods that generate net benefits for users are financed by taxes or philanthropic contributions in lieu of user charges. If these services were provided through the for-profit market, we would find greater use of fees and price rationing, and less reliance on taxation and philanthropy, to cover the cost. It is therefore useful to look at the distribution of taxes and donations as well as the distribution of consumption. It may well be that the upper classes consume a disproportionate share of a service, but they may contribute a still larger share of taxes and donations, in which case the poor are better off than they would be if a shift occurred to the private for-profit price-financed market. Dick Netzer's chapter makes this comparison between share of financing and share of consumption, but most of the others do not. Chapter 1 provides information on the distribution of contributions and taxes that could be used to make similar comparisons for other subsectors.

II. Theoretical Predictions about the Redistributional Effects of the Nonprofit Sector

Besides thinking about the measure of net benefits, and how the results of these studies might change if a more accurate measure were used, I also thought about what we might expect the distributional consequences of the nonprofit sector to be, on a priori grounds. My starting point is an industry with 100 percent fee-financing and free entry. Since pure profits = 0 in the long run, firms in this industry must use price rationing whether they are nonprofit or for-profit, so net benefits are zero for everyone, at the margin. The distribution of usage will depend on the income elasticity of these goods, but there is no redistribution.

Now suppose that there are barriers to entry, so profits exist. Profit-maximizing firms will continue to use price rationing and will generate zero marginal net benefits. Nonprofits, however, must use up these profits in some way, within the organization. For example, they may produce beyond the profit-maximizing quantity or quality or they may charge some or all people less than they are willing to pay, thereby generating positive net benefits. A similar situation arises when selected nonprofits get access to donations or government grants that other firms in the industry do not have. Again, potential profits exist, net benefits may be generated, and we are asking how these net benefits are distributed among income groups.

Of course, the choice by nonprofits about whether to use potential profits to increase quantity or quality or nonprice rationing, and if the latter, how the discount should be distributed, depends on the objective function of the organization. And this, in turn, depends upon the founders and current managers. The desire to help the poor is only one among many competing objectives and there is no a priori reason for it to be a dominant motivation. The distributional consequences of nonprofits is therefore an empirical rather than a theoretical question. (But for further theoretical predictions, see my later comments on Salamon's chapter, particularly my discussion of the objectives of nonprofits that are founded due to government failure or cultural heterogeneity—for example, religious competition.)

Given all of the above, I would expect to find net benefits for the poor only when there are large government grants or barriers to entry, and even then I would not expect to find such redistributions as an important or typical occurrence. In fact, some nonprofits may actually engage in perverse redistributions to the rich, while for-profits could not do this and survive. The evidence presented seems consistent with these expectations about the relative distributional effects of nonprofits versus for-profits. For example, in the health industry, where both institutional forms co-exist, usage patterns are not very different between them, nor does one consistently serve a wealthier clientele than the other.

If we compare nonprofits with public agencies, it is even more difficult to make predictions, since we do not have a generally accepted theory of the state. If a large group of lower- and middle-class people form a dominant coalition, they may indeed be able to redistribute away from the very wealthy, and public services will have a pro-poor bias. On the other hand, if the middle class forms a coalition with the wealthy, public service may be heavily consumed by the rich. Perhaps most likely is a small amount of tax-financed redistribution, since this helps the poor directly and also helps the rich indirectly by reducing the probability of crime or revolution. One way to provide a small amount of redistribution is to do so through publicly produced services for the poor, which are constrained both in quantity and quality, while the rich purchase better quality substitutes from for-profits or nonprofits (as in the fields of health and education). Another way is to give small grants to public agencies and nonprofits which enable them to serve the poor, but only to a limited extent, as in the social services field. In both examples, redistribution is positively associated with public funding, but the political equilibrium makes a relatively small amount of public funding available for this purpose. Moreover, in both examples public agencies are more likely to serve the poor than nonprofits, but the latter have a well-defined role in the institutional arrangements that permit some redistribution to take place. This seems to be the pattern in the United States, judging by the evidence in this volume.

I move on now to the two chapters on foundations and human service organizations, which I was specifically asked to discuss.

III. Margo on Foundations

The chapter on foundations was heroic, in view of the data problems. I think Margo made surprisingly good use of the limited information available. His study left me with the view that foundation grants are less favorable to upper-income groups and more tilted toward social welfare activities than I would have expected.

I have a small question about the determinants of the payout rate and its changes through time. Suppose that annual foundation expenditures depend, in part, on the current rate of return, which may deviate from the long-term rate. Then, in periods when the rate of return is high, foundations would have a high payout rate (ratio of grants to assets), because they would be spending (part of) their transitory income, and vice-versa. Would incorporating this variable help explain changes in the payout rate over the time period covered here?

I also have a further thought regarding the regional distribution of grant recipients. It seems likely to me that this is strongly influenced by the prior location of organizations, such as colleges and museums, that are major recipient categories. That is, grants may go to the Northeast not because foundations are located there, but because many private colleges and museums were located there long before they got foundation grants and constitute a "demand for foundation grants" variable. Furthermore, perhaps foundations and recipient nonprofits were both motivated by the same unobserved forces—such as cultural heterogeneity, an ethic of self-reliance, etc.—while other (more homogeneous) regions provide similar services to their residents through the public sector and have a lower "demand for foundation grants." If this is the case, regional inequalities in foundation assets and grants will remain in long-run equilibrium, even if they are somewhat diminished in magnitude.

IV. SALAMON ON SOCIAL SERVICES

Salamon makes several very important points:

1. Relatively few clients of nonprofit human service organizations are poor; over one half of all agencies in the Urban Institute survey reported few or no low-income clients (see table 5.7).

2. The government is the single largest funder of nonprofit human service agencies. (Incidentally, in other countries government plays an even larger role.)

3. There is a positive relationship between public funding and provision of services for the poor, suggesting that public funding is more pro-poor than private funding and that the poor would suffer disproportionately if public funding were cut.

I have a minor quibble with Salamon's interpretation of his data. He claims that "government spending . . . outdistances the spending of nonprofit organizations by a factor of 2.5 to 1." But if we subtract income transfers and look only at provision of social services, we find that the government spends $25 billion while nonprofit human service agencies spend $37 billion, of which $10 billion comes from private philanthropy (see table 5.4). From table 5.5, I estimate that about $14 of the $25 billion in public funds goes to nonprofit agencies and is therefore included in the $37 billion which they spend. I would summarize this situation by stating that government provides most of the finances within the category that Salamon calls "human services," but the bulk of this is used for income transfers while, in contrast, most of the services are delivered by nonprofits. Although government is the single biggest source of nonprofit funds in this area, philanthropy is a close second. This is a much more favorable view than Salamon's of the nonprofit sector's role in providing human services and mobilizing private funds.

My more serious problem with Salamon's paper, however, concerns the section which presents and tests alternative theoretical explanations for his findings. The theories he presents are not mutually exclusive; it is possible that they might all contribute some explanatory power. I applaud his efforts to test theory, which is exactly what should be done, but I disagree with his interpretation of these theories and his specification of tests; consequently, I believe that this analysis does not allow us to draw the stated conclusions.

Let me start by restating what Salamon calls "voluntary failure theory," which is really very close to "market failure." The argument is that voluntary contributions will not provide an efficient or Pareto-optimal amount of redistribution because of the free rider problem. In addition, some people may want to force others to redistribute on equity grounds beyond the amount dictated on efficiency grounds, and that obviously won't take place on a voluntary basis. Government intervention is one way societies have of overcoming free rider problems, as well as the desire of the rich to retain what they have, and compelling redistribution. This is a classical welfare theory argument for public finance.

Although voluntary or market failure arguments are designed to tell us what governments *should* do, one problem is that they do not tell us what governments *will* do. For example, voluntary failure does not guarantee government desire to redistribute to the poor; in many countries it turns out that government spending is pro-rich rather than pro-poor (see Birdsall and James 1990). Also, voluntary failure does not tell us how important redistribution is versus other reasons for government spending. Even if redistribution is one goal, we may observe income-neutral spending overall because other goals conflict. Finally, voluntary failure does not tell us whether governments will achieve their redistributive goals by providing services or cash, by spending through public agencies, or by subsidizing private agencies. Thus we could observe a wide range of public spending on the poor and nonprofit involvement with the poor, none of which would be incompatible with voluntary failure theory. Nevertheless, while not testing a theory, Salamon's data are consistent with the view that public spending on human services is motivated, in part, by the desire to alter the income distribution achieved by the voluntary market, and one of the major mechanisms used is service delivery through nonprofits. (This should be placed in the broader context that most other types of government spending, such as defense, education, health, probably benefit other income groups more heavily.)

I move on to a second theory, which Salamon labels market failure/government failure. It should be clear that "voluntary failure," as just described, subsumes the concept of "market failure." Therefore I shall concentrate here on the "government failure" part of the argument. This theory was developed first by Weisbrod (1977); further theoretical elaborations and empirical tests are cited in James and Rose-Ackerman (1986). The main point is that, since people are not all identical, and perfect compensation is not practiced in the real world, some people will not be completely satisfied with what government is doing to remedy market failure. Government spending replaces some private spending but does not crowd out all private spending if the marginal private benefit from additional spending exceeds the price for some people. Those who derive private utility from redistributing to the poor, for example, may be willing to make voluntary contributions to supplement government contributions. They are likely to make these contributions to nonprofit organizations, rather than to for-profits or governments, to facilitate monitoring and enhance the probability that their contributions will indeed reach the intended beneficiaries. This theory does not predict that nonprofits will be more redistributive than government but it does predict greater use of private charity where government support to the poor is lowest, *ceteris paribus*.

The *ceteris paribus* condition is essential, but unfortunately it is forgotten in Salamon's analysis. This theory could be tested in a multiple regression analysis across localities and/or over time, with total private contributions to nonprofit agencies that primarily serve the poor (expressed per capita or as a percentage of disposable income) as the dependent variable; the main independent variable would then be government spending on the poor, with various indicators of poverty and other social problems (for example, percentage of families living below the poverty line, percentage of families with single female heads of household, crime rate, drug rate, etc.) as control variables. Holding these poverty and problem indicators constant, government failure theory predicts a negative relationship between pro-poor public spending and pro-poor private contributions (unless an observable "taste for redistribution" causes both of these to move together, as it might if the Tiebout hypothesis[2] is operating).

Salamon's first empirical test of the theory, however, is quite different from this multiple regression test and is based on the simple differences

2. The Tiebout hypothesis argues that different communities will offer different packages of taxes and local public goods and people will choose to live in the community offering the package they most prefer, together with other people who have similar tastes. In that case, people with strong redistributive preferences may live in communities that have high amounts both of public spending and private contributions, so these two would be positively, not negatively related (see Tiebout 1956).

between urban and rural areas. Public social welfare programs are less generous in rural areas; Salamon claims that government failure theory would therefore predict greater nonprofit attention to the poor in rural areas (as measured by the percent of human service agencies serving clients with low or no income). In fact, nonprofits are not more attentive to the poor in rural areas, so this version of the theory is not supported. Unfortunately, this test is quite different from the one proposed above, both in its choice of dependent variable and, even more so, in its lack of controls for any poverty indicators. Rural areas may have less pro-poor public and private spending precisely because they have fewer poverty problems. I don't believe the urban-rural comparison, as presented, tells us anything about the validity of government failure theory.

As a second test, Salamon looks at the relationship between source of income and probability that the agency is serving the poor. He claims that the government failure paradigm would predict greater nonprofit attention to the poor in agencies with less government support and more private support. Since his data show a positive relationship between degree of government support and poverty of clientele, and no relationship between degree of government support and poverty of clientele, he claims this further invalidates the government failure argument.

However, I question this interpretation. Government failure theory does not dispute the possibility that public spending may be redistributive, nor does it say anything about the mix of public and private funds at agencies serving the poor. I will give a little example to illustrate this point. Suppose that some people are dissatisfied with government spending for the poor and also with government spending for low-income working groups and therefore make voluntary contributions for both of these purposes, in equal proportions, spread across many agencies. This action fits the government failure paradigm. Public spending, too, serves many purposes and many different groups (for example, in higher education it benefits the middle and upper classes), but in the human service area it is strictly targeted toward agencies serving the poor and does not serve lower-income workers. This would produce the pattern we observe in tables 5.11 and 5.12. These data, therefore, are entirely consistent with government failure theory (as well as with voluntary failure theory).

The "supply-side" theory of nonprofit formation is the third theory considered in Salamon's paper. One supply-side theory, with which I have worked, predicts that religious heterogeneity and, to a lesser extent, other types of cultural heterogeneity (along linguistic or nationality lines) will lead to more nonprofit service providers in contrast to public providers, as each religious (cultural) community tries to retain its own members and attract new members. This theory does not make any prediction as to whether the resulting nonprofit activities will be progressive or regressive. Data from many countries, including the United States, confirm that nonprofit activity in the field of education is indeed greater in areas with more cultural, particularly religious, heterogeneity and that these nonprofits serve a very mixed income clientele (see James and Rose-Ackerman [1986] for a fuller description of this theory; see James [1987 and 1991], and James and Benjamin [1987], for empirical tests). It would have been interesting to use Salamon's data, together with information about the cultural composition of different communities, to test whether there is also greater reliance on nonprofit human service agencies (as opposed to public human service agencies) in areas with greater religious (or linguistic or ethnic) heterogeneity. However, this was not done in the present study.

While Salamon does not test this supply-side theory, he does propose and test another theory: that religious nonprofits are more likely than secular nonprofits to be pro-poor. The motivation for this theory is not clear to me and, on a priori grounds, I would argue for something quite different. Since the "religious heterogeneity" supply-side theory mentioned above posits that religious organizations found nonprofits in a competition for members, group identification and loyalty, I would expect them to serve all income groups and not to focus on the poor. In fact, these founders might be more interested in attracting and retaining the rich and middle class, who are powerful and prestigious, than the poor (as in elite schools and universities in other countries that are run by religious orders), although some pro-poor activities might be implemented as a kind of social insurance for the group as a whole. Consistent with my expectations and contrary to his, Salamon finds a weak negative relationship between religious affiliation and pro-poor client focus.

I also have some questions about Salamon's test of organization theory, with which I am less familiar. This theory (according to Salamon) states that professionals are less likely than amateurs to be pro-poor. Let us assume for a moment that this is true. But suppose that, due to market failure, public funds are needed for pro-poor activities. Suppose further that agencies with public funds are more likely (indeed are often required) to hire professionals. Then, at the very least, this test of organization theory would have to control for government funding. In other words, I believe the entire discussion that looks at bivariate relationships is not very helpful and one must immediately go to multivariate regression, as in table 5.18. But even here problems arise. For example, if there is a high degree of multicollinearity between professionalization and government funding, it would be difficult to separate out these effects.

V. Final Thoughts

In sum, Salamon has collected valuable data and has moved us in the right direction by testing theories with these data. His data provide convincing evidence that we cannot rely on voluntary actions and organizations to bring about substantial redistributions to the poor; government funding seems to be necessary for that (although it also seems that government funding for this purpose is very limited in the United States, probably because voters who "have" don't favor policies that give generously to "have-nots"). This evidence is consistent with the theoretical predictions developed in the first part of my comment.

The clear implication of Salamon's chapter, as well as of the others in this volume, is that when people make voluntary payments to nonprofit organizations, they generally do so with the object of getting some private benefit in return. A minority of people may contribute altruistically to organizations serving the poor, and some nonaltruistic activities may generate externalities as a byproduct, but redistributive externalities are not the primary aim of a voluntaristic system. Thus, while government failure and supply-side theories help explain what nonprofits do and where they are found, these theories do not predict that privately funded nonprofits will be very redistributive, and indeed, empirically, privately funded nonprofits do not seem to be as redistributive as publicly funded activities, even in the social service field. However, publicly funded nonprofits play an important role in delivering social services (as well as educational and health services) to the poor and, in that sense, are crucial components of the complex institutional structure in this country that permits some (limited) redistribution to take place.

Commentary

Frank Levy

I was, I think, chosen to be a commentator for this volume because I know something about the income distribution. I know little, however, about the nonprofit sector; so reviewing these studies required me to try to think through the nature of the sector, the nature of the outputs, and the goals one might have for these chapters. A good starting point was the objective Charlie Clotfelter laid out in chapter 1: "the studies in this volume should be seen as relevant to incremental changes in the size of the nonprofit sector or its components. . . . What would be the distributional effects of such incremental changes in the extent of the sector?"

The answer to this question varies substantially across "components" (Charlie's word), because the alternatives to a nonprofit provider differ so much from one component to the next. In the case of secondary education, the alternative to a nonprofit is typically a neighborhood public school with near monopoly power. In the case of postsecondary education, the alternative to a nonprofit is a much wider array of public institutions as well as some private schools. In the case of organized religion, the alternative is . . . ? A cup of coffee with a friend? Volunteer service at the Red Cross? A visit to a local tavern? A session with a psychiatrist? I recognize, however, that the difficulty in commenting on this volume is dwarfed by the difficulty in writing it, so I press on.

I. Schwartz and Baum on Education
Secondary Education

For my own benefit (if not for the rest of you), it is useful to begin with the basics of secondary education. For the purposes of this volume, secondary education is best thought of as a commodity like an undergraduate's meal. Some undergraduates don't care much about food (or do care, but are income constrained). They will eat whatever the dorm serves them. Others will spend the extra money to eat off-campus or to cook in their own apartments. Similarly with education, some parents take the local school's offering because they want to or because they cannot afford to do otherwise. Others will spend significant amounts of money to move to a favored school district or to place their child in a nonpublic school. In this view, the nonprofit nature of schools subsidizes the price of the nonpublic producer. The subsidy, such as it is, comes through the encouragement of charitable contributions. The tax-exempt status of school profits is of little concern, since there aren't many profits to begin with.

What, then, are the hedonic components of this commodity that parents want to purchase? Three aspects are apparent:

1. A course of instruction (including, possibly, the teaching of moral or religious precepts).
2. A level of skill in instruction.
3. A set of governing expectations for the school, covering areas as diverse as the amount of homework, appropriate dress, aspirations for graduates, and the likelihood that a student can go to the bathroom without being mugged.[1]

I suspect (without much knowledge) that secondary schools vary at least as much on the third aspect as on the first two. How does a school produce this third aspect? We have all heard stories about principals who can create high expectations in the worst of circumstances.[2] But high expectations are much easier if the students (and, equally important, the parents) have high expectations at the outset. In this sense, the nonprofit nature of nonpublic schools is subsidizing the price of segregation with likeminded persons. (The much noted ability of such schools to expel undesirable pupils is a reenforcement of this process.)

What do they get for their money (besides the expectations)? The evidence on Catholic schools, reviewed by Schwartz and Baum, suggests they get some amount of at least three outputs. In presenting these outputs, it is useful to define an "adjusted public school rate" as an output (such as a

---

1. These items, of course, can vary independently. Last year, our family was on leave and my two children went to a private school that had an outstanding academic program, that was entirely safe, and that prohibited flashy, "competitive" clothes. But the dress code only extended as far as the ankles and my 11-year-old son and each of his friends knew precisely where their sneakers stood in the social hierarchy.

2. See, most recently, Richard Louv, "Hope in Hell's Classroom," *New York Times Sunday Magazine*, November 25, 1990, p. 30 ff.

dropout rate) in which the public school rates within income classes have been reweighted by the income distribution of Catholic school students.[3]

1. A higher chance of completing high school.
   Public School Dropout Rate = 14.4 percent
   Adjusted Public School Dropout Rate = 11.6 percent
   Catholic School Dropout Rate = 3.3 percent

2. Higher Postsecondary matriculation rate (two-year and four-year colleges).
   Public School Matriculation Rate = 45.2 percent
   Adjusted Public School Matriculation Rate = 48.8 percent
   Catholic School Matriculation Rate = 67.4.

One can argue, of course, that these outputs should be credited to the self-selected students rather than to the Catholic schools themselves. The simple version of this argument carries over from the evaluation of a manpower training program with volunteer applicants. There, it is properly argued, one cannot automatically credit the participants' success to the program. The fact that the participants volunteered for the program suggests they may have particularly high motivation and they would have succeeded in any case.[4] Applying this reasoning to the case of Catholic schools has several implications, not all of them necessarily correct:

1. The students in Catholic secondary schools (and/or their parents) are particularly interested in education, holding observable characteristics constant.

2. These students would have done better in public schools than one would have predicted on the basis of observable characteristics.

3. Catholic schools would not have shown comparable gains if they had to work with a random selection of public school students (that is, random with respect to their interest in education).

The first and third statements are undoubtedly true. The second statement is open to question. Many people who have recently spent time in high schools (including me) would argue that "going with the flow" is a powerful force and a student in a demoralized school who wants to study

---

3. In an earlier version of the Schwartz-Baum paper, Catholic schools also showed small positive differentials in writing and with math gains even when family income was held constant.

4. More precisely, these volunteer applicants may be far more motivated than eligible persons who don't volunteer, but the two groups may be identical in their age, education, and other observable characteristics that might be recorded by the agency. A standard statistical analysis would not be able to observe the motivation and would credit all successes to participation in the program.

must be very strong because he or she will have to give up many of his or her friends.[5]

In sum, I am arguing that expectations are an important part of schools, that expectations involve substantial externalities, and so when people purchase segregation with likeminded students, they are purchasing real output.[6]

Allowing my argument that the benefit is real, what then is its distribution across income classes? As I read Schwartz and Baum, they do not attempt to address this question. Not that it is an easy question to answer. If a Catholic school education were free, one could simply look at the income distribution of enrollees, perhaps adjusting for the fact that the education *may* have more benefits for lower- than higher-income students. But, of course, a Catholic School education is far from free. To the contrary, it has been a long grievance of many Catholic school parents that they pay for schooling twice: once through taxes for the public schools, which their children don't use, and again for the Catholic schools, which their children attend. At the same time, I have heard many anecdotes about dioceses that maintain schools in poor areas out of social responsibility at the cost of large subsidies. Unless Schwartz and Baum can come up with evidence, even in one metropolitan area, as to who pays what, the distribution of benefits will remain a mystery.

Postsecondary Education

Here, unlike the case of secondary education, Schwartz and Baum are much closer to the volume's stated goals. The difference, of course, is that in this case the data exists (or can be put together) that begin to answer the questions they are asking.

First, it is easier to conceptualize what the output is. Postsecondary education has always been characterized by much more choice than secondary education. Putting aside, for a moment, the utility of psychic income, it is reasonable to postulate that people go to college to make money and they choose one college over another because it appears to make more sense to them on a benefit-cost calculation. Some persons argue, for example, that

5. After the conference was held, George Akerlof made a similar point in his Richard T. Ely Lecture at the 1990 American Economic Association Meetings. Applying concepts of psychology, Akerlof argues that the "salience" (that is, the vividness) of immediate disapproval of friends may make it appear to outweigh the benefits of academic rewards in the future.

6. As one of the conference participants put it, a school's enrollment is partly endogenous—that is, created by its students—rather than entirely external to them.

people are willing to pay Ivy League tuitions for the signal an Ivy League college attaches to them and the connections they will make (self-segregation again). But both the signal and the valued connections ought to show up in earnings differentials. The authors note that no data set is ideal for this purpose—where ideal means both long work histories (to observe stabilized earnings patterns) and details regarding the institution attended. But as the authors also note, Estelle James and her colleagues have done one good study of this kind and others may be forthcoming (see James et al. 1989).

At the same time, and again unlike secondary schools, studies exist which begin to nail down the kind of subsidy received by different kinds of college students at different institutions. Without asking the impossible, it is worth trying to get as finegrained a distinction as possible in this regard. As the authors say in their review of earnings studies, a simple public versus private comparison is unlikely to have significant effects in part because it lumps too many things together.

In sum, it appears that Schwartz and Baum are on their way to being able to say something about the distribution of both subsidies and benefits of postsecondary education. There is, however, one caution I would raise. At two points, they quote a finding by Leslie and Brinkman (1988) to the effect that "the relative progressivity of the higher education is highest in states where there is a large private sector, attracting students from higher-income families. In other words, the existence of the private sector increases the progressivity of publicly funded institutional subsidies."

The authors seem to interpret this as a bonus byproduct of the nonprofit sector. I am not so certain. My own sense is that these results are driven by New England and Middle Atlantic states where the private universities got there first, as it were. While the public universities in these states may be relatively progressive, it is worth nothing that none of these states contain a crown jewel public campus on the order of a Michigan-Ann Arbor, a Wisconsin-Madison, or a California-Berkeley.

II. Biddle on Religion

Let me turn to the chapter on religion, where Jeff Biddle has done a nice job of beginning to lay out what religious organizations do. In his study, he finds that religious organizations perform two broad kinds of activities: "club" activities that largely benefit members and charitable activities that typically benefit persons outside the organization. He estimates that approximately 70 percent of church activities are of the club kind. These benefit church membership whose income distribution is not much different than that of the population as a whole, so these activities involve little redistribution. Charitable activities make up the other 30 percent of church budgets and, to the extent they can be measured, are significantly focused on lower-income groups.

In the end, however, I am not sure what to make of all of this. Suppose that churches practiced no philanthropy and that there was no redistribution in the standard way we measure such things. Would that mean that there would be no adverse consequences of eliminating the tax break for religion? Biddle begins to touch on this point in his section on externalities. He cannot cite many respectable social science studies on these externalities—that doesn't surprise me—but it proves very little. Think about the institutions that transmit values in this society: religion is one, certain kinds of schools may be another, the market is a third, politics is a fourth. As I see it, we are now concluding a ten-year experiment in taking moral direction from a particular version of the market. According to some, it has involved a movement toward self-reliance, and I am all for that. But mixed in with that self-reliance has been a kind of hypercompetitive ethos that has focused on short-run gain.

The term "short run" is important here. An individual interested in long-term growth is, by necessity, interested in the development and maintenance of institutions. In the 1980s, by contrast, it became fashionable to recontract frequently, moving to the highest bidder of the moment, while allowing institutions to somehow take care of themselves. Given what I view as the consequences of this behavior, I believe society benefits from exposure to other behavioral models—in particular, a model emphasizing a longer-term view of life—even if it is to no one's immediate profit to expound such views. In this sense, religious institutions play a useful role regardless of their distributive impact.

To sum up, it seems that in education, churches, and most other "components" of the nonprofit sector, the distribution of outputs is interesting insofar as they highlight abuses—for example, museums that really serve only as tax write-offs for rich art collectors—but redistribution is neither a necessary nor sufficient condition for such organizations to be useful to society.

References

Aaron, Henry, and Martin McGuire. 1970. "Public Goods and Income Distribution." *Econometrica* 38: 907–20.

Allport, G. W. 1966. "The Religious Context of Prejudice." *Journal for the Scientific Study of Religion* 5: 447–57.

American Association of Fund-Raising Counsel. 1990. *Giving USA: The Annual Report on Philanthropy for the Year 1989*. New York: AAFRC Trust for Philanthropy, Inc.

American Hospital Association. 1983. *Hospital Statistics*. Chicago: American Hospital Association.

———. 1988. *Hospital Statistics*. Chicago: American Hospital Association.

———. 1989. *Hospital Statistics*. Chicago: American Hospital Association.

Anderson, James, 1987. *The Education of Blacks in the South, 1860–1935*. Chapel Hill: University of North Carolina Press.

Andreoni, James. 1988. "Privately Provided Public Goods in a Large Economy: The Limits of Altruism." *Journal of Political Economy* 35: 57–73.

Andrews, F. Emerson. 1956. *Philanthropic Foundations*. New York: Russell Sage Foundation.

Bailey, Anne. 1989. "Private Health Clubs Assail Tax Exemptions of 'Yuppie' YMCA's with Fancy Facilities." *Chronicle of Philanthropy* (May 30).

Baum, Sandra, and Saul Schwartz. 1986. "Equity, Envy and Higher Education." *Social Science Quarterly* 67, no. 3 (September): 491–503.

Baumol, William J., and William G. Bowen. 1966. *Performing Arts—The Economic Dilemma*. New York: Twentieth Century Fund.

Beatty, K. M., and O. Walter. 1984. "Religious Preference and Practice: Reevaluating Their Impact on Political Tolerance." *Public Opinion Quarterly* 48: 318–29.

Beck, Dorothy Fahs, and Mary Ann Jones. 1973. *Progress on Family Problems: A Nationwide Study of Clients' and Counselor's Views on Family Agency Services*. New York: Family Service Association of America.

Benson, John M. 1981. "The Polls: A Rebirth of Religion?" *Public Opinion Quarterly* 45: 576–85.

Bethell, Tom. 1978. "Welfare Arts." *The Public Interest* 53: 134–38.

Birdsall, Nancy, and Estelle James. 1990. "Efficiency and Equity in Social Spending: How and Why Governments Misbehave." Washington, D.C.: World Bank Working Paper WP5 274.

Bixby, Ann Kalman. 1990. "Public Social Welfare Expenditures, Fiscal Years 1965–1987." *Social Security Bulletin* 53 (2):10–26.

Boris, Elizabeth. 1987. "Creation and Growth: A Survey of Private Foundations." In *America's Wealthy and the Future of Foundations,* ed. Teresa Odendahl, pp. 66–92. New York: The Foundation Center.

Brennan, Geoffrey. 1976. "The Distributional Implications of Public Goods." *Econometrica* 44: 391–99.

Brenton, Maria. 1985. *The Voluntary Sector in British Social Services.* London: Longman.

Carey, Sarah. 1977. "Philanthropy and the Powerless." In *Research Papers,* Commission on Private Philanthropy and Public Needs, Vol. 2, pp. 1109–64. Washington, D.C.: Treasury Department.

Carson, Emmett D. 1990. "Patterns of Giving in Black Churches." In *Faith and Philanthropy in America,* ed. Robert Wuthnow, Virginia A. Hodgkinson, and associates, pp. 232–52. San Francisco: Jossey-Bass.

Catholic Charities USA. 1990. *1989 Annual Survey Report.* Washington, D.C.: Catholic Charities USA.

Chubb, John E., and Terry M. Moe. 1990. *Politics, Markets and America's Schools.* Washington, D.C.: The Brookings Institution.

Clotfelter, Charles. 1985. *Federal Tax Policy and Charitable Giving.* Chicago: University of Chicago Press.

———. 1990. "The Impact of Tax Reform on Charitable Giving: A 1989 Perspective." In *Do Taxes Matter? The Impact of the Tax Reform Act of 1986,* ed. Joel Slemrod, pp. 203–35. Cambridge, MA: MIT Press, 1990.

Clotfelter, Charles T., and C. Eugene Steuerle. 1981. "Charitable Contributions." In *How Taxes Affect Economic Behavior,* ed. Henry J. Aaron and Joseph A. Pechman, pp. 403–37, Washington, D.C.: The Brookings Institution.

Cloward, Richard A., and I. Epstein. 1965. "Private Social Welfare's Disengagement from the Poor: The Case of Family Adjustment Agencies." In *Social Welfare Institutions: A Sociological Reader,* in M. N. Zald, pp. 623–43. New York: John Wiley and Sons, Inc.

Coleman, James S., and Thomas Hoffer. 1987. *Public and Private High Schools.* New York: Basic Books.

Coleman, James S., Thomas Hoffer, and Sally Kilgore. 1982a. "Cognitive Outcomes in Public and Private Schools." *Sociology of Education* 55 (April/July): 65–76.

———. 1982b. "Achievement and Segregation in Secondary Schools: A Further Look at Public and Private School Differences." *Sociology of Education* 55 (April/July): 162–82.

———. 1982c. *High School Achievement: Public, Catholic and Private Schools Compared.* New York: Basic Books.

College Board. 1988. *Trends in Student Aid: 1980 to 1988.* Washington, D.C.: The College Board.

Commission on Private Philanthropy and Public Needs. 1975. *Giving in America.* Washington: The Commission.

Congressional Research Service. 1988. *Medicaid Source Book: Background Data and Analysis.* A Report Prepared for the Subcommittee on Health and the Environment of the Committee on Energy and Commerce, U.S. House of Representatives; 100th Congress, 2d session, Committee Print 100-AA, November 1988. Washington: U.S. Government Printing Office.

Cooperative Institutional Research Program. 1989. *The American Freshman: National Norms for Fall 1989.* Los Angeles: UCLA Higher Education Research Institute.

Crean, J. 1975. "The Income Redistributive Effects of Public Spending on Higher Education." *Journal of Human Resources* 10: 116–23.

Dess, Gregory C., and Donald W. Beard. 1984. "Dimensions of Organizational Task Environments." *Administrative Science Quarterly* 29 (1): 52–73.

DiMaggio, Paul J. 1986. "Support for the Arts from Independent Foundations." In *Nonprofit Enterprise in the Arts: Studies in Mission and Contrast,* ed. Paul J. DiMaggio, pp. 113–39. New York and Oxford: Oxford University Press.

DiMaggio, Paul J., Michael Useem, and Paul Brown. 1978. *Audience Studies of the Performing Arts and Museums: A Critical Review.* Washington: National Endowment for the Arts.

Donee Group. 1977. "Private Philanthropy: Vital and Innovative or Passive and Irrelevant?" In *Research Papers,* Commission on Private Philanthropy and Public Needs, vol. 1, pp. 49–85. Washington, D.C.: Treasury Department.

Douglass, Merrill E., and Joyce McNally. 1980. "How Ministers Use Time." *Christian Ministry* 11: 22–26.

Dudley, Roger L., Patricia B. Mutch, and Robert J. Cruise. 1987. "Religious Factors and Drug Usage among Seventh-Day Adventist Youth in North America." *Journal for the Scientific Study of Religion* 26: 218–33.

Etzioni, Amitai. 1964. *Modern Organization.* Englewood Cliffs, NJ: Prentice-Hall, Inc.

Feder, Judith, and Jack Hadley. 1987. "A Threat or a Promise: Acquisition of Teaching Hospitals by Investor-Owned Chains." *Journal of Health Policy, Politics and Law* 12: 325–42.

Feld, Alan L., Michael O'Hare, and J. Mark Davidson Schuster. 1983. *Patrons Despite Themselves: Taxpayers and Arts Policy.* New York: New York University Press.

Filer, Randall K. 1986. "The 'Starving Artist'—Myth or Reality? Earnings of Artists in the United States." *Journal of Political Economy* 94: 56–75.

Fisher, Donald. 1983. "The Role of Philanthropic Foundations in the Reproduction and Production of Hegemony." *Sociology* 17: 206–33.

Foundation Center. 1960–66. *The Foundation Directory.* New York: Russell Sage Foundation.

———. 1971–89. *The Foundation Directory.* New York: The Foundation Center.

———. 1990a. *The Foundation Directory 1991.* New York: The Foundation Center.

————. 1990b. *The Foundation Grants Index*. New York: The Foundation Center.

Frank, R. G., and D. S. Salkever. 1991. "The Supply of Charity Services by Non-profit Hospitals: Motives and Market Structure." *RAND Journal of Economics* 22, no. 3 (Autumn).

————. 1990. "Do Public Mental Hospitals Crowd Out the Supply of Indigent Psychiatric Care by Nonprofit General Hospitals?" Unpublished Johns Hopkins University Working Paper.

Frank, R. G., D. S. Salkever, and J. Mitchell. 1990. "Market Forces and the Public Good: Competition among Hospitals and Provision of Indigent Care." In *Advances in Health Economics and Health Services Research,* ed. R. Scheffler and L. Rossiter, pp. 159–83. Greenwich, CT: JAI Press.

Frank, Richard, David Salkever, and Fitzhugh Mullan. 1990. "Hospital Ownership and the Care of Uninsured and Medicaid Patients: Findings from the National Hospital Discharge Survey, 1979–1984." *Health Policy* 14: 1–11.

Freemont-Smith, Marion R. 1965. *Foundations and Government*. New York: Russell Sage Foundation.

Frey, Bruno S., and Werner W. Pommerehne. 1989. *Muses & Markets: Explorations in the Economics of the Arts*. Oxford, England, and Cambridge, MA: Basil Blackwell.

Friedman, Bernard, and Mark V. Pauly. 1983. "A New Approach to Hospital Cost Functions and Some Issues in Revenue Regulation." *Health Care Financing Review* 4: 105–14.

Gallup Organization. 1987. *Religion in America 1987*. Princeton, NJ: Gallup Organization.

Gapinski, James H. 1986. "The Lively Arts as Substitutes for the Lively Arts." *American Economic Review* 76: 20–25.

General Accounting Office. 1989. *Health Insurance: An Overview of the Working Uninsured*. Report GAO/HRD-89-45. Washington: U.S. General Accounting Office.

————. 1990. *Nonprofit Hospitals: Better Standards Needed for Tax Exemption*. Report GAO/HRD-90-84. Washington: U.S. General Accounting Office.

George, Y. S., V. Richardson, M. Lakes Matyas, and F. Blake. 1989. *Saving Minds: Black Churches and Education*. Washington, D.C.: American Association for the Advancement of Science.

Gilbert, Neil, and Harry Sprecht, eds. 1981. *Handbook of the Social Services*. Englewood Cliffs, NJ: Prentice-Hall, Inc.

Ginzburg, Eli. 1962. "Hospitals and Philanthropy." In *Philanthropy and Public Policy,* ed. Frank G. Dickinson, pp. 73–101. New York: National Bureau of Economic Research.

Giving USA, 35th Annual Edition. 1990. Edited by Nathan Weber. New York: AAFRC Trust for Philanthropy.

Goldberger, Arthur S., and Glen G. Cain. 1982. "The Causal Analysis of Cognitive Outcomes in the Coleman, Hoffer and Kilgore Report." *Sociology of Education* 55 (April/July): 103–22.

Goss, Kristin. 1990. "Churches Lead Big Effort to Rebuild after Hurricane Hugo." *Chronicle of Philanthropy,* 20 March, p. 1.

Hadley, Jack, and Judith Feder. 1985. "Hospital Cost Shifting and Care for the Uninsured." *Health Affairs* 4(3): 67–80.

Hansen, W. Lee. 1970. "Income Distribution Effects of Higher Education." *American Economic Review* 60(2): 335–40.

Hansen, W. Lee, and B. A. Weisbrod. 1969. "The Distribution of Costs and Direct Benefits of Public Higher Education: The Case of California." *Journal of Human Resources* 4: 176–91.

Hansmann, Henry B. 1980. "The Role of Nonprofit Enterprise." *Yale Law Journal* 89: 835–98.

Hanushek, Eric. 1986. "The Economics of Schooling: Production and Efficiency in Public Schools." *Journal of Economic Literature* 24 (September): 1141–77.

Harrison, Shelby M., and F. Emerson Andrews. 1946. *American Foundations for Social Welfare.* New York: Russell Sage Foundation.

Hasenfeld, Yeheskel, and Richard A. English, eds. 1974. *Human Service Organizations: A Book of Readings.* Ann Arbor: The University of Michigan Press.

Health Care Financing Administration, Office of National Cost Estimates. 1990. "National Health Expenditures, 1988." *Health Care Financing Review* 11 (4): 1–41.

Hill, C. Russell. 1981. "Education and Earnings: A Review of the Evidence." *Economics of Education Review* 1(4): 403–20.

Hodgkinson, Virginia A. 1990. *Giving and Volunteering in the United States.* Washington, D.C.: The Independent Sector.

Hodgkinson, Virginia A., and Richard W. Lyman, eds. 1989. *The Future of the Nonprofit Sector.* San Francisco: Jossey-Bass Publishers.

Hodgkinson, Virginia A., and Murray S. Weitzman. 1989. *Dimensions of the Independent Sector: A Statistical Profile.* Washington, D.C.: Independent Sector.

Hoffer, Thomas, Andrew M. Greeley, and James S. Coleman. 1985. "Achievement Growth in Public and Catholic Schools." *Sociology of Education* 58 (April): 74–97.

Hollingshead, August B., and Frederick C. Redlich. 1965. "Social Class and the Treatment of Neurotics." In *Social Welfare Institutions: A Sociological Reader,* ed. Mayer N. Zald, pp. 609–22. New York: John Wiley and Sons, Inc.

Independent Sector. 1986. *Dimensions of the Independent Sector,* 2d ed. Washington, D.C.: Independent Sector.

———. 1988a. *From Belief to Commitment: The Activities and Finances of Religious Congregations in the United States.* Washington, D.C.: Independent Sector.

———. 1988b. *Giving and Volunteering in the United States.* 1988 ed. Washington, D.C.: Independent Sector.

———. 1989. *Dimensions of the Independent Sector.* 3d ed. Washington, D.C.: Independent Sector.

———. 1990. *Giving and Volunteering in the United States.* 1990 ed. Washington, D.C.: Independent Sector.

Interfaith Research Committee. 1977. "A Study of Religious Receipts and Expenditures in the United States." In *Research Papers, Commission on Private Phi-*

lanthropy and Public Needs 1: 365–449. Washington, D.C.: Treasury Department.

Internal Revenue Service. 1989. *Statistics of Income—1986 Individual Tax Returns.* Washington, D.C.: Treasury Department.

James, Estelle. 1987a. "The Nonprofit Sector in Comparative Perspective." In *The Nonprofit Sector: A Research Handbook,* ed. Walter W. Powell, pp. 397–415. New Haven: Yale University Press.

———. 1987b. "The Public/Private Division of Responsibility for Education: An International Comparison." *Economics of Education Review* 6 (1): 1–14.

———. 1987c. "The Political Economy of Private Education in Developed and Developing Countries." World Bank Discussion Paper EDT81. Washington, D.C.

———. 1991. "Why Do Different Countries Choose a Different Public-Private Mix of Educational Services?" Unpublished manuscript.

James, Estelle, Nabeel Alsalam, Joseph Conaty, and Duc-Le To. 1989. "College Quality and Future Earnings: Where Should You Send Your Child to College?" *American Economic Review* 79 (2): 247–52.

James, Estelle, and Gail Benjamin. 1987. "Educational Distribution and Redistribution Through Education in Japan." *Journal of Human Resources* 22 (4): 469–89.

James, Estelle, and Susan Rose-Ackerman. 1986. *The Nonprofit Enterprise in Market Economies.* New York: Harwood Academic Publishers.

Jencks, Christopher. 1985. "How Much Do High School Students Learn?" *Sociology of Education* 58 (April): 128–35.

———. 1987. "Who Gives to What?" In *The Nonprofit Sector: A Research Handbook,* ed. Walter W. Powell, pp. 321–39. New Haven: Yale University Press.

Johnstone, D. Bruce. 1986. *Sharing the Costs of Higher Education.* New York: The College Entrance Examination Board.

Jones, Alison S., and David S. Salkever. 1988. "Trends in Health Insurance Coverage and Utilization of Health Care Services by the Poor and Uninsured: 1976–1984." Unpublished report. Health Services Research and Development Center, Department of Health Policy and Management, The Johns Hopkins University, Baltimore (June 2).

Judy, Marvin T. 1969. *The Multiple Staff Ministry.* Nashville, TN: Abingdon Press.

Juster, F. I., P. Courant, G. Duncan, J. P. Robinson, and F. Stafford. 1979. *Time Use in Economic and Social Accounts.* Ann Arbor, MI: Inter-University Consortium for Political and Social Research.

Juster, F. I., M. S. Hill, F. Stafford, and J. E. Parsons. 1983. *Time Use Longitudinal Panel Study, 1975–1981.* Ann Arbor, MI: Inter-University Consortium for Political and Social Research.

Juster, F. I., and Frank Stafford. 1985. *Time, Goods, and Well-Being.* Ann Arbor, MI: Institute for Social Research.

Kamerman, Sheila B., and Alfred J. Kahn. 1976. *Social Services in the United States: Policies and Programs.* Philadelphia: Temple University Press.

Karl, Barry D., and Stanley N. Katz. 1981. "The American Private Philanthropic Foundation and the Public Sphere, 1890–1930." *Minerva* 19: 236–70.

————. 1987. "Foundations and Ruling Class Elites." *Daedalus* 116: 1–40.

Kessel, Reuben. 1958. "Price Discrimination in Medicine." *Journal of Law and Economics* 1: 20–53.

Lagermann, Ellen C. 1989. *The Politics of Knowledge: The Carnegie Corporation, Philanthropy, and Public Knowledge.* Middletown, CT: Wesleyan University Press.

Lee, John B. 1987. "The Equity of Higher Education Subsidies." Proceedings of the Fourth Annual NASSGP/NCHELP Research Conference on Student Financial Aid Research. Albany, NY: New York State Higher Education Services Corporation.

Lee, John B., and Marilyn Sango-Jordan. 1988. "Further Exploration of the Distribution of Higher Education Subsidies." National Center for Postsecondary Governance and Finance. University of Maryland. Copy.

————. 1989. "Evidence on the Distribution of Direct Student Subsidies to Undergraduates from the National Postsecondary Student Aid Study." National Center for Postsecondary Governance and Finance. University of Maryland. Copy.

Leslie, Larry L., and Paul T. Brinkman. 1987. "Student Price Response in Higher Education." *Journal of Higher Education* 58 (March/April): 181–202.

————. 1988. *The Economic Value of Higher Education.* New York: American Council on Education and Macmillan Publishing Co.

Levy, Frank. 1987. *Dollars and Dreams: The Changing American Income Distribution.* New York: Russell Sage Foundation.

Lewin, Lawrence, Timothy Eckels, and Linda Miller. 1988. "The Provision of Uncompensated Care by Not-For-Profit Hospitals." *New England Journal of Medicine* 318: 1212–15.

Lewis, Gwendolyn. 1989. "Trends in Student Aid: 1980–1988." Washington, D.C.: The College Board.

Lincoln, C. Eric, and Lawrence H. Mamiya. 1988. "In the Receding Shadow of the Black Plantation: A Profile of Rural Clergy and Churches in the Black Belt." *Review of Religious Research* 29: 349–69.

Lumsdon, Kevin. 1981. "Pressure Growing in the Fight to Stay Tax Exempt." *Healthcare Financial Management.* January: 21–28.

MacDonald, Jean. 1985. *The Philanthropy of Organized Religion.* Washington, D.C.: The Council on Foundations.

McDonald, M. B. 1980. "Educational Equity and the Fiscal Incidence of Public Education." *National Tax Journal* 13: 45–54.

McGuire, J. W. 1976. "The Distribution of Subsidy to Students in California Public Higher Education." *Journal of Human Resources* 11: 343–53.

McGuire, Martin C., and Henry Aaron. 1969. "Efficiency and Equity in the Optimal Supply of a Public Good." *Review of Economics and Statistics* 51: 31–39.

Menchik, Paul, and Burton A. Weisbrod. 1981. "Volunteer Labor Supply in the Provision of Collective Goods." In *Nonprofit Firms in a Three Sector Economy,* ed. Michelle J. White, pp. 163–81. Washington, D.C.: Urban Institute.

Menchik, Paul, and Burton Weisbrod. 1987. "Volunteer Labor Supply." *Journal of Public Economics* 32: 159–202.

Moore, G. A. 1982. "Income Redistribution from Public Higher Education Finance within Relevant Age Cohorts." *Economics of Education Review* 2: 175–87.

Morgan, James, and Greg Duncan. 1979. "College Quality and Earnings." In *Research in Human Capital and Development,* ed. Ismail Sirageldin, pp. 103–23. Greenwich, CT: JAI Press.

Morgan, James N., Richard F. Dye, and Judith H. Hybels. 1977. "Results from Two National Surveys of Philanthropic Activity." In *Research Papers,* Commission on Private Philanthropy and Public Needs, vol. 1, pp. 157–323. Washington, D.C.: Treasury Department.

Mortenson, Thomas G., and Zhijun Wu. 1990. "High School Graduation and College Participation of Young Adults by Family Income Backgrounds, 1970 to 1989." ACT Student Financial Aid Research Report 90-3. Iowa City: American College Testing Program. September.

Murnane, Richard J. 1984. "A Review Essay—Comparison of Public and Private Schools: Lessons from the Uproar." *Journal of Human Resources* 19 (Spring): 263–77.

Murnane, Richard J., Stuart Newstead, and Randall J. Olsen. 1985. "Comparing Public and Private Schools: The Puzzling Role of Selectivity Bias." *Journal of Business and Economic Statistics* 3 (1): 23–33.

Musgrave, Richard A., and Peggy B. Musgrave. 1989. *Public Finance in Theory and Practice,* 5th ed. New York: McGraw-Hill.

National Assembly of State Arts Agencies. 1990. *State Arts Agencies Legislative Appropriations Annual Survey.* Washington, D.C.: the author.

National Association of Church Business Administration. 1990. National Church Staff Compensation Survey 1990–1991. Fort Worth, TX: National Association of Church Business Administration.

National Center for Health Statistics, E. Hing, E. Sekscenski, and G. Strahan. 1989. "The National Nursing Home Survey: 1985 Summary for the United States." *Vital and Health Statistics.* Series 13, no. 97. DHHS Pub. no. (PHS) 89-1758, Public Health Service. Washington: U.S. Government Printing Office.

National Council of La Raza. 1977. "Philanthropic Foundations of the U.S. and Their Responsiveness to the Special Needs, Problems, and Concerns of the Hispanic Community, 1960–1971." In *Research Papers,* Commission on Private Philanthropy and Public Needs, vol. 2, part 2, pp. 157–323. Washington, D.C.: Treasury Department.

National Institute on Drug Abuse and National Institute on Alcohol Abuse and Alcoholism. 1989. *Highlights from the 1987 National Drug and Alcoholism Treatment Unit Survey (NDATUS).* Unpublished paper, Division of Epidemiology and Statistical Analysis, NIDA and Division of Biometry and Epidemiology, NIAAA (February 9).

National Institute of Mental Health. 1990. *Mental Health, United States, 1990,* ed. R. W. Manderscheid, and M. A. Sonnenschein. DHHS Pub. no. (ADM)) 90-1708. Washington: U.S. Government Printing Office.

National Research Center of the Arts. 1975. *Americans and the Arts: A Survey of Public Opinion.* New York: Associated Councils of the Arts.

Nelson, Ralph L. 1987. "An Economic History of Large Foundations." In *America's Wealthy and the Future of Foundations,* ed. Teresa Odendahl, pp. 126–77. New York: The Foundation Center.

Nerlove, Marc. 1972. "On Tuition and the Costs of Higher Education: Prolegomena to a Conceptual Framework." *Journal of Political Economy* 80: pp. S178–S218.

Netzer, Dick. 1978. *The Subsidized Muse: Public Support of the Arts in the United States.* New York: Cambridge University Press.

———. 1986. "Dance in New York: Market and Subsidy Changes." *American Economic Review Proceedings* 76: 15–19.

———. 1987. "Changing Economic Fortunes of Dance in the U.S." In *Economic Efficiency in the Performing Arts,* ed. Nancy K. Grant, William S. Hendon, and Virginia Owen, pp. 86–99. Akron, Ohio: Association for Cultural Economics. Volume I of the Proceedings of the Fourth International Conference on Cultural Economics.

———. 1990. "Cultural Policy in an Era of Budgetary Stringency and Fiscal Decentralization: The U.S. Experience." Paper presented at the Sixth International Conference on Cultural Economics, Umea, Sweden, June 1990. (Proceedings to be published by the Association for Cultural Economics in 1992.)

Nielsen, Waldemar A. 1972. *The Big Foundations.* New York: Columbia University Press.

———. 1985. *The Golden Donors.* New York: E. P. Dutton.

Noell, Jay. 1982. "Public and Catholic Schools: A Reanalysis of 'Public and Private Schools.'" *Sociology of Education* 55 (April/July): 123–32.

Odendahl, Teresa. 1989. "The Culture of Elite Philanthropy in the Reagan Years." *Nonprofit and Voluntary Sector Quarterly* 18: 237–48.

———. 1990. *Charity Begins at Home: Generosity and Self-Interest among the Philanthropic Elite.* New York: Basic Books.

Pechman, Joseph A. 1970. "The Distributional Effects of Public Higher Education in California." *Journal of Human Resources* 5(Summer): 361–70.

———. 1985. *Who Paid the Taxes, 1966–85?* Washington: The Brookings Institution.

Pechman, Joseph A., and Benjamin A. Okner. 1974. *Who Bears the Tax Burden?* Washington, D.C.: The Brookings Institution.

Powell, Walter W., ed. 1987. *The Nonprofit Sector: A Research Handbook.* New Haven, CT: Yale University Press.

Radich, Anthony J., ed. 1987. *Economic Impact of the Arts: A Sourcebook.* Denver, CO: National Conference of State Legislatures.

The Random House Dictionary. 1978. New York: Ballantine Books.

Reece, W. S. 1979. "Charitable Contributions: New Evidence on Household Behavior." *American Economic Review* 69: 142–51.

Reed, Ritchie, and Herman P. Miller. 1970. "Some Determinants of the Variation in Earnings for College Men." *Journal of Human Resources* 5(2): 177–90.

Rich, Wilmer Shields. 1955. *American Foundations and Their Fields.* New York: Raymond Rich Associates.

Riley, Margaret. 1989. "Private Foundation Returns, 1985." In Department of the Treasury, *Statistics of Income Bulletin* 9(1): 27–43. Washington, D.C.: U.S. Government Printing Office.

Riley, Patrick. 1981. "Family Services." In *Handbook of the Social Services,* ed. Neil Gilbert and Harry Sprecht, pp. 82–101. Englewood Cliffs, NJ: Prentice-Hall, Inc.

Robinson, John P., Carol A. Keegan, Marcia Karth, and Timothy A. Triplett. 1987. *Survey of Public Participation in the Arts: Volume I, Project Report.* College Park, MD: University of Maryland. Final report to the National Endowment for the Arts on the 1985 survey.

Rudney, Gabriel. 1987. "Creation of Foundations and Their Wealth." In *America's Wealthy and the Future of Foundations,* ed. Teresa Odendahl, pp. 179–201. New York: The Foundation Center.

Salamon, Lester M. 1987. "Of Market Failure, Voluntary Failure, and Third-Party Government: The Theory of Government-Nonprofit Relations in the Modern Welfare State." *Journal of Voluntary Action Research* 16 (1–2): 29–49.

Salamon, Lester M. and Alan J. Abramson. 1982. *The Federal Budget and the Nonprofit Sector.* Washington, D.C.: The Urban Institute Press.

Salamon, Lester M.,and Fred Teitelbaum. 1984. "Religious Congregations as Social Service Agencies: How Extensive Are They?" *Foundation News* 25: 62–65.

Salamon, Lester M., and Kenneth P. Voytek. 1989. *Managing Foundation Assets: An Analysis of Foundation Investment and Payout Procedures and Performance.* New York: The Foundation Center.

Sapp, Gary L., and Logan Jones. 1986. "Religious Orientation and Moral Judgement." *Journal for the Scientific Study of Religion* 25: 208–14.

Savas, E. S. 1982. *Privatizing the Public Sector.* Chatham, NJ: Chatham House.

Schaefer, Jeffrey. 1968. "Philanthropic Contributions: Their Equity and Efficiency." *Quarterly Review of Economics* 8: 25–35.

Schapiro, Morton O., Michael P. O'Malley, and Larry H. Litten. 1990. "Tracing the Economic Backgrounds of COFHE Students: Has There Been a 'Middle-Income Melt'?" Boston: Consortium on Financing Education. (Photocopy).

Schlesinger, Mark. 1990. "Privatization and Change: Organizational Ownership and the Diffusion of Innovations in Human Services." Unpublished paper. Kennedy School of Government, Harvard University.

Schuster, J. Mark Davidson. 1988. *Perspectives on the American Audience for Art Museums.* Research monograph based on the 1985 Survey of Public Participation in the Arts. Unpublished monograph on file in the Educational Resources Information Center (ERIC).

Scott, Robert A. 1974. "The Selection of Clients by Social Welfare Agencies: The Case of the Blind." In *Human Service Organizations: A Book of Readings,* ed. Yeheskel Hasenfeld and Richard A. English, pp. 485–98. Ann Arbor: University of Michigan Press.

Seidman, R. L. n.d. Unpublished tabulations from the hospital financial data of the California Health Facilities Commission.

Seidman, R. L., and S. B. Pollock. 1991. "Trends in Hospital Deductions from Revenue." *Hospital Topics* 69, no. 1 (Winter): 19–26.

Sen, Amartya K. 1977. "Rational Fools: A Critique of the Behavioral Foundations of Economic Theory." *Philosophy and Public Affairs* 6: 317–44.

Sewell, W., and R. Hauser. 1975. *Education, Occupation and Earnings: Achievement in the Early Career.* New York: Academic Press.

Seybold, Geneva. 1939–42. *American Foundations and Their Fields.* New York: Raymond Rich Associates.

Shils, Edward. 1973. "The American Private University." *Minerva* 11: 6–29.

Siegfried, John J., and Katherine M. McElroy. 1981. "Corporate Philanthropy in the U.S., 1980." Department of Economics Working Paper no. 81-W26. Nashville, TN: Vanderbilt University.

Simon, John G. 1987. "The Tax Treatment of Nonprofit Organizations: A Review of Federal and State Policies." In *The Nonprofit Sector: A Research Handbook,* edited by Walter W. Powell, pp. 67–98. New Haven, CT: Yale University Press.

Sloan F. A., M. A. Morrisey, and J. Valvona. 1988. "Hospital Care for the 'Self-Pay' Patient." *Journal of Health Politics, Policy and Law* 13: 83–102.

Sloan, Frank A., Joseph Valvona, and Ross Mullner. 1986. "Identifying the Issues: A Statistical Profile." In *Uncompensated Hospital Care: Rights and Responsibilities,* edited by Frank Sloan, James Blumstein, and James Perrin, pp. 16–53. Baltimore: The Johns Hopkins University Press.

Sloane, Douglas M., and Raymond H. Potvin. 1986. "Religion and Delinquency: Cutting Through the Maze." *Social Forces* 65: 87–105.

Smart, John. 1988. "College Influences on Graduates' Income Levels." *Research in Higher Education* 29(1): 41–59.

Solmon, Lewis, and Paul Wachtel. 1975. "The Effects on Income of Type of College Attended." *Sociology of Education* 48 (Winter): 75–90.

Sosin, Michael. 1986. *Private Benefits: Material Assistance in the Private Sector.* Orlando, FL: Academic Press.

Southern, David W. 1987. *Gunnar Myrdal and Black-White Relations: The Use and Abuse of An American Dilemma, 1944–1969.* Baton Rouge, LA: Louisiana State University Press.

State of Maryland. 1986. Health Services Cost Review Commission, "1986 Study of 818 Bills at Eight Maryland Hospitals." Unpublished report.

Steuerle, Eugene. 1977. "Payout Requirements for Foundations." In Department of the Treasury, *Research Papers Sponsored by the Commission on Private Philanthropy and Public Needs,* pp. 1663–77. Washington, D.C.: U.S. Government Printing Office.

Sullivan, Dennis H. 1985. "Simultaneous Determination of Church Contributions and Church Attendance." *Economic Inquiry* 23: 309–20.

Sulvetta, Margaret. 1985. "Dimensions of the Uncompensated Care Problem." In *Uncompensated Care: Issues and Options.* Waltham, MA: Brandeis University Health Policy Research Consortium (March).

Thorpe, K. E., and C. E. Phelps. 1988. "The Social Role of Not-For-Profit Organizations: Hospital Provision of Charity Care." Unpublished paper, Harvard
School of Public Health (January).

Throsby, C. D., and G. A. Withers. 1983. "Measuring the Demand for the Arts as
a Public Good: Theory and Empirical Results." In *Economics of Cultural Decisions,* ed. William S. Hendon and James L. Shanahan, 177–91. Cambridge,
MA: Abt Books.

Tiebout, C. 1956. "A Pure Theory of Local Expenditures." *Journal of Political
Economy* 64 (no. 5): 416–24.

Tierney, Michael. 1982. "The Impact of Institutional Net Price on Student Demand
for Public and Private Higher Education." *Economics of Education Review* 2
(4): 363–83.

Trusheim, Dale, and James Crouse. 1981. "Effects of College Prestige on Men's
Occupational Status and Income." *Research in Higher Education* 14 (4):
283–304.

U.S. Bureau of the Census. 1975. *Historical Statistics of the United States.* Washington, D.C.: U.S. Government Printing Office.

———. 1985. *1982 Census of Service Industries.* Geographic Area Series: United
States; SC82-A-52. Washington, D.C.: U.S. Government Printing Office.

———. 1985. *School Enrollment: Social and Economic Characteristics of Students, October 1985 and 1984.* Washington, D.C.: U.S. Government Printing
Office.

———. 1989. *Statistical Abstract of the United States.* Washington, D.C.: U.S.
Government Printing Office.

———. 1975–89. *Statistical Abstract of the United States.* Washington, D.C.: U.S.
Government Printing Office.

U.S. Council of Economic Advisers. 1990. *Economic Report of the President.*
Washington, D.C.: U.S. Government Printing Office.

U.S. Department of Commerce. Various years. See entries under U.S. Bureau of the
Census, *Statistical Abstract of the United States.*

U.S. Department of Education, National Center for Educational Statistics. 1981.
High School and Beyond, 1980. Washington, D.C.: U.S. Government Printing
Office.

———. 1987a. *National Postsecondary Student Aid Study.* Washington, D.C.:
U.S. Government Printing Office.

———. 1987b. *The Condition of Education.* Washington, D.C.: U.S. Government
Printing Office.

———. 1989. *Digest of Education Statistics, 1989.* Washington, D.C.: U.S. Government Printing Office.

U.S. Department of Education. 1985–86. *Digest of Education Statistics.* Washington, D.C.: U.S. Government Printing Office.

———. 1986. *Higher Education General Information Survey (HEGIS).* Washington, D.C.: U.S. Government Printing Office.

U.S. Department of Education, Office of Educational Research and Improvement.
1990. *The American Eighth Grader: NELS: 88 Student Descriptive Summary.*
Washington, D.C.: U.S. Government Printing Office.

U.S. Department of Health and Human Services. 1983. *The Medicare and Medicaid Data Book, 1983.* Baltimore, MD: Health Care Financing Administration, Pub. no. 03156.

U.S. National Endowment for the Arts. 1975. *Museums USA: A Survey Report.* Washington: U.S. Government Printing Office.

U.S. News and World Report. 1989. "America's Best Colleges." 107 (October 16): 53–58.

United Way of America. 1990. *Fund Distribution Results, by Agency, by Program, 1988 Metros I–VIII.* Alexandria, VA: United Way of America.

Vickrey, William. 1962. "One Economist's View of Philanthropy." In *Philanthropy and Public Policy,* ed. Frank G. Dickinson, pp. 31–56. New York: National Bureau of Economic Research.

Vredeveld, George. 1974. "Income Inequality and Subsidizing Higher Education." In *Costs and Benefits of Education,* edited by R. Leiter. Boston: Twayne Publishers.

Wachtel, Paul. 1976. "The Effect on Earnings of School and College Investment Expenditure." *Review of Economics and Statistics* 58: 326–31.

Wales, Terence J. 1973. "The Effect of College Quality on Earnings: Results from the NBER-Thorndike Data." *Journal of Human Resources* 8 (3): 306–17.

Weaver, Warren. 1967. *U.S. Philanthropic Foundations: Their History, Management and Record.* New York: Harper and Row.

Weisbrod, Burton. 1977. "Toward a Theory of Voluntary Nonprofit Sector in a Three-Sector Economy." In B. Weisbrod, *The Voluntary Nonprofit Sector,* pp. 51–76. Lexington, MA: D. C. Heath.

———. 1988. *The Nonprofit Economy.* Cambridge: Harvard University Press.

Westat, Inc. 1990. *A Sourcebook of Arts Statistics: 1989.* Rockville, MD: the author. Referred to in text and tables as *1989 Sourcebook.*

Wickenden, Elizabeth. 1976. "A Perspective on Social Services: A Review Essay." *Social Service Review* 50 (4): 570–85.

Williamson, J. Peter. 1977. "Reasonable Investment Expectations and the Payout of Private Foundations." In Department of the Treasury, *Research Papers Sponsored by the Commission on Private Philanthropy and Public Needs,* pp. 1648–52. Washington, D.C.: U.S. Government Printing Office.

Williamson, Jeffrey, and Peter Lindert. 1980. *American Inequality: A Macroeconomic History.* New York: Academic Press.

Willms, J. Douglas. 1985. "Catholic-School Effects on Academic Achievement: New Evidence from the *High School and Beyond Follow-up Study." Sociology of Education* 58 (April): 98–114.

Windham, D. M. 1970. *Education, Equality and Income Redistribution.* Lexington, MA: D. C. Heath.

Withers, Glenn A. 1908. "Unbalanced Growth and the Demand for Performing Arts: An Econometric Analysis." *Southern Economic Journal* 46: 735–42.

Wuthnow, Robert. 1990. "Religion and the Voluntary Spirit in the United States: Mapping the Terrain." In *Faith and Philanthropy in America,* eds. Robert Wuthnow and Virginia Hodgkinson, pp. 3–21. San Francisco: Jossey-Bass.

Wuthnow, Robert, and Clifford Nass. 1988. "Government Activity and Civil Privatism: Evidence from Voluntary Church Membership." *Journal for the Scientific Study of Religion* 27: 157–74.

Ylvisaker, Paul N. 1987. "Foundations and Nonprofit Organizations." In *The Nonprofit Sector: A Research Handbook,* ed. Walter W. Powell, pp. 360–79. New Haven, CT: Yale University Press.

Zald, Mayer N. 1965. *Social Welfare Institutions: A Sociological Reader.* New York: John Wiley and Sons, Inc.

Contributors

HENRY J. AARON
 The Brookings Institution
SANDY BAUM
 Skidmore College
JEFF E. BIDDLE
 Michigan State University
CHARLES T. CLOTFELTER
 Duke University
RICHARD G. FRANK
 Johns Hopkins University
ESTELLE JAMES
 State University of New York at
 Stony Brook

FRANK LEVY
 University of Maryland
ROBERT A. MARGO
 Vanderbilt University
DICK NETZER
 New York University
LESTER M. SALAMON
 Johns Hopkins University
DAVID S. SALKEVER
 Johns Hopkins University
SAUL SCHWARTZ
 Tufts University and Carlton
 University

Index

279